FROM CAIRO to BEIRUT

In the Footsteps of an 1839 Expedition
through the Holy Land

to Monica,
for putting up with
all my crazy ideas...

FROM CAIRO TO BEIRUT

In the Footsteps of an 1839 Expedition
through the Holy Land

~~~~~~

WRITTEN & ILLUSTRATED BY
SUNIL SHINDE

DESIGNED BY
LILIANA GUIA

CHIN MUSIC
PRESS

www.fromcairotobeirut.com
IG: @sunshinde

Published by:
Chin Music Press
1501 Pike Place #329
Seattle, WA 9810-1542
www.chinmusicpress.com

Editor: Tatiana Wilde
Design: Liliana Guia

ISBN: 9781634050241
Library of Congress Control Number: 2021942231

CONTENTS

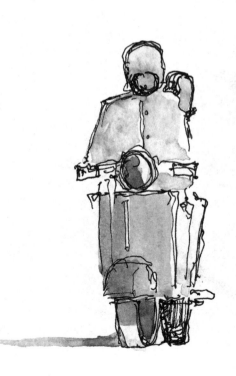

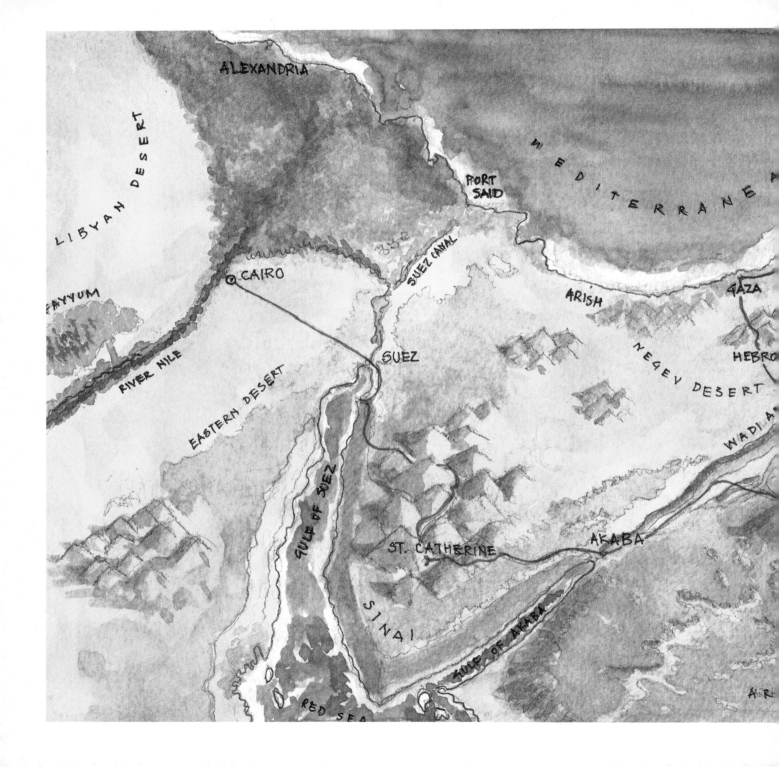

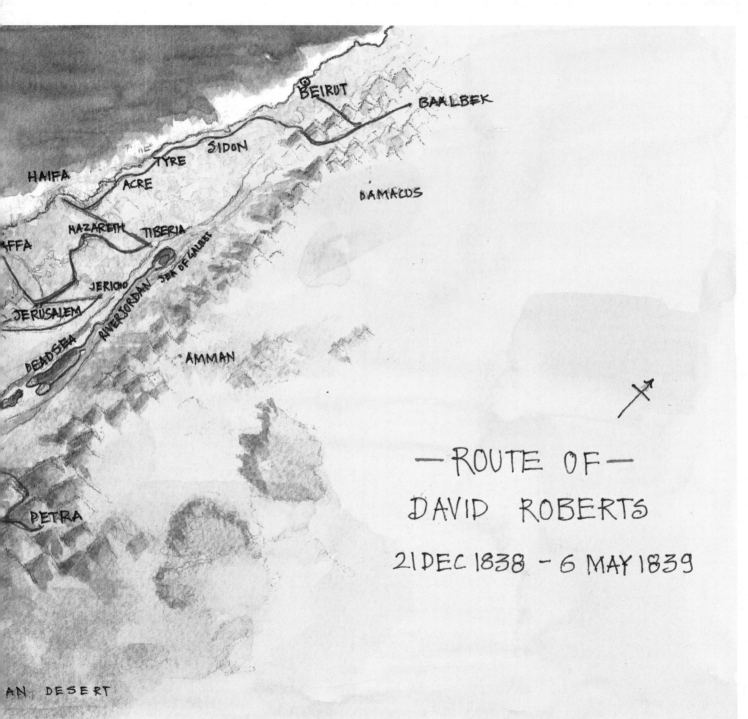

BEIRUT • BAALBEK

SIDON

TYRE

HAIFA

ACRE

NAZARETH   TIBERIA

FFA

JERICHO   SEA OF GALILEE

JERUSALEM

DEAD SEA   RIVER JORDAN

AMMAN

DAMACUS

PETRA

AN DESERT

—ROUTE OF—
DAVID ROBERTS
21 DEC 1838 — 6 MAY 1839

FOREWORD

~~~~~

Was David Roberts an early influencer? An Instagrammer from a century and a half before the word and the requisite equipment had even been thought of? His epic almost-six-month-long trek from Cairo to Beirut certainly generated plenty of admirers and, whereas today they are simply numbered in their tens of thousands, David Roberts' followers – and even then there were certainly plenty of them – were also notable for their importance. An archbishop, a prime minister, even Queen Victoria were loyal advocates.

Today Instagram followers like to find their way to the iconic location and pay homage to the original photographic creation via selfies. That may not have been an option for nineteenth-century collectors of Roberts' delightful lithographs, but fast forward to today, and Sunil Shinde is certainly an enthusiastic follower, although fortunately he pays his respect not with instant selfies, but in a much more respectful fashion: a sketch. Selfie or sketch, it's delightful how often the steps from David Roberts' 1838 original to Sunil Shinde's two-centuries-later illustration is often almost as seamless as the jump from your inspirational Instagram to my quick selfie. "Look," Sunil is often thinking, "the view today is just as Roberts captured it all those years ago." Indeed the ladder is still there, propped against a window in the Holy Sepulchre.

There's something else that hasn't changed from when David Roberts made his journey: the overriding jumble of politics in the region. Of course they're entirely different politics; today we're worrying about the sad follow up to the Arab Spring, the smoldering embers of ISIS, the chaos in Lebanon, and the insoluble differences between Israel and Palestine. But even in 1838 there were plenty of political, cultural, and big power problems for Roberts to tangle with. Back then it was local uprisings versus the collapsing Ottomans and for super-power influence, it was Britain, the arch-imperialist, hovering menacingly in the background.

Despite which, Sunil's travels reinforce all the unchangeable reasons why travel is so important and why it's going to be essential to get back to it once we've got this pandemic out of the way. He has plenty of kindness-of-stranger experiences, plenty of "wow, it is amazing being right here at exactly this moment" incidents. And in a region where there's absolutely no shortage of alternative views of the truth, it's reassuring that he regularly underlines that there are always two ways of seeing the same picture.

Personally, it was also wonderful to regularly be reminded of how much I've enjoyed the region myself. That ranges from trekking up Mt Sinai from St Catherine's Monastery with my children, aged six and nine at the time, to noting how life in Hebron is definitely wedged between a rock and a hard place, to, just a year ago, sipping tea in Fishawi in Cairo, only a week before the pandemic brought my travel world tumbling down. I look forward to normal service resuming and slotting myself back into another David Roberts lithograph, preferably, just like Sunil, with some interesting food as an important distraction.

TONY WHEELER
CO-FOUNDER, LONELY PLANET PUBLICATIONS

PROLOGUE

~~~~~

"You *must* be David Roberts," said the Bedouin.

In the Middle East, one often hears the street vendors shout a provocative word or two to grab your attention. They seem to have figured out the right combination of words and names to hook any nationality. I was used to hearing, "Hi there India!" or, "Hello to Shah Rukh Khan!" But here was a Bedouin who looked like Jack Sparrow – kohl-lined eyes, pointed beard, tight fitting black clothes, black bandana, referencing my favorite Orientalist painter. What are the chances?

I was in Petra. My 14-year-old daughter Rhea and I had chosen the desert ruins of Jordan for our father-daughter spring-break trip in 2015. I had found a spot to settle down and sketch in front of the incredible façade of Al-Khazneh, arguably Petra's most recognizable monument. Rhea had chased down a stray puppy and was attempting to teach him to sit on command. A steaming cup of sweet tea sat beside my open sketchbook and the ancient courtyard I was sitting in was bathed in glorious morning sunlight. Tourists were starting to arrive, their heads craned at impossible angles, drinking in the sight of the monument carved into the pink limestone cliffside. Bedouin children wearing mismatched bathroom slippers flitted between the tourists, displaying a knack for salesmanship far exceeding their age. My pencil hovered over an unfinished sketch of the Khazneh as I struggled to depict the Corinthian columns carved twenty-one centuries ago. The Bedouin had been patiently squatting next to me long enough that I had forgotten he was still there.

"You must be David Roberts," he repeated. "Look." He placed in front of me a print wrapped in cellophane. "Did you make this?"

I was aware of the painting, which was made by David Roberts during his own visit to Petra in 1839. The print showed Khazneh as Roberts saw it when he sat in this courtyard himself. Other than one or two prominent details – a broken column of the portico was lying askance, and a brook ran in the middle of the canyon floor – it seemed as though nothing had changed in the last 175 years. In fact, I was consciously imitating the very angle and composition of Roberts' painting in my travel journal. I admit that I was somewhat irritated to be caught red-handed in the act of copying, but the Bedouin's words lit a bulb in my head. The bulb burned bright all day as we roamed the city "half as old as time."

I had accidently discovered David Roberts on an earlier trip to Egypt in 2006. I had been sitting in the courtyard of the Temple of Edfu when a local enticed me into buying a postcard booklet from him. Flipping through the postcards, Ahmet, our Egyptologist guide, paused on one that depicted the sunny courtyard of a ruined temple, framed by giant crumbling columns. Sand choked the entrance, the walls were disintegrating – but despite being devoured by the desert, the scintillating beauty of the temple and its evident antiquity was unmistakable. To my amazement and delight, Ahmet pointed out that I was sitting in the very courtyard that was shown in the postcard. On closer inspection, I could make out details in the painting that I could trace in front of me on the walls of the temple. Until that moment, it had never occurred to me that places shown in such paintings existed anywhere outside the artist's imagination.

For the rest of the trip, I spotted David Roberts' paintings reproduced frequently on kitsch souvenirs – calendars,

El Khazneh, Petra

TEMPLE CALLED KHAZNEH, PETRA

RIGHT: BY DAVID ROBERTS, R.A.
MARCH 1839

ABOVE: BY SUNIL SHINDE, JANUARY
2018

postcards, mugs, keychains, wall hangings, booklets, and even papyrus. I asked Ahmet to identify the locations amidst the tremendous pharaonic sites of Upper Egypt that were depicted. Roberts had an unmistakable style. His compositions captured monumental architecture set against glorious landscapes and accentuated by vividly colored figures in the foreground. His choice of location, composition, treatment, and color scheme inspired my own formative art palette. I did not know it then, but I was already on the trail of David Roberts.

Back in the warmth of our hotel room in Petra in 2015, Hillary Clinton had just announced her candidacy for President of the United States and I was browsing David Roberts on the internet. I read a line that caught my attention: Roberts traveled to the Orient, funding the trip himself, *with the express purpose of sketching*. That sounded like somebody I saw every morning in the mirror. After several years of toting expensive digital cameras around with me on my travel adventures, I had switched to sketching as a means of documenting my experiences. Without the digital paraphernalia to lug around, I packed light, traveled slow and sketched fast. It seemed like David Roberts had pioneered this style of travel all those years ago. Curious, I dug further – Roberts used his travels to build a portfolio that he would later publish. His seminal work – *The Holy Land, Syria, Idumea, Arabia, Egypt, and Nubia*, lavishly produced volumes of lithographic prints based on the eleven months he spent in the region – was popular with two very diverse audiences. Art lovers adored the color and the drama of his works, while archaeologists and anthropologists used them to study nineteenth century Palestine.

How much fun would it be to follow David Roberts' footsteps through the Near East, I thought. I was so excited by the idea that I threw it away. If it were any good, it would come back knocking, as good ideas do. So, I switched off the bulb that had burned bright all day and went to bed.

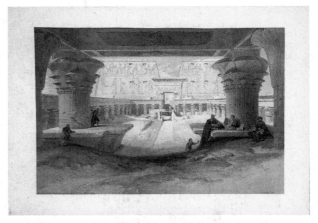

VIEW FROM UNDER THE PORTICO OF TEMPLE OF EDFOU
BY DAVID ROBERTS, R.A. 23RD NOVEMBER 1838

Two years later, I was driving Asha – my younger daughter, then 9 – to her school. The fall colors of the Pacific Northwest were enveloped in a dense fog, the car stereo was tuned to NPR and the newscaster announced the liberation of Raqqa from the clutches of ISIS. Raqqa had been the last remaining city in Syria under ISIS control. With the threat of ISIS neutralized in the region, at least temporarily, the last piece of the jigsaw of my Near East journey fell into place.

Raqqa is four hundred kilometers (two hundred fifty miles) northeast of Ba'albec, which was as far north and east as David Roberts had reached in his expedition of 1839. Ba'albec was too far away from Raqqa for the victory over ISIS to impact the day-to-day situation, but the bulb had lit up again.

I was on a sabbatical. A calendar jam-packed with back-to-back business meetings had been replaced by soul-fueling activities. A second cup of *masala* tea in front of a roaring fire. Dropping

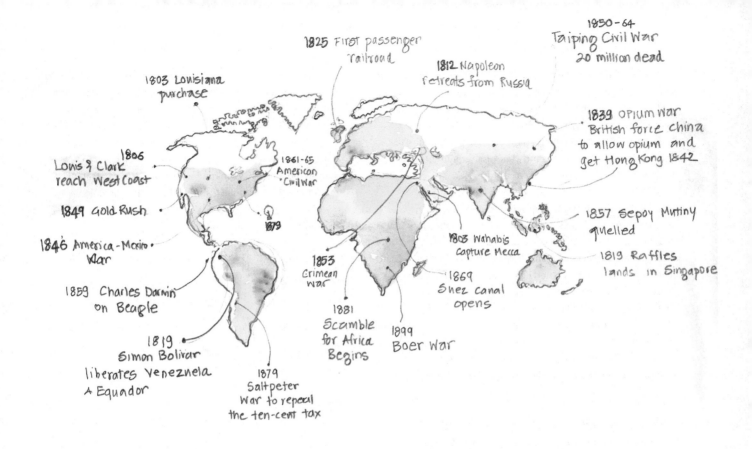

1825 First passenger railroad

1850-64 Taiping Civil War 20 million dead

1812 Napoleon retreats from Russia

1803 Louisiana purchase

1839 Opium War British force china to allow opium and get Hong Kong 1842

1806 Louis & Clark reach West Coast

1861-65 American Civil War

1879

1849 Gold Rush

1857 Sepoy Mutiny quelled

1846 America-Mexico War

1803 Wahabis capture Mecca

1819 Raffles lands in Singapore

1859 Charles Darwin on Beagle

1853 Crimean War

1869 Suez canal opens

1819 Simon Bolivar liberates Venezuela & Equador

1881 Scramble for Africa Begins

1899 Boer War

1879 Saltpeter War to repeal the ten-cent tax

THE WORLD IN THE NINETEENTH CENTURY

off my daughters at their schools. Late morning naps. Afternoon runs to the grocer for fresh produce. Playing tug with Oscar, our golden retriever. Whipping up spicy recipes for the family. Devouring half a book in a single sitting at the neighborhood bookstore. Returning the next day to finish it. If I wanted to undertake an extended journey, there wouldn't be a better

time. I realized I had a narrow window to make things happen if I moved fast. So, I moved fast.

I traced David Roberts' itinerary onto a map. Roberts had arrived in Cairo in Sept 1838; after obtaining the necessary permissions and equipment, he chartered a cutter with a crew at £15 per month. He hoisted a Union Jack onto its mast and sailed up and down the Nile for ten weeks, living out his fantasy of being an explorer in an unexplored land. Roberts scouted and sketched the ruins of ancient Egypt – temples, courtyards, statues. Some of the sketches he made happened to become the last documentation of two-thousand-year-old monuments that disappeared under Lake Naseer a century later.

When Roberts returned to Cairo in December 1838, he procured a *firman* for his journey onwards into the Holy Land. Despite a plague in Jerusalem, clouds of war in Syria, and unrest amongst the Egyptian civilians, Roberts started out from Cairo in February 1839. He traveled east across the Sinai Peninsula, stopping at the ancient monastery of St. Catherine before heading over the tip of the Arabian desert to the ruins of the lost city of Petra. From there he crossed the desert and biblical sites of Palestine, passed through the walled city of Jerusalem, and traveled up through the Syrian wilderness to explore the Roman ruins at Ba'albec before finally reaching Beirut three months later, in May 1839.

David Roberts prodigiously sketched the sights and scenes he came across during this journey. Very few Europeans had laid their eyes on the landscape Roberts navigated in 1839 and no independent professional artist had ever documented it. Upon returning home to London with several sketchbooks containing detailed images of the Holy Land, Roberts published them. His depiction of the Holy Land set him apart from the horde of explorers, scholars, treasure hunters, historians, antiquarians, amateur archaeologists, and adrenalin junkies who made similar journeys in early nineteenth century. His book, the title shortened in modern times to *The Holy Land and Egypt*, was published in two three-volume sets in the 1840s and became an instant bestseller. Until the advent of the camera, Roberts' work was considered the most accurate visual guide of the region.

I made up my mind to retrace Roberts' footsteps from Cairo to Beirut. The plan was to follow his route as closely as possible with the intention of standing in as many places he had stood, to sketch what he had sketched – and what he had missed.

The journey came together in a few days because it was several years in the making. Within six weeks of the Syrian Defense Force liberating Raqqa, I was in Cairo, at the starting line.

Operation David Roberts was a go.

EGYPT

〜〜〜

"...a city unequalled in the world for the picturesque."
— DAVID ROBERTS, 24TH DECEMBER 1838, CAIRO.

CAIRO

〜〜〜〜

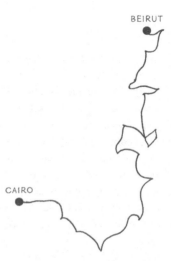

The city of Cairo after sunset is like the attic of my childhood home in rural India: it is dark, dusty, and smelly. It brims with mysterious objects and wonderful stories. It is scary and inviting all at the same time.

When the taxi drops me outside a colonial-era building on a crisp December evening in 2017, domes, minarets, and a million satellite dishes are already silhouetted against a red sky. A broom-closet elevator takes me up to the sparsely furnished lobby of the Hostel Grand Pharaoh. It dawns on me that while I had been imagining the luxury that the name "Grand Pharaoh" evoked, the online booking site was pricing a hostel. The guy manning reception has a wide grin. He takes me to my room, which features a large window overlooking a crowded street. The water in the shower is steaming hot and drums with a therapeutic force on the back of my neck.

In the morning, I enjoy the brief and delicious sensation of not knowing which part of the world I am in. I follow the smell of freshly brewed coffee through a labyrinth of corridors to a tiny kitchen. A woman with a big toothy smile seats me by a window that looks down over the still sleepy street. I move my chair to catch a warm square of early morning Cairene sun on my face. She pours me a mug of thick Arabic coffee, which warms my hands and the cockles of my heart.

John joins me at the table at 8 o'clock. He has arrived on time. An Egyptian who arrives on time is a very rare thing. John maneuvers his chair to avoid the sunlight. The toothy woman pours John a coffee as he sits down. She asks if I want a glass of mango juice.

"Yes," I say. "If the juice is fresh."

"Yes, it is," she says. "I just poured it out of the box."

I search her face for sarcasm. None. I look at John, who is smiling sheepishly. Only later will I realize that John always smiles sheepishly.

"Welcome to Cairo," he says. Still no hint of sarcasm.

John, whose last name, thankfully, is not Smith, is to be my guide and companion for the next several days in Egypt. From my home in Seattle, I exchanged emails with him to try and condense David Roberts' thirty-seven-day Cairo stay into the six days available to me. John worked patiently to build a plan that I was happy with – not an easy feat. Now, sitting across from me, he speaks softly, with the measured tone of a teacher who knows that every word is being written down by a class full of students. The breakfast plates have been cleared. The coffee mugs have been refilled. A handwritten checklist lies in front of me and every item is checked. John patiently answers all my questions and I listen attentively as his delicate finger traces the lines of our route on the well-thumbed map lying between us, occasionally pausing in midair and then tapping a location, delicately hammering in a detail.

After exploring Cairo for a week, following closely in Roberts' footsteps, I plan to travel due east, through the hinterlands of the desert to Suez. I will cross the canal that connects the Orient and the Occident and head south into the mountains of the Sinai Peninsula to St. Catherine's Monastery. I will then continue into the wilderness of the Peninsula, traveling further east to Taba where I will encounter the Egypt–Israel border. That is how far east I can go and still be on Egyptian soil.

Taba is as far as John plans to go with me. I will then change travel companions at Aqaba, in present day Jordan, just like Roberts, who also changed guides there before heading to the famed ruins of Petra. I let my finger follow a geological fault on the map in his wake. After Petra, Roberts crossed over into Palestine, just south of the Dead Sea. He proceeded on to Hebron, then Gaza, traversing up the eastern coast of the Mediterranean until Jaffa – present day Tel Aviv. From there he went to Jerusalem, exploring the surrounding Judaean desert and several sites mentioned in the Bible. He then traversed Palestine and traveled north to Syria, to the parts that are today in Lebanon, until he reached Ba'albec. Then, rather than continuing to Damascus, he turned to Beirut. This would be my route over the next three months.

John looks at me, "How are you going to do all this, Sunil?" he asks. He is asking me *how*, but his tone telegraphs why. "How are you going to get into Gaza? How will you go from Israel to Lebanon?"

My family asked me these questions, too, and I managed to skillfully duck. I did not know the answers myself. An exasperated friend blurted out, "*You should not do this. It is too dangerous. Nobody does these things anymore.*" In one breath, three buttons inside me had been pressed–this journey was forbidden, unfamiliar, and dangerous.

John looks worried. I try to assuage him. "I'll pull an ancient Hindu trick," I say, my index fingers curling to meet my thumbs. I inhale deeply, trying to project my inner yogi-like calm. "I'll summon a magic carpet. Or something."

John taps the map. He asks, "Aren't you going to ask me if Sinai is dangerous?"

"I'm afraid you'll say it isn't."

Mosque of Sultan Hassan

Citadel

THE CITADEL

The rickety elevator of my hostel clatters to the ground floor. In the United States, such a nineteenth-century colonial building would be on the US historic registry. In Cairo, it is just another ugly "modern" construction. I am in a city where even a five-hundred-year-old building is often not the oldest structure on the block.

John flags down a taxi. One or two slow down; the drivers check us out and speed away. In Cairo, you don't pick a cab, the cabbie picks you. Eventually a vintage cab pulls over. It probably slowed down and couldn't pick up speed in time. John is surprisingly nimble as he swiftly ducks into the passenger seat.

Despite the early hour, traffic is already snarling and the cab belches tremendous plumes of diesel fumes as it struggles to keep pace with the slow-moving flow. Oblivious to the din outside, our taxi-driver noisily sips mint tea from a Styrofoam cup balanced on an ashtray brimming with stubs of knock-off Marlboros. The cab fishtails on a flyover with a vantage view of Cairo. The driver pulls deeply on his cigarette before gesturing at the jumble of domes and minarets on his left, his fingers moving as if casting a spell.

"That's old Cairo," he says in remarkably good English. He then points through the other window and says, "And that's older Cairo."

He cackles in a manner that suggests he has enjoyed telling this joke a few times before. But he is right – no other city of this magnitude has been continuously inhabited for so long and yet changed so little. Not Rome, not Varanasi, not Luoyang. Take away the few vestiges of modern development – the Cairo Tower, the high-rise hotels along the Nile, the stadium, the airport, the bridges and the flyovers – and Cairo would be as recognizable as at any time in the last thousand years.

"Very little has changed since December 1838 when Roberts was here," I say excitedly to John.

"Yes, very little has changed," the driver says. "Especially this red light. It seems like it has been stuck on red since Napoleon was here."

Our Cairene itinerary starts at the Citadel, exactly where Roberts started his. The magnificent medieval fortress sits in the shadow of the Mukattam hills that dot the eastern border of the city. Before Roberts could begin his own journey, he had to visit the Citadel with his liaison, Colonel Campbell, to get himself a *firman* – an Ottoman-era visa to travel to Palestine and Syria. Such a document would provide him the necessary permission to traverse the territory held under Mohammed Ali Pasha, the ruler of Egypt, without fear of being robbed or persecuted. After long hours daily spent lobbying the bureaucrats at the Citadel, Roberts would sit down in the vicinity of the fortress to sketch local scenes.

John and I walk past machine-gun-toting commandoes dressed in desert fatigues and mirrored Ray Ban sunglasses. A throng of elementary school kids in blue and white uniforms swarm around us. They are on a field trip to the Citadel and their unadulterated joy is not shared by the Citadel guards. The kids squeal in delight every time the airport-style metal detector at the entrance to the Citadel goes off, and they seem to keep discovering new ways to trigger it. They are in no hurry to enter the Citadel – after all, who in their right mind needs a lesson in history?

The maze of old Cairo sprawls beneath the citadel walls and disappears into a haze of smog that now permanently blankets the city. Somewhere under the dust, the Nile snakes towards the Mediterranean. The founders of Cairo chose the east bank of the Nile to settle. The powerful river, which halted the sands of the Sahara on its west bank, was used to create distance from the ancient Pharaohs and their cult of death. In the eleventh century, Cairo was a new start. These days, it is difficult to associate the word "new" with anything in Cairo, but no city as old is as beautiful, as atmospheric and alive.

When Roberts stood on the ramparts of Saladin's Citadel in Cairo and stared out at hundreds of minarets poking into the sky, he was probably reminded of a delightful phase in his life. At the age of 20, he had joined a traveling circus, "a troupe of traveling pantomimists," as a scene painter. Every night, after he finished his work, he would go and sit in the circus theatre, which played *Ali Baba and the Forty Thieves*. The oriental scenery of the lavishly painted backdrop fascinated him. He sat there, spellbound, memorizing the details so he could sketch the scenes later from memory until Baghdad with its countless minarets was quite familiar to him.

Roberts wrote in his journal on 24th December 1838:

"THE EFFECT TONIGHT WAS GRAND: THE SKY WAS CLOUDED AND OVERCAST – THE SETTING SUN FROM TIME TO TIME BURSTING THROUGH THE HAZE – THE PYRAMIDS TOWERING BLACK AS THE CLOUDS THAT OVERHUNG THEM; THE NILE REFLECTED THE GLIMPSES OF THE SUN, WHILE THE CITY EXTENDED AS FAR AS THE EYE COULD REACH, STUDDED WITH MINARETS OF THE MOST VARIED AND FANTASTIC SHAPES, THAT OF SULTAN HASSAN RISING IN ALL ITS MAJESTY."

SALAH AL-DIN SQUARE, CAIRO, DEC 2017

THE COURTYARD OF THE ALABASTER MOSQUE, CAIRO

The Pasha undertook ambitious projects in the first two of decades of the 1800s. He overhauled Egypt's education system, nationalized agriculture, introduced new crops using modern techniques and technologies, built a modern army and navy and developed a force of fresh, young, foreign-educated, well-traveled diplomats. He spent lavish amounts of money on importing technology and know-how from the West. What could not be bought with gold was acquired by seducing the West into believing a vision of the mystical and exotic land of the Orient.

Pioneers, dreamers, industrialists, entrepreneurs, scientists, adventurers, artists, theologists, historians, mystics, and looters rushed through the portals of the Orient that were being cracked open. Roberts was one of them.

The Alabaster Mosque was still under construction when Roberts visited. He called the mosque, "an ugly symbol of global homogeneous architecture." He considered the carvings, "...barbarous and show[ing] the degraded state of modern art," an appellate I would go so far as to use for the Cairo Holiday Inn – certainly not the crown jewel of Old Cairo's skyline. Perhaps Roberts was disappointed that the general plan and appearance of the mosque borrowed heavily from the Blue Mosque of Istanbul, whose atmosphere and antiquity is legendary and unsurpassable. Perhaps it was in keeping with the habit of the day for the "civilized visitors" from the Western world to denigrate Islamic Egypt whilst simultaneously waxing eloquent about the Pharaonic era. For hundreds of years, Egypt had been an unbreachable black box for the rest of the world. When the box opened, the West was surprised to find stupendous buildings and monuments, enormous feats of engineering and artistry and an unparalleled demonstration of wealth and manpower to instantly invalidate notions of a barbaric, uneducated, unkempt civilization of lazy people of an unknown faith.

That Christmas Eve Roberts was lonely but in excellent health, preparing for the journey of his lifetime to Palestine and Syria. He was in good spirits. I am in good spirits too. I am on his trail.

Shafts of midday sun filter through latticed windows and crisscross the dark interior of the Alabaster Mosque. I stop in front of the tomb of Muhammed Ali Pasha to pay my respects. Without his blessing, Roberts' journey would not have been possible. The Pasha had ruled over Egypt with an iron fist for thirty-five years. He had correctly sensed the waning power of the Ottoman Empire and realized that Egypt needed to modernize to be independent. Such a project required vision and an unrelenting will, both of which the Pasha had plenty of.

The beautiful courtyard of the Alabaster Mosque reverberates with the flapping of hundreds of pigeons taking off. The enclosure, surrounded by arcades topped with domes, is adorned with a clock tower presented by King Louis-Philippe of France as a reciprocation of Muhammed Ali's gift of the 3,000-year-old Luxor obelisk, which had been installed at the Place de la Concorde in Paris.

"Doesn't this symbolize Ali Pasha getting the modern technologies he needed from the west in exchange for Pharaonic tidbits, which he had in abundance?" I ask John. The Pasha's plans to modernize Egypt were in full swing at the time of Roberts' visit. Egypt was spending lavishly and purchasing modern machinery, technology, and knowledge from the west.

"The clock never worked," John replies, in his usual matter-of-fact manner, "like most of the technology he imported."

A typical coffeeshop, Cairo

AL QARAFA

~~~~~

By the end of the thirteenth century, Cairo was already overcrowded. The Mamluks, the new Sultans of Egypt, designated a large parcel of land on the eastern outskirts of the city as a cemetery – al-Qarafa. East of it, the desert extends all the way to Mecca. In al-Qarafa the Mamluk Sultans built their elaborate funerary estates. A royal funerary estate would cover several city-blocks and consist of a mosque, a *madrassa*, a mausoleum, a loggia or two, gardens, water troughs for animals, water fountains for travelers, apartment complexes for paying tenants, storage spaces, and living areas for the caretakers of the complex. The larger estates had their own compound walls and gates. A funerary estate would have dedicated staff for the upkeep of the premises.

Death has always been a good business in Egypt.

The noblemen emulated royalty and built their own mortuary estates on a scale that matched their stature and standing in society. The smallest of mausoleums had a tomb and living space for the caretakers. Al Qarafa, on the outskirts of a Cairo, soon became a destination for military parades, public ceremonies, trade fairs, seasonal bazaars – anything and everything that could not be accommodated in the Old City. It became a place for the outrageous and the outcasts to converge. Sufi saints built humble shelters. As their congregations grew, their abodes became religious compounds. Tombs of dead saints became sacred places, drawing religious visitors. Eateries followed visitors. Khans – inns – sprung up. The cemetery came to life.

Sun-beaten caravans, having crossed the sands of the Arabian desert, stopped at al-Qarafa before proceeding to the

TOMBS OF THE KHALIFS, CAIRO BY DAVID ROBERTS, R.A. JANUARY 1839

metropolitan hubbub of medieval Cairo. Caravanserai – ancient truck stops – sprung up. Caravans that ferried pilgrims to Mecca started at al-Qarafa. Roberts witnessed the launch of such a caravan on 13th January 1839. His journal entry of that day, longer than his usual, captured the event vividly:

"TO-DAY THE GRAND CARAVAN STARTS FOR MECCA. WITH SOME FRIENDS LEFT CAIRO AT SUNRISE, AND PROCEEDING TEN OR TWELVE MILES INTO THE DESERT, WE REACHED THE ENCAMPMENT BEFORE IT HAD BROKEN UP. THERE WERE ABOUT TWO THOUSAND CAMELS AND TWO OR THREE HUNDRED HORSES. IN THE CENTRE WAS THE EMIR'S TENT, SURROUNDED BY AN IMMENSE GATHERING OF ALL TRIBES AND NATIONS IN THE MOST PICTURESQUE DERANGEMENT, THOSE FROM CONSTANTINOPLE BEING MOST CONSPICUOUS. AT MID-DAY OR NOON PRAYERS, ALL THE CAMELS, AS WELL AS THE WORSHIPPERS, FACED THE EAST, AND ON A SIGNAL FROM A GUN THE WHOLE MASS OF HUMAN BEINGS, WHICH STRETCHED AS FAR AS THE EYE COULD REACH, BEGAN TO MOVE — THE GUAHMAL WITH ITS SACRED LOAD BEING IN THE CENTRE — RECALLING VIVIDLY THE CHILDREN OF ISRAEL BEARING THE ARK THROUGH THE WILDERNESS. THE HARNESS, THE RICH TRAPPINGS, AND GAY COVERINGS OF THE TENTS, BORN ON THE BACKS OF CAMELS, GAVE THE WHOLE A GAY RATHER THAN A SOLEMN APPEARANCE."

Roberts visited al-Qarafa many times during his stay in Cairo. Al-Qarafa is overflowing with stunning Mamluk architecture and was known to be uncrowded, both great news for Roberts. On 16th January Roberts wrote in his diary:

> "MADE TWO DRAWINGS OF THE TOMBS OF THE CALIPHS. SUBJECTS VERY GOOD; THE DAY DELIGHTFUL."

I head to al-Qarafa in search of Sultan Qaitbey.

~~~~~~

When your taxi driver stops to ask for directions, you know you are really, really lost.

We have pulled over beside a tomb. A man leans against it, scraping wax from his ears using a ballpoint pen. After a rapid exchange in Arabic, the man points in the general direction of a jumble of buildings. The driver slaps the steering wheel in frustration. Clicking his tongue, he says,

"I know where it is. I need to know how to get there." With that, he floors the gas pedal, and the taxi peels off, wheels kicking dust.

John is embarrassed that we are having trouble getting to our destination. "I have not been here in twenty-five years," he confesses.

After driving through narrow dusty roads for a few minutes without the destination in sight, good sense eventually prevails. An address is punched into a smartphone. Once the driver follows the turn-by-turn directions provided by Google Maps, we find the complex of Sultan Al-Ashraf Qaitbey in a jiffy. (John says to me *sotto voce* that Arab drivers do not like to take directions from the "Google girl.")

A rash of single-storied buildings surround the mosque. Garage style steel shutters are being pushed up to reveal workshops

under asbestos roofs. Dogs lie in the middle of the road warming themselves in the early morning December sun. Weather-beaten early-year cars line the roadside, used as immovable storage units. If you could see through the layers of grime covering the metal, the cars would be a collector's delight in the West. In Egypt, old is not gold – unless you are in the tourism industry.

I pull out a binder from my khaki bag. It contains color printouts of Roberts' lithographs based on the sketches he made in Cairo. I flip through the sheaf of printouts until I find the lithograph titled *The Mosque of Sultan Qaitbey*. The portrait-oriented lithograph depicts an imposing Mamluk-era mosque with an intricately decorated dome and a minaret hemmed-in by ordinary buildings. In the foreground, people are going about their daily lives. Men are transacting business, seated on the back of mules. A small crowd has gathered to inspect goods imported from exotic regions. A sad soul shares his worries with a friend, receiving counsel and a friendly pat on the shoulder. Men enjoy the December sun, pulling on their waterpipes.

I hold the printout in my right hand, which is fully extended. It takes me a couple of minutes of shuffling back and forth until I find a spot where all the angles in the painting line up with the scene in front of me. I am now standing within a five-foot radius of the exact spot Roberts must have sat down to sketch the scene. John curiously peeps over my shoulder comparing the Roberts composition with the real-life scene. The Mamluk-era building on the left is now gone, replaced by a concrete building with a workshop named Mamluk Glass Works. Robert's lithograph shows a second building butting against the edifice of the mosque on the right. Glancing up, I can see a discolored patch on the front wall of the mosque, exactly where the second story would have leaned, the walls now gone, along with the lower wooden balconies. The mosque is in a splendid state of preservation – the elaborately carved three-tiered balconies of the minaret over the entrance, the double barrel vault recess at the entrance with the muqarnas, the ablaq façade, the vegetal and geometric motifs of the exquisitely carved dome, the carved wooden balconies of the loggia on the upper floor, matching Robert's description in his journal:

"...THOUGH MUCH DILAPIDATED, IS BEAUTIFUL IN FORM, AND ITS INTERNAL DECORATIONS ARE GORGEOUS."

"As a guide I am trained to see details that a visitor would miss," John whispers behind me. "Roberts sees details that I may miss."

In other words, John is having a David Roberts moment.

A boy of 10 or 11 years watches me sketch, my book ensconced in the crook of my arm. He fetches me a metal chair from the workshop. Fifteen minutes later he is back, balancing cups of mint tea on a shiny tray. He squats on his haunches next to me and watches me sketch like an American toddler watches YouTube. He waits patiently until I am done before asking, "Do you want to go inside the mosque? My uncle has a key."

The lad goes in search of his uncle, who is located with some old-school hollering, hands cupped to the lips. An old man with a long beard pulls a key from a keyring as large as a dinner plate. The door squeaks on unoiled hinges and we are let into the mosque, the ancient prayer hall quiet and sacred. The sun peeps through stained windows high on the walls – like a cardiac surgeon looking inside a heart, peering into a holy, unreachable space, a privilege afforded to a chosen few. As dust mites dance in the sun beam, I remind myself that this is the resting place of powerful Egyptian Sultans. Sultan Al-Ashraf Qaitbey ruled Egypt during times of economic upheavals with the enemies beating down at the gate. He was a patron of art and he built some of the most memorable monuments in Syria, Palestine and Egypt. He constructed for himself this elaborate funerary complex.

I wonder if the obscurity of his mausoleum is a philosopher's resounding success or a narcissist's abject failure.

Mosque of Sultan Hasan @ Cairo

SULTAN HASSAN

~~~~~~

The Sultan Hassan Mosque is situated a stone's throw away from Bab El Azab, the principal gate to the Citadel in the 1800s. The square outside the mosque, which is really a circle, has a lush green lawn that provides a rare vegetal spot for the eye to rest in the otherwise bone-dry Cairene cityscape.

At the mouth of the narrow alleyway in the entrance of the mosque, the binder comes out of my khaki bag again. The lithographs in the binder are arranged chronologically – a feat requiring good old sleuthing, since Roberts failed to date his sketches in Cairo. I flip to a painting, which had been the easiest to match to an entry in his journal.

On 1st January 1839, Roberts writes:

> "TWO DRAWINGS DONE TODAY — 'ENTRANCE TO THE MOSQUE OF SULTAN HASSAN', AND THE 'SUMMIT OF A MOSQUE.'"

I shuffle around until I have lined up the scene in front of me with the lines in the lithograph titled *Entrance to the Mosque of Sultan Hassan*. The composition is a typical Roberts street sketch – monumental architecture framing colorful local characters. It shows a crowded street: a Turkish merchant runs a roadside eatery under a striped canvas tent brimming with customers; a carpet seller convinces a young couple to take home a handspun beauty; tall Bedouins gossip dressed in the traditional kaftan and carry long-barreled muskets; *fellahin* wearing tattered *kamis* smoke the ubiquitous long chabouk. Above the day-to-day bustle rises the massive portal of the mosque, towering over neighboring multi-storied residential buildings. With his characteristic flair, Roberts managed to deftly convey the sheer size of the entrance, the intricate geometric design of the Mamluk period, and the half-dome stalactite vaultings.

The real-life scene in front of me has been dusted with modernity, but it hasn't structurally changed. The residential buildings are taller, the street level has risen. Smoke sticks have become shorter, texting on mobile phones has replaced conversation.

Inside the cavernous vestibule of Sultan Hassan, we surrender our shoes to the attendant. John switches to guide-mode and points out the salient architectural characteristics that make Sultan Hassan a gem of Mamluk religious design: the elaborate façade with stone *muqarnas* (stalactite work) in the half-dome above the entrance, the striped masonry of cream-colored limestone, the interlacing stones in different colors laid in intertwining fashion, the inscriptions in calligraphic Arabic script quoting the Qur'an.

Sultan Hassan looks like a fortress and it is built like one too. So large and sturdy is the mosque, and so close to the fortification walls of the citadel, that the Ottoman commanders in the fifteenth and sixteenth centuries were wary of the threat the mosque posed. They were especially worried that the minarets had a line of sight over the top of the citadel walls and could be potential sniper's nests.

A narrow dark passageway twists us to the right and then to the left. The street bustle quiets as we go deeper into the belly of the mosque. We pass a room that rings with the sounds of young boys repeating the verses of the Qur'an in unison. The passageway leads to a brightly lit courtyard open to the sky. The Friday prayers are still an hour away and the courtyard is empty. A woman in grey hijab sits on a plastic chair under a soaring arch, reading a Qur'an. A boy in trousers and a shirt two sizes too big works a vacuum cleaner as tall as him. A grandma in a black abaya watches two toddlers wrestle on the carpet. Under the shadow of the soaring hallway walls, away from all sight and sound of the city beyond, the courtyard is a perfect bubble in time and space.

I bring out another page from my binder and once again hold it up at eye level, maneuvering myself until all the elements in the painting line up with the scene in front of me. I find myself standing inches in front of a nook tucked into the northeast wall of the mosque. The nook promises a quiet sanctuary from probing eyes, where my sketchbook will not be conspicuous. I feel my two-day stubble bristle when I realize Roberts must have had the same thought too. Not only am I in Roberts' footsteps, but a little bit in his head too.

Roberts chose to compose what he sketched that day because it was the best possible composition *from the first good seat he found*. I perch in the nook myself and sketch. The azaan for the Friday prayer sounds. As I pack up, John, who has been patiently waiting in the shadows, asks to see my sketch.

"Will you be adding more details later?" he asks me, his eyes darting back and forth between my sketch and Roberts'.

I can hear loudly what John is *not* saying. Roberts' painting abounds in detail. Like a camera, it captures every intricate detail of the courtyard. My sketch, on the other hand, looks almost like a caricature.

Roberts was introducing the Western world to the interiors of Sultan Hassan. A civilization that grew up considering the Parthenon as the pinnacle of architectural achievement was about to see a completely unique and unknown style of architecture. The towering arches, the intricately carved wooden *minbars*, the flowing Arabic calligraphy, the holy men of Islam – their attitudes and mannerisms inside the mosque – were being unveiled to the west. Roberts had no choice but to be detailed. I, on the other hand, had no such obligation. Several books and

THE MOSQUE OF SULTAN HASSAN, CAIRO BY DAVID ROBERTS, R.A. 12TH JANUARY 1839

thousands of webpages, replete with color photographs of the courtyard, have done that task for me.

Roberts' painting is also a selfie. It establishes his presence in the courtyard as much as it establishes the courtyard itself. His eyes frame the point of view. He is telling the world that David Roberts saw this scene with his very own eyes. David Roberts was here. Whereas my sketch captures the memory of a few fleeting minutes spent in the five-hundred-year-old mosque. It is a little doodle in the margin of the notebook of my life. A note to self, meant to be forgotten almost as soon as it is written.

David Roberts journal entry of 12th January 1839:

"DREW THE MOSQUE OF SULTAN HASSAN. MADE ONLY ONE DRAWING OF THE COURT."

As it so happened, on the exact day that Roberts sat in that nook at the mosque of Sultan Hassan, an article was printed in the *Literary Gazette* in London. The article, titled "Fine Arts: The Daguerreotype," was authored by Hippolyte Gaucheraud, a journalist and a historian who described a demonstration he had witnessed that would forever change the history of human documentation.

Earlier that week, a motley crowd of scientists had gathered at Collège des Quatre-Nations, across from the Louvre, on the Left Bank of River Seine. In a large room with a vaulted ceiling and stained-glass windows opening onto a lovely garden, François Arago, a well renowned scientist, was presenting an invention to the Académie des Sciences. A *camera obscura* had been set up by covering all windows and doors of the room and allowing a tiny beam of light to pierce through a pinhole. The beam traveled across the darkness and created an upside-down mirror image within the chamber.

Mr. Arago proceeded to place a chemically treated copper plate under the image projected by the pinhole camera. After a few minutes, he plugged the pinhole. Once their eyes had adjusted to the new light, the crowd gasped. The image persisted on the copper plate. Photography had been born.

Louis Daguerre had been working on the technique to permanently capture the fleeting image of the *camera obscura* using light and chemistry. The show-and-tell in Paris was Louis Daguerre's attempt to find an investor for the invention that would forever change the world. The daguerreotype, as the photograph came to be known, writes the Met Museum on its website, "is a remarkably detailed, one-of-a-kind photographic image on a highly polished, silver-plated sheet of copper, sensitized with iodine vapors, exposed in a large box camera, developed in mercury fumes, and stabilized with saltwater."

Mr. Arago's sales pitch included a long list of the practical uses of photography in the fields of art and science. With remarkable foresight, and in keeping with the times during which travel to the Orient was on the rise, Mr. Arago included in his list, "a labor-saving means to copy the millions and millions of hieroglyphics, which entirely cover the great monuments at Thebes, Memphis and Carnac, etc."

Auguste Salzmann, an artist and an archaeologist, was an early pioneer of photography who visited the Holy Land in 1853. However, the earliest images he shot were unable to compete with the riot of colors the romantic painters put out. His images were sepia, the camera was bulky, and the processing tedious. Furthermore, assembling compositions that resembled the painted images – wide-angle views with strong foregrounds and scenic backgrounds – was difficult because of cultural and logistical hurdles. Hence, rather than being artistic, the early images of the Holy Land turned out to be documentary in nature, merely evidence to support Western assumptions of how the Holy Land looked.

David Roberts' paintings were the benchmark of the Middle Eastern image – colorful, exotic, and unchanged since the days of Nativity. When Francis Frith, another pioneer of photography who made some of the earliest images of the Holy Land, traveled to Egypt between 1857 and 1860, he was traveling in Roberts' footsteps. "For Frith, the impetus towards Egypt must have been its artistic presentation by David Roberts," writes Caroline Williams in an essay titled *A nineteenth century photographer: Francis Frith*. "Frith often photographed the same scenes that David Roberts had drawn." That is because Roberts' sketches of the Holy Land were the best and most accurate representation of the Holy Land, as is evident from a caption Francis Frith wrote under a photo of the fallen

colossus at the Ramesseum in Thebes. "David
Roberts in his splendid work has bestowed
upon it a very respectable and recognizable
profile, but my picture shows that the face
is so mutilated as scarcely to leave a feature
traceable." Unable to match the opulence
of David Roberts' painting using early-stage
cameras, he instead chose to demonstrate
the technology's ability to record accuracy.
Ruefully he added "A truthful record is of
more value than the most elaborate beautiful
picture."

AL FISHAWI

~~~~~

John and I are sitting at a table in a narrow alley outside El-Fishawi, Cairo's oldest coffee shop, situated in Khan el Khalili, Cairo's oldest public bazaar. El Fishawi has been around for two hundred and fifty years – the Khan el Khalili, twice as long. People from all walks of life stop here for a spot of coffee and a pull on the *sheeshas*. Napoleon's soldiers would often come here for a shot of their favorite Turkish mud. Roberts' 1838 residence in Cairo is nearby and he must have passed through here daily. His portfolio has one lithograph of a Cairene coffee shop. Was it made at El Fishawi?

I am already feeling a sense of achievement within the first two days of the adventure. It is abundantly evident to me that Cairo is architecturally unchanged since Roberts' visit eighteen decades ago. The vagaries of time have been very kind to the city, or very cruel depending on the point of view. Monuments, buildings, streets and squares in Cairo are intact. There are neighborhoods in India where I grew up that I cannot recognize after thirty years, my eyes unable to find traces of places indelibly etched in my childhood memories, so fast has modernization changed them. I had braced myself to have to stretch my imagination to see Roberts' Cairo.

Inside the well-preserved Islamic Cairo, I had pinpointed the exact spot from which Roberts sketched the courtyard of Sultan Hassan. Only standing in that courtyard was I able understand why Roberts had chosen to sit where he sat. In doing so I felt like I had peeped into Roberts' psyche across all the intervening years. My reason for following in Roberts' footsteps was to learn from a master travel sketcher. And I had been given the first lesson in composition. "Photography is first and foremost the art of seeing," Ansel Adam was known to say, a philosophy that can be easily applied to sketching. The art of seeing ergo framing the subject or deciding what to compose defines an artist's style as much as his color palette and brush strokes. I had imagined Roberts scoping out a variety of angles under different light conditions before settling on one he was happy with. Except once inside the courtyard of Sultan Hassan, the bashful Roberts had ensconced himself in the first nook he found where his back was against a wall, nobody could peep into his sketchbook, and he was tucked away from glaring eyes. From that safe spot, Roberts made the best of the scene in front of him. His seat had determined the composition, not the other way around.

My journey in Roberts' footsteps is a quest to follow and learn from the earliest known travel sketchers of all times. Stand where he stood and sketch what he sketched – my goal is now clear to me. The goal also automatically, and inadvertently, simplifies the logistics of traveling in one of the most complicated regions in the world. So quickly had the trip come together, that I had not taken time to think through the nitty-gritty details. Figuring out the trip was to be part of the trip. And now I no longer have to figure out how to get into Gaza or enter Lebanon from Israel. Against the contemporary travel philosophy, the destination is going to be the journey.

With that detail sorted in my head, I can finally concentrate on the waiter gliding between the tables at El Fishawi, balancing a brass tray on his fingers. He has half the elegance of a Ritz Carlton waiter but twice the hustle. As he moves rapidly from table to table, dropping frosted bottles of water for his customers, he puts an open cup of water in front of me.

"That's because you look Egyptian," John laughs. "Only the tourists get bottled water."

The air is laden with the aroma of fresh coffee and burning tobacco. I look around. There are as many cups of water on tables as bottles, a heartening sign that locals are returning to their favorite coffee shop after the tourist onslaught of pre-Arab Spring days. That was the good news.

"Tourists are no longer coming to Egypt," John sounds the bad news.

Waves of tourists have come to Egypt in the years since Napoleon opened the doors to the Orient. The decoding of Egypt's hieroglyphics in the 1820s brought the scholars and the early explorers. Thomas Cook's tours in the 1860s made the Nile accessible to the average traveler. Howard Carter's discovery of Tutankhamun's treasures in 1920s proved that Egypt was not a sucked orange. In the 1990s *National Geographic* produced a series of spectacular documentaries focused on discovery and decoding of Egypt in collaboration with Egypt's Head of Antiquities, Zahi Hawass, triggering another wave. Each wave greedily bought into the mysticism of the Orient accompanied by the inimitable sounds and flavors of Islamic Africa, the awe-inspiring grandeur of the pharaonic monuments and the romance of ruins in the desert.

In 2010, Egypt saw the arrival of 15 million visitors – the most ever. Then came the revolution of 2011. Thousands died in bloody protests to unseat the

El-Fishawi, OldCairo

El Fishawy, Khan el-Khalili

president-dictator Hosni Mubarak, who had governed Egypt for thirty years. Protests erupted again in 2013 to unseat his successor, President Morsi. In 2015 a Russian airliner was downed in the wilderness of the Sinai, killing all 224 passengers on board. That same year, the Egyptian armed forces fired rockets and 30mm machine guns from Apache helicopters at a tour group in the Bahariya oasis, killing six. The touring group, despite taking all necessary precautions including procuring the correct permits and traveling with state-provided security, had been mistaken for Islamic jihadists.

Terror and tourism do not mix. Tourists suffer from sheep mentality. The meek followers are sent scurrying by the slightest uncertainty. Globally, 2015 was the biggest year for tourism. Over one billion people, almost a fifth of the world's population, traveled that year on the back of a roaring economy, global peace, cheap air travel, the advent of social media, and a generation that bought into the mantra of investing in experiences that create memories. Notably, Egypt and parts of the Middle East missed this boom. The region was and remains in the troughs of a tourist recession. Ninety percent of the people whose livelihoods depend on tourism have lost their revenue stream.

From Cairo to Beirut, I experienced the tourist paucity at close quarters. The Middle East is looking for ideas to figure its way out of the recession.

"Every time the economy was in recession, Zahi Hawass would come to the rescue," John says. "He would find a lost mummy or eke out a hidden chamber in the pyramid. He knew how to keep the Egyptian story alive." Zahi Hawass was part of President Mubarak's circle, and the new regime has Zahi cooling his heel on the sidelines.

"Mark my words. Zahi Hawass is not yet history," John roots for the famous Egyptologist.

A glass stuffed with fresh mint leaves is placed in front of me. Piping hot tea is poured into it from a blue teapot held three feet above the table. Sipping the sweet treat through the froth, John recognizes a senior cabinet minister entertaining a guest at a nearby table. The minister's security detail occupies nearby tables – well-built, clean shaven youngsters trying to blend into a crowd of swarthy, bearded El Fishawi regulars. The bodyguards all bulge at the waist, hiding their service revolvers; the rest flaunt their penchant for falafel.

A group of women occupies a cluster of tables in a different part of the coffee shop. Aged between sixteen and sixty, they are dressed in a variety of veils and scarves that display the full spectrum of Islamic dress code. The elders wear the draconian *niqaab*, which covers the whole body with just a fishnet rectangle for the eyes. The middle-aged women are draped in *hijabs*, which expose only the oval of their faces. The youngest sport bandanas that barely touch their hair, the cloth more a fashion accessory than conformance to religious code. The *hijabs* are worn with an assortment of dresses: traditional Arabic kaftans, loose trousers, long tops, ripped jeans and short skirts. It is a collection of The United Burkhas of Cairo, a beautiful lineup of *muhajabat* (veiled women). The women pull on long tubes of *sheesha*, dragging hot air over burning charcoal, vaporizing the flavored tobacco without burning it, bubbling it through water, gurgling like children slurping soda. In Hindi, India's national language, the verb form of "the act of smoking" is drinking. The phrase "smoking a cigarette" is "cigarette *peena*," which translates back as "drinking" a cigarette. I now understand how the Arabic cultural nuance has traveled across geography and languages.

"El Fishawi is one of the few places in Cairo where women can let their hair down." John says, and on cue, the women break into a song. A musician materializes from the souks as if an invisible hand has rubbed an invisible lamp. He brings with him a mandolin that he plays vigorously and encourages the group to sing more. Their singing grows louder, the songs more raucous, the words coarse and lewd. The women ululate and clap. Many customers in the café join them, feet stomping and cheering.

There is something heartening about this scene. Two days before, President Trump had formally recognized Jerusalem as the capital of Israel. He ordered the relocation of the US embassy from Tel Aviv to the holy city. The announcement sounded like a match being struck inside a gunpowder warehouse. A violent reaction from the Arab world would light the fuse. Retaliation from any of the hundreds of fringe Islamic militants would set this region ablaze. The Western world, especially the United States, held its collective breath, not knowing what to expect.

And here, sitting in the oldest part of the old city of Cairo – as conservative a neighborhood as it gets anywhere in the world – I am witnessing a "live and let live" moment. Inclusion and tolerance are on display, confidently rubbing shoulders with tradition and faith. My sweet tea tastes sweeter.

~~~~~

In the fourteenth century, global trade was booming despite the plague – Black Death – having devastated Europe. Many trade routes converged in Cairo. From Sudan came ivory and gold; from Arabia came myrrh and frankincense; from India came cloves, pepper, and cardamom; from Ethiopia came slaves. The goods proceeded from Cairo to the ports of Alexandria and Gaza on the Mediterranean and from there traveled to Venice and Genoa for their onward journey deeper into Europe. The Ottoman conquered Istanbul in 1453 and easterly trade routes came under their control. The price of goods skyrocketed under the Muslim monopoly and *khans* along the trade routes prospered. The khan in Cairo was the pulsating center of the city, where traders traded during the day and slept amidst their camel trains at night, a medieval motel for the medieval traveling salesman.

The West was getting desperate. Neither could they afford the price of the spices nor the thought of eating their meat and potatoes without it. Vasco Da Gama sailed around the horn of Africa at the end of the fifteenth century and forged a route that was free of the tariff. As commercial traffic switched to the new route, the caravans rolling into Cairo dwindled and the markets in Cairo crashed. The trade-centered ecosystem quickly buckled, affecting every citizen of Cairo directly or indirectly. The khan was the ground zero of the recession. In a last-ditch attempt to revive Cairo's economy, the Sultan ordered the demolition of the open-air khan and in its place a covered structure was built. The new bazaar – Khan el Khalili – was secured with strong gates in the hope that the covered bazaar would attract a trade of precious goods. Ancient Cairo had done what cities in trouble do even today – demolished a strip mall to erect a supermarket to attract higher value trade.

Back in the day, Khan el Khalili was a maze of streets, an ancient supermarket with well-demarcated areas for copper, cotton, silk, spices, weapons, jewelry, fortune-telling, fruit, fresh vegetables, household utensils, birds, animals, and slaves. As much a place for traders as for the citizens to procure their daily essentials: that was how it was when Roberts visited and that is how it is still.

BAYN AL-QASRAYN

~~~~~~

"Honest, god-fearing citizens can buy everything on their *begum's* grocery list in the open market of the khan," John says, "The not-so-honest only need to know where to knock." John manages to utter a suggestive statement without suggesting anything untoward. Weaving through waves of humanity, we cross a busy street. The rush hour traffic is snarling, impatience and aggression locked in a vicious cycle. At the head of a tiny street that dips between two massive Mamluk-style buildings, John steps aside to make a phone call.

Something about this location feels very familiar. Am I getting a flashback from my 2006 visit or is this just a glitch in the matrix? Like scratching the general area to pinpoint an elusive itch, I look around searching for clues. The tiny street pinched between the buildings. Pop-up shops selling cheap clothes. A wooden staircase leading to a mosque. Lamps hanging from a wooden lintel. A wooden roof with a skylight. Lamps…wooden lintel …wooden roof … skylight!

The piaster finally drops!

I know where I am! I am standing in the middle of a famous Roberts painting titled *The Bazaar of the Silk Merchants in Cairo*. The composition is typical

BAZAAR OF THE SILK MERCERS, CAIRO BY DAVID ROBERTS, R.A.
JANUARY 1839

Roberts fare: monumental architecture framing a colorful, local street scene. It captures a typical winter afternoon in North Africa – sunny but cold. Merchants have set up stalls under a wooden roof installed between the two Mamluk roofs. The shopkeepers, dressed in traditional winter coats, take a breather as the onslaught of customers has subsided in the hour after lunch. Oriental handspun carpets, camel leather shoes, and other wares are on display. Roberts accurately captures the intricate details of the Islamic buildings – the latticed windows, the lamps hanging from the doorway, the massive half-domed niches, the beautiful calligraphy that depicts verses of the Qur'an.

John sees me smile. He wraps up his phone call and says, "I knew you would get a kick out of it." He is beaming from ear to ear. He has set up this moment thoughtfully. He led me to the location and waited patiently, allowing me the delicious sensation of discovery.

The Bayn al-Qasrayn is several feet lower than it was in 1839, undoubtedly the result of successive excavations for modern construction. The shopkeepers smoke cigarettes instead of *shisha*, wear faux leather bomber jackets instead of the long, striped robes as they hawk knick-knacks in their shops. Otherwise, the street hasn't changed much.

I lean against a wooden post and balance the sketchbook in the nook of my arm. I sketch fast. The Cairene hustle and bustle carefully curves around me as I sketch for the next hour to my heart's content. Occasionally, a passerby slows down to peep at my sketchbook. A question or two is thrown at me, which I field with a smile and a nod of my head.

"They think you are Egyptian," John laughs and translates the Arabic queries of the passersby. "They are wondering how you have so much free time to stand and stare." A passing woman scowls at me and hides her toddler daughter in the folds of her black *burkha* as if I were pointing a camera at them. An orange-seller looks quaint in his jute robe, so I add him to my composition. Halfway through, I look up and he is gone, leaving his oranges behind. I hear a grunt of approval at my right elbow and there he is, watching me sketch. For an incurable introvert like me, these languageless interactions with the locals is a big part of the fun of street sketching. I dip a brush in the humanity around me and apply it to the sketchbook. I capture a cross section of people's lives, snatch a moment in the fast-flowing river of time and put it onto the page. Every line is soaked with everyday stories, every stroke a strand of DNA carrying memories of a society.

Roberts did not share my philosophy. He writes about being interrupted, pushed, touched and having his sketchbook knocked out of his hands by a half-eaten orange tossed from one of the overhanging windows. He finds, "...drawing (is) a most arduous undertaking in these narrow stinking streets..." He further adds, "...I have stood working in the crowded streets of Cairo, jostled and stared at till I came home sick." His eye for detail, his expert draftsmanship, and the sense of drama he brings to his sketches and paintings shine despite the considerable discomfort he felt while sketching. His private space, a thoroughly Western concept, was repeatedly invaded by the pushing and shoving – an oriental routine.

"NO ONE LOOKING OVER MY SKETCHES WILL EVER THINK OF THE TROUBLE THE COLLECTION OF THEM HAS COST ME."

What else would a European gentleman, disguised as a Turk, toting a sketchbook, standing in the middle of one of the busiest streets of Cairo in the nineteenth century, expect? Roberts detested but innately understood his situation when he wrote:

"FANCY AN ARAB IN AN ENGLISH COUNTRY TOWN. WOULD THE PEOPLE BEHAVE BETTER... IF THE SAID ARAB WERE TO SPREAD HIS CARPET AND GO TO PRAYERS, WHICH IS THEIR CUSTOM 5 OR 6 TIMES A DAY."

~~~~~

Napoleon's invasion was the first time Egyptians encountered Europeans *en masse*. During Napoleon's short stay, the Franks – as the Westerners were called – were pork-eating, idol-worshipping, technology-laced intruders, whose women were scandalously uncovered. The white men, for once, did not enjoy the god-like status that was bestowed on them by the Incas in Southern America or by the tribes of central Africa. The artifacts of the Islamic golden age were ubiquitous and a living proof that the white man was modern but less cultured. After Napoleon hastily retreated, his military campaign in shambles, Mohamed Ali Pasha stepped into the power vacuum. The Pasha had cleverly understood the need to modernize the country as a means of displacing the waning Ottoman empire. Modernization needed technology and know-how from the West. The Pasha opened his arms wide to welcome the West to the Orient. Sighting a Frank in the streets of Cairo was no longer a rarity. But in the 1830s and 1840s, they were still rank outsiders and considered Pasha's stooges: pale skinned people of strange faith and interests. People who did not understand the local customs and made no effort to do so. People who could not stand the heat or the dust or the desert. People interested in ruins. Weak. Meek, yet strangely powerful. Everything about the white man was as foreign as foreign could be.

AL GHURI

~~~~~

The first mosque Roberts entered almost turned out to be his last.

In January 1839, dressed as a Turkish army officer, Roberts stepped into the mosque of Al-Ghuri. He was accompanied by a bodyguard assigned by the Pasha and was the first Christian to ever set his foot inside the sixteenth century mosque, a fact that Robert must have been acutely aware of. A special one-time *firman* from Mohammed Ali Pasha had allowed Roberts the privilege to enter and sketch in any of the 400 mosques in Cairo as long as he complied with two rules: he had to dress and behave as a Turk would – cultured and sophisticated – and could not use paintbrushes made of pig hair, as pigs are considered *haram* in the Islamic world. So thrilled was Roberts at this prospect that he even agreed to shave his facial hair, writing in his journal this line about applying the straight razor to his mutton chops:

> "THIS IS TOO BAD; BUT HAVING TAKEN SUCH
> A LONG JOURNEY, I MUST NOT STICK AT
> TRIFLES."

One can only imagine the mixture of terror and excitement Roberts must have felt at stepping inside the mosque, crossing the threshold into a domain so foreign and uncontrolled. Since his arrival in Egypt, Roberts had walked in the footsteps of explorers that had come before him. He had followed their itineraries judiciously, carefully working within the known boundaries of safety. For the very first time, there was no precedent to what he was about to experience.

Roberts must have tried to find solace in the experience he had with mosques. In 1832, he had traveled to Spain, a country that wasn't widely visited at the time (because "everybody else had been painting Italy"). He traveled to every major city in Spain and experienced a variety of European architecture, which he sketched to put together a wonderful portfolio. In Cadiz and Cordoba, Roberts made hundreds of sketches and studies inside the mosques, an investment that was starting to pay him rich dividends in Cairo.

Once the initial excitement of stepping inside a North African mosque subsided, Roberts became the keen observer he was. Known for his powerful visual memory, Roberts could recall intricate details of a scene after just a cursory glance. Roberts' sensory perceptions must have been in overdrive by the profusion of elaborate Mamluk art and architecture that surrounded him in Cairo. As his eyes hungrily absorbed the details, he relaxed. He forgot the instructions given to him – *Act like a local at all times*. Emboldened temporarily by the dimly lit interiors and the false safety of the Turkish uniform, he joined a small crowd gathered around a green silk cloth in one of the side rooms of the mosque. Going with the flow, he knelt in front of the cloth, which had designs made with golden thread. Others around him kissed the cloth in devotion but a wide-eyed Roberts reached out for the cloth, his fingers feeling the texture of the material.

He writes in his journal:

> "ON LIFTING MY EYES, I SAW MY ATTENDANT
> FIRST PUT HIS FINGER ON HIS LIP AND THEN
> ACROSS HIS THROAT... HIS GESTURE TOLD ME
> THAT IF I DID NOT FOLLOW HIM THE RESULT
> MIGHT BE FATAL."

Roberts showed remarkable presence of mind. He calmly prostrated before the cloth one more time, this time kissing it, then rising unhurriedly he made his way out of the mosque. Once outside, he ran pell-mell through the streets of Cairo, glad to have made it out alive. The cloth was being prepared for a journey to Mecca where it would cover the tomb of the prophet. Roberts' childlike curiosity and impulsive action had ousted him both as a foreigner and a non-believer. Roberts would have been lynched on the spot for contaminating the holy cloth. His bodyguard stood no chance of saving him.

This story is fresh in my mind as I hand over my shoes at the entrance and feel the ice-cold five-hundred-year-old marble floors suck the body heat out of me though my socks. John stops to pay his respect to the Imam, a striking man with a long, beautiful beard. The hand the Imam proffers is soft and smooth. It is a hand that has never lifted an object heavier than a holy Qur'an. He patiently listens to me talk about my project, but it becomes apparent that he has never heard of David Roberts. I show the Imam Roberts' sketch of the interiors of the al-Ghuri mosque, like the proud parent of an overachieving student meeting the class teacher at school.

The painting, titled the *Interiors of the Mosque of the Sultan El Ghouree,* beautifully captures minute details of the interior of the mosque: the qibla iwan with the decorated *minbar,* the details of the stained-glass windows, the Qur'anic verses in *Thuluth* script under the wooden muqarnas. Roberts could not have possibly sketched any of this on that fateful day at al-Ghuri, as he was too busy escaping before his actions became known. He must have either reproduced the scene completely from memory or, more likely, he returned to the mosque later to sketch, an act of daring that should earn him some kudos.

INTERIOR OF THE MOSQUE OF THE SULTAN EL GHOREE
BY DAVID ROBERTS, R.A. JANUARY 1939

"What do you think?" I ask, anticipating nothing but words of praise.

The Imam clucks his tongue and shakes his head in disapproval. He points to the figure of a man kneeling in a red shirt.

"He is praying in the wrong direction."

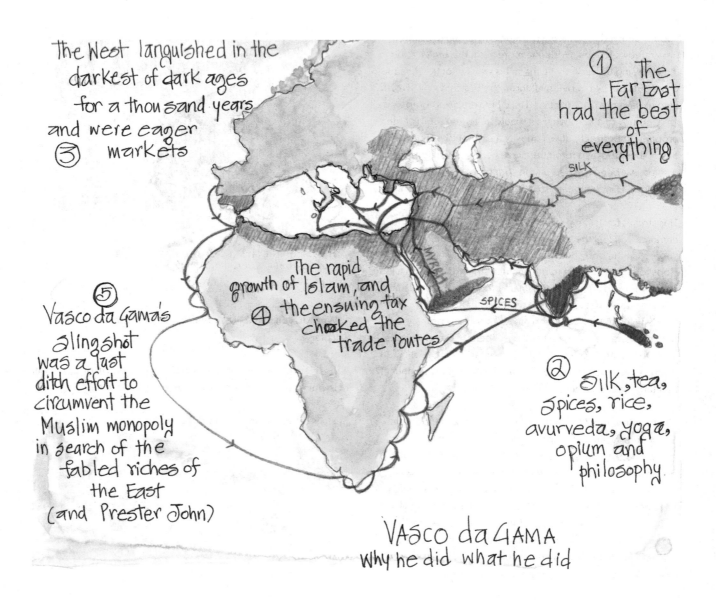

The West languished in the darkest of dark ages for a thousand years and were eager ③ markets

① The Far East had the best of everything

SILK

MYRRH

The rapid growth of Islam, and ④ the ensuing tax choked the trade routes

SPICES

⑤ Vasco da Gama's slingshot was a last ditch effort to circumvent the Muslim monopoly in search of the fabled riches of the East (and Prester John)

② Silk, tea, spices, rice, avurveda, yoga, opium and philosophy.

VASCO da GAMA
Why he did what he did

Sultan Qansuh al-Ghuri, the patron of the mosque and the second-to-last Sultan of the Mamluk dynasty, was a lover of art and architecture, as is evident in the attention lavished on decorating the interior of the beautiful mosque. Great art comes at a great price. The price was paid by Sultan's subjects, who felt harassed by the extravagant taxes imposed on them.

The Sultan, in turn, was being harassed by the Portuguese in the second decade of the sixteenth century. Vasco De Gama's sea route to India bypassed the Muslim world disrupting the Sultan's revenues. When diplomacy and war did not help to reinstate the trade routes, the Sultan used his last leverage: he threatened to lay waste to those Christian holy sites that remained on Muslim-controlled territory after the failed Crusades. When that ploy did not work either, Sultan Ghuri reached out to the Ottoman, an emerging power in eastern Europe. The Sultan invited the Ottoman, who had an axe to grind with the Christians, the proverbial enemy of the enemies, to build a navy and neutralize the Portuguese armada in the Indian ocean. That plan failed too, but not before the Ottoman had gained a foothold on Egyptian soil. The Ottoman continued to gnaw on Sultan Ghuri's empire from the north and soon annexed Syria. Ghuri rushed into a battle with the Ottoman in the Northern Desert, never to return. His body never made it back to the beautiful mausoleum he had constructed in Cairo. With Ghuri out of the way, the Mamluk dynasty extinguished. The Ottoman rode into Egypt and ruled for the next three hundred years.

With the Imam's permission, we push open a heavy door at the back of the mosque and slip into a dark corridor. Our footsteps echo as we cross the roof of the sixteenth century construction. We are already several stories above the street, and still climbing. We pass through a labyrinth of doors and corridors before the staircase narrows and spirals upwards. My breath becomes shallow and urgent, my flashlight illuminating discarded cans of coke and empty packets of Lays chips. When there are no more steps to climb, we exit onto a balcony high up on the minaret.

A sea of sand-colored buildings stretches all the way to the horizon. The twin minarets of Bab Zuweila. The twin minarets of Sultan Hassan. The spiral minaret of Ibn Tulun. The gigantic mass of the Citadel. The hubbub of Muizz Street. The minarets of al-Azhar, the university older than Cairo. From this elevation, Cairo is a map, not a city. From here the city looks permanent. Infallible. The city has withstood the last one thousand years with grace and from here it looks capable of withstanding ten thousand more.

GIZA

〜〜〜〜

A beige sky hangs over a beige city. A stiff, cold wind from the desert huffs and puffs at the clouds, to no avail. The bridge over the River Nile connects the ancient city of Cairo to the antiquity of Giza. The traffic is already crawling at this early hour. The pyramids, bathed in the pre-sunrise light, fill the windscreen as the taxi descends the ramp to leave the highway. There is not much left to say about the first sight of the Pyramids that has not already been said more eloquently by more qualified people. I choose to gape in rapt silence.

John has a prior engagement, and I am on my own. He has left me with more instructions than the father of a teenager on her first evening out at the mall. The taxi drops me in front of a roadside coffee shop. A man in a flowing jute robe pours me a cup of muddy Turkish coffee from a brass *kanaka*. I nurse the scalding hot cup and wait for the ticket office to open.

I am the only person at the ticket window when it finally squeaks opens, a telltale sign of the dwindled tourist footfall since the Arab Spring of 2011. When I was here in 2006, the courtyard was jostling with several hundred camera-toting tourists. After buying my ticket, I follow a long line of flatulent camels who don't look happy to be up so early in the morning; their manners mirror those of their owners. The clouds clear as I walk towards the pyramids. The sun makes an appearance. The plateau heats up quickly. I am the only tourist at the oldest and longest surviving tourist spot in the history of human civilization.

In ancient times, the silhouette of the pyramids, visible several miles into the open desert, would be a sight to behold for a traveler approaching the Nile through the undulating sand dunes of the Western Desert. Fatigued, hungry, his parched tongue sticking to the roof of his mouth, he would squint at the horizon – blurry behind heat eddies and dust storms. The razor-sharp lines of the pyramids piercing the sky would look like an act of God. Even in modern times, with advanced know-how and technology, the monumental constructions seem beyond the capacity of the human race, their existence connected to God or extra-terrestrials, the two indistinguishable in the mist of ignorance and faith.

A bearded Egyptian has captured a spot of shade and a patch of *Khafre* to lean against. His neck craned upwards; he is perhaps the only *other* human being on the plateau looking at the pyramids. I set myself up a few feet away from him, allowing the Saharan sun to warm my back. I would have thought he was asleep had his right hand not moved like a well-oiled piston to feed a cigarette into his mouth periodically.

Salaam-alaikum. A camel-riding cop on his daily beat greets him. A man selling tea places a glass next to him without being asked. The guide leading the first tourist litter of the day waves at him enthusiastically and shouts, "Gamal, I have some questions for you. I will come see you later." Nobody asks Gamal if he wants a camel ride. Nobody tries to sell him hand-made beads made from the clay of the Nile. Nobody disturbs Gamal's reverie. Clearly, Gamal is a frequent flier around here. And, by sheer proximity, I have inadvertently wrapped myself in his invisible bubble, keeping the plateau pests away.

The pyramids can be underwhelming to some. Firstly, because everything that can be said about them has been said. Very little is left to imagine. Secondly, the pyramid has been described in numbers that are not understood easily: It is as tall as a forty-five-story building (approximately 450 ft). An average block of the pyramid stone weighs as much as a Humvee (about 2.5 tons.) The base area of the pyramid equals that of the Windsor

Castle. The truth of the matter is that a forty-five-story building is not too tall for a New Yorker, nobody has tried to lift an armored truck, and where is Windsor Castle anyway?

A visitor standing at a certain distance from the face of the pyramid realizes that every thin, unwavering, horizontal line is a row of granite blocks about five feet tall. As the gaze traverses up the pyramid, the monolithic pile breaks down into individual stones until the neck is bent at an uncomfortable angle and the sun is shining in the eyes. Then, the mind is blown.

"So why did they build it?" I hear Gamal say at the exact moment I am overtaken by amazement, my neck bent at an obtuse angle, discerning the size of the stone blocks of the topmost layers.

"Excuse me?"

"It looked like you were about to ask that question."

"There are some interesting theories making the rounds," I reply. I reel off a few: electricity generator, Alexander the Great's burial

place, grain silo, antennae capable of reaching a civilization far, far away, the Egyptian Book of the Dead symbolized in stone. Storm bunker for mankind. Firesafe of human knowledge. A sonic machine.

"Never judge a man by the cover of the book he is pretending to read," Gamal says, tapping the book lying face down by his side. I had spotted it earlier. It is the kind of book that gets tagged as a pioneering study, a reinterpretation of sacred architecture, a controversial investigation, a series of explosive findings, an alternate theory, sensational. Archaeologists and scientists would call it "Yellow Egyptology."

We have a good laugh. He orders a glass of mint tea for me. He asks about my sketchbook. We talk about Roberts for a few minutes. I read out Roberts' terse entry dated 17th January 1839 from his journal:

"VISITED THE PYRAMIDS OF GEEZEH. MADE THREE SKETCHES. I CANNOT EXPRESS MY FEELINGS ON SEEING THESE VAST MONUMENTS."

Roberts writes precisely as many lines as the number of sketches he made on that day. I pull out of my backpack a copy of the very sketches – probably the driest and stiffest of all Robert's lithographs in his Egypt and Holy Land portfolio. Roberts was unable to employ his hitherto successful device of posing colorful local people against the monumental edifices in the background – the scale of the pyramids is so massive that the foreground loses all definition.

I share with Gamal my other gripe: Robert's journal is also tantalizingly silent about the most startling and recent archaeological discovery in Egypt at the time. (Not that one. Howard Carter would not stumble upon Tutankhamen's tomb for another 88 years.) Colonel Howard Vyse, a distinguished

British military man, parliamentarian, and amateur Egyptologist, had used gunpowder a few months before Roberts' visit to blast open four cavities located above the King's chamber of the Great Pyramid, cavities that had been hermetically sealed since the time the Great Pyramid was built. No royal treasure was found – no gold, no gems, no glittering riches, but instead the only tangible link ever found between the pharaoh and the pyramid named after him was discovered. Colonel Vyse had found graffiti in tight confines and inscriptions or quarry marks of the work-gangs whose names included variants of Pharaoh Khufu's name. During his stay in Cairo, Roberts had rubbed shoulders with many people who had played a role in the discovery of the graffiti, including a certain Mr. Hill, whose hotel in Cairo Roberts frequented, and Colonel Campbell, who was responsible for getting both Colonel Vyse and Roberts the necessary *firman*. But, alas, Roberts stays silent on the subject. It is the equivalent of being in New York in the second half of September 2001 without mentioning airplanes flying into tall buildings.

Gamal opens the book he is reading to a page that uses one of Roberts' lesser-known sketches of upper Egypt without giving Roberts photo credit. That brings the topic back to the book and pyramidology. Gamal claims, without making it sound like a boast, to have read every theory about the origin, construction, and purpose of the pyramids. I ask him, without making it sound too much like a challenge, for his favorite alternate theory. After some persuasion, he tells me.

The story goes as follows: Caliph al-Ma'mun of Baghdad, son of Harun al-Rashid of One Thousand and One Nights fame, is exploring the pyramids in search of the fabled treasures of the pharaoh. Failing to find the entrance to the Great Pyramid, his men blast a hole on the seventh level of the north face. After digging several feet into the belly of the pyramid, his men hear a rock rolling deep inside the pyramid. Intrigued, they turn the tunnel in the direction of the sound and make a breakthrough.

The tunnel emerges inside the pyramid exactly at the intersection of an ascending and a descending passage. The excited men explore further and find plugs set in the ascending passage, which they clear to discover the Grand Gallery. Al-Ma'mun is called to the dig and he personally enters the King's Chamber. He finds nothing but an empty sarcophagus. No traces of the fabled pharaonic treasures.

Gamal uses his finger to draws a schematic of the two passages, the Grand Gallery and the Kings Chamber, in the dust. Then he asks a rhetorical question: what are the mathematical chances of al-Mamun's men serendipitously, and blindly, finding the exact intersection of the ascending and descending passage?

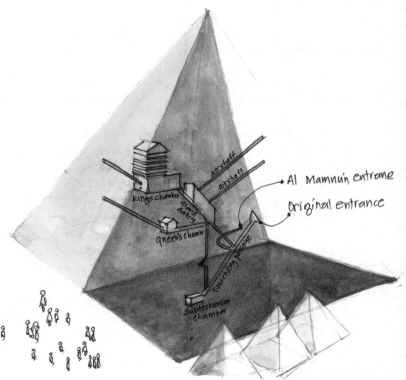

Then he describes a theory that explains how the tunnel so accurately breaches such a critical spot. A more palatable logical sequence of events would be as follows:

The workers enter the pyramid through the formal entrance of the Great Pyramid, which was well known at the time. The explorers descend the passage and discover the limestone plug that seals the ascending passage. They find a way around the plug and discover the Grand Gallery. Al-Ma'mun is summoned. Al-Ma'mun enters the King's Chamber and makes a startling discovery: an artifact of great historical value. The artifact is too large to navigate the awkward angle of the ascending and the descending passages. As a last resort, al-Ma'mun's men dig a passage from the inside and the tunnel emerges at the seventh level of the pyramid. That is how the tunnel perfectly intercepts the very spot where the ascending and descending passages meet.

But it leaves a big question unanswered. I ask because somebody has to. "What do you think they found?"

"That's a sixty-four thousand ducat question, my friend," Gamal replies, not implicating himself any further in the theory.

In the fifth century BC, the Greek mathematician Thales used a stick to calculate the height of the Great Pyramid using basic trigonometry. The ratio of the length of the stick to the length of its shadow would apply to the height of the pyramid and the length of its shadow at the same time of day. In the seventeenth century, John Greaves, an English mathematician and antiquarian, accurately measured the pyramid using the best equipment available to him. He used the measurements to propose an Egyptian unit of measure, which he called the Royal Cubit. In the middle of eighteenth century, Sir Isaac Newton used the Royal Cubit to calculate the circumference of the earth while proving his Theory of Gravity. His hypothesis was that

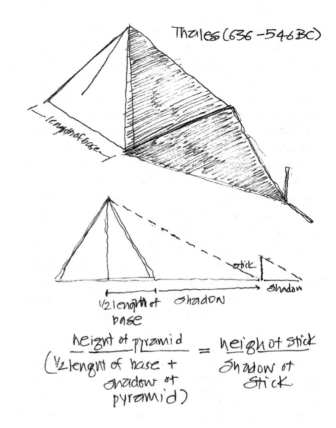

a structure as stupendous as the Great Pyramid would most certainly enshrine geographical and celestial measurements – lengths, angles and ratios. In the middle of the nineteenth century an essayist, John Taylor, figured out that the ratio of the perimeter of the pyramid to the height approached the value of pi. Around the same time, Charles Smyth, Astronomer Royal of Scotland, published the first cross-sectional view of the pyramid that accurately showed the location and angles of the passages inside. He believed that the pyramid-inch was a divine unit of measurement, handed over by the Gods to humankind and that God himself had played a role in its construction. After that publication, Pyramidomania exploded.

I ask Gamal if he has formed his own pyramid theory. He pins me with his thousand-meter stare for a few moments, deciding if I am qualified to hear what he was about to say. He takes a long drag of his cigarette and blows a thick smoke ring into the desert air. Then he launches into it.

"The Great Pyramid is an ode to Pythagoras, not a pharaoh," Gamal says, in a tone that reminds me of my childhood story-time hour that started with the phrase *Once upon a time...*

"It is estimated that a few trillion human hours have been spent solving a Rubik's cube. Twenty-seven interlocking cubes have kept human race busy for a long time. Yet it took Erno Rubik just eighteen months to perfect the mechanism of the puzzle. A couple of thousand hours of one ingenious mind kept millions of human beings busy for millions of hours."

Gamal pushes the cigarette stub into the sand, opens the pack with his thumb, and pulls out a fresh stick with lips he has moistened with the flick of his tongue. The flint wheel of his lighter rasps a couple of times, and he dips the cigarette into the flame. He inhales deeply before continuing.

"We have spent a lot of time trying to figure out the pyramids. Aerial photography, x-rays, spectrometry, robotics, LIDAR – every new technology brings the scientists and the Egyptologists scurrying back to the pyramids to mull over the same questions: whodunit, whydunit, howdunit. Hundreds of thousands of hours have been spent discovering the passages and vacuums and subterranean chambers and shafts and apartments inside the pyramids. Every time you tap somewhere,

you find something new. Every time you find something new, the research restarts. Over and over and over."

Now my mind is racing ahead trying to connect the dots that I cannot yet see, "So if human beings are not kept busy, they design iron maidens or atomic bombs or bubonic plagues?"

"... or the internet," Gamal says.

"And puzzles are the best way to keep humans busy?"

"The pyramid is a ten million cube puzzle." If Gamal is impressed with my powers of deduction, he does not show it, "If we human beings spent a trillion hours on a twenty-seven-cube puzzle that was built in eighteen months, how many hours will be spent on a puzzle that has millions of cubes built over a thousand months?"

I start to piece it together myself.

I realize Gamal and I are no longer in the shade. The sun had peeped around the corner looking for us. I sense the build up towards the QED moment.

"So why this – this rubimid?" Watson asks Holmes, Hastings to Poirot.

"It is a device designed and executed by an advanced civilization that knew the importance of keeping human beings curious and busy. An infinitely huge ball of yarn for us kittens. An elaborately-designed treasure hunt with infinite clues." Gamal blows out a tremendous cloud of smoke. "The pyramid is a professionally designed time-waster."

SHARIA AL-MUIZZ

〜〜〜〜〜

Mohamed Wahba Elshenawy is an artist trapped in a boxer's body. He is wearing a military green canvas jacket, a green hat and is carrying a military surplus rucksack when we meet in a coffee shop in *al-Muizz*. Mohamed is part of the Cairo chapter of the Urban Sketchers, an international group of artists that meets locally once a month on a Sunday to sketch in the streets.

Photography had been my passion for several years, the camera a constant companion, almost an extension of me. There was point in my life when travel, photography, and history were the cornerstones of my leisure time. History made me travel, travel encouraged photography, documenting my photographs made me read more – it was a beautiful interminable cycle that kept me busy and happy, until one day I realized that the camera came too much between me and my subject. In 2013, as part of a conscious effort to reduce my dependence on electronics, I put down the camera and picked up a sketchbook. The Urban Sketching movement, founded by the Seattle-based Gabi Campanario, was gaining momentum. After joining the Urban Sketchers of Seattle, I had the opportunity to sketch with Gabi and learn the tricks of the trade. Sketching in the street had quickly gone global – I had connected with Mohamed online after becoming enamored by his inimitable style.

Cobbled streets lined with quaint coffee shops and falafel stalls, filigreed *mashrabiya*, overhanging galleries hovering over narrow streets, intricately carved domes and minarets visible against the sky – al-Gamaliya seems like scene straight out of a Naguib Mahfouz novel, whose childhood home is coincidentally not too far from where we are seated, on the edge of Khan el Khalili.

After a cup of coffee and introductions – we are meeting for the first time – Mohamed and I walk and sketch the northern part of the Sharia al-Muizz street, from Khan el-Khalili up to Bab Al-Fotouh. In existence since the foundation of the Fatimid city in the tenth century, the street epitomizes organic growth over hundreds of years, oriented roughly north but not aligned to the cardinal directions like the Mayan or Harappan grids. Like roots of a gigantic tree growing haphazardly in search of moisture and nutrition, the street meanders to the right or the left, gobbling any available footage. No two consecutive buildings are in a straight line, giving Sharia al-Muizz a phenomenally craggy and ragged texture.

Even a frequent passerby is guaranteed to discover something new on every trip through this jumble of mosques, schools, mansions, minarets, water fountains, courtyards, crusader-era portals, caravanserais, and hospitals.

"These are glorious subjects, but difficult to draw in the crowded streets," writes Roberts in his journal. He had rented a house in an area known as El Moski, a district just east of here, its architecture heavily influenced by the French[1]. According to John Murray's 1867 Handbook for Travelers in Egypt, the Franks were permitted to reside at el Moski since the time of Saladin in the twelfth century. Judging by the large number of sketches he executed in this area, Roberts walked through the street regularly, going south through Khan el Khalili, past al-Ghuri mosque and al-Azhar

---

[1] The house rented by Roberts belonged to Osman Effendi – a Scottish youth who was really called William Taylor and who had been captured in Egypt in 1807. Sold into slavery and compelled to convert to Islam, he readily adjusted to his new way of life, gained his freedom, and became a successful member of the elite Turkish community in Cairo. He also served as an intermediary between Egyptian society and many British travelers, scholars, businessmen and government officials who traveled to the country in the early nineteenth century. "Osman Effendi: A Scottish Convert to Islam in Early Nineteenth-Century Egypt" by Jason Thompson, *Journal of World History*, vol. 5, no. 1, 1994, pp. 99–123.

university, headed either towards the Citadel or the cemeteries of the Sultans.

Al-Muizz street is now an open-air museum. Cars are not allowed, which allows me to walk in the center of the narrow street, my head turning to capture a detail here and a nuance there, like a country bumpkin in Times Square, overwhelmed by the wonders around me. Mohammed points out a stone weaved into the column of a mosque built in the 1500s. The pharaonic hieroglyphics on the stone are a pleasant surprise – like finding a $20 bill tucked into an old book.

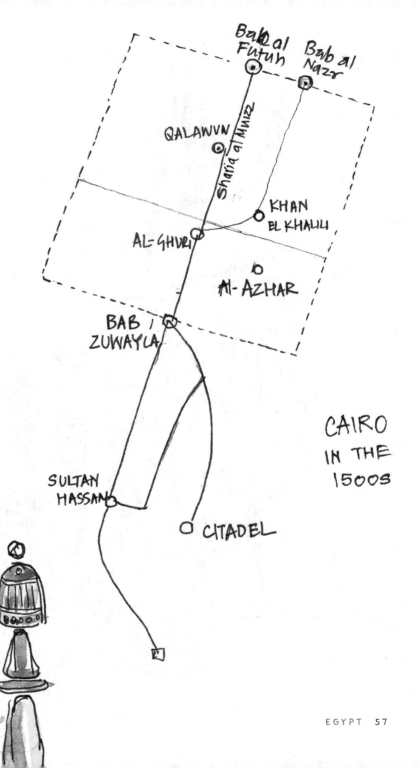

Bab al Futuh

Bab al Nazr

QALAWUN

Sharia al Muizz

KHAN EL KHALILI

AL-GHURI

AL-AZHAR

BAB ZUWAYLA

SULTAN HASSAN

CITADEL

CAIRO IN THE 1500s

QALAWUN COMPLEX, MOIZZ STREET, CAIRO

"Ancient recycling," he says, finding a spot for us to sit down opposite a public fountain built by Muhammed Ali Pasha in memory of his son who passed away in 1822. Around us, Cairenes move at Cairene pace. A girl leans into her mom, her young head laid on the elder's shoulder, teen worries being consoled. Elsewhere, a girl in faded jeans with her head covered in a traditional scarf perches on ancient steps with a group of boys and guffaws with wild abandon. A five-year-old who has been wailing and shrieking for the last few minutes suddenly finds himself lying on the ground, the wind knocked out of him by his father's lightning-fast strike. While the tiny eyes are wide in surprise, nobody else raises an eyebrow, the father's action considered par-for-course, a timely life lesson for the tot. "If the father does not spank his young son, the world will do it repeatedly later on." A voice from my past echoes in my head, bringing me a smile.

We sketch late into the evening. Mohammed and I capture these moments in our respective sketchbooks, interpreting the world around us though our own filters until we are unable to see what we are doing in the dark.

〰〰〰

"BOUGHT SEVERAL ARTICLES WANTED ON MY JOURNEY TO SYRIA: PISTOLS, SABRE, ETC."

When Roberts wrote the line in his journal on the 14th of January, he had procured the Syrian visa. On the 21st, Roberts was all set to head eastward, having hired four camels for the journey when he received news of plague in Jerusalem. The holy city was under quarantine. He decided to wait until he received better news. Robert wrote in his journal that the thought of omitting Jerusalem from a journey through the Levant was…

"…AS BAD AS GOING TO ENGLAND AND NOT SEEING LONDON."

He waited productively. He worked the streets of Cairo to fill up his sketchbooks. He set up his easel at high spots to paint panoramas of the city. He kept his journal up to date and wrote long letters to his sixteen-year-old daughter and his friends in Scotland. He made new acquaintances and hobnobbed with the European crowd in Cairo.

Roberts met Hanafee Ismail Effendi at the Sultan Hassan mosque in the courtyard with the beautiful ablution fountain. Ismail had studied in Scotland for several years and spoke immaculate English. His affable manner and smiling countenance rubbed off easily on Roberts. Young, well-bred, and charming – Ismail, who worked as a senior manager in the manufacturing enterprises, was a poster child for Pasha's cadre of modern civil service.

Roberts was also introduced to John Pell, a wanderer who traveled to distant lands in search of undiscovered ruins for sheer pleasure. He came from Devonshire, studied at Oxford and was known for his fondness for fine arts and antiquities. For both men, the meeting was fortuitous. In 1837 Pell had joined a caravan in Damascus to travel to Palmyra. From there he had hitched a ride to Ba'albec and Lebanon and was in Cairo in search of a caravan that would go to Petra. Pell found in Roberts the companion (and the caravan) he needed to travel to Petra, if only he could persuade Roberts to make the detour. The desert city that had been discovered in 1812 by Burckhardt had never been properly explored. Petra was the fix Pell needed. And the plague in Jerusalem gave Pell opportunity to work on Roberts.

Pell set out to work. He was acquainted with Linant de Bellefonde, who worked as the chief engineer of the public works of Egypt and was in charge of modernizing Egypt's irrigation canal infrastructure. Linant was contemplating a way to connect the Red Sea with the Mediterranean, an idea that had flustered engineers in the region for several thousand years. In his previous life, Linant had explored Egypt and traveled with Léon de Laborde to Petra in 1828. Pell got himself and Roberts invited to Linant's house for dinner. Over spiced kebabs, Roberts got a chance to see firsthand Linant's sketches of the Nabatean city. Linant's illustrations were the only visual representation of Petra available to the Western world at the time. Roberts immediately recognized the opportunity to better the product available in the market and to add to the handsome portfolio he has put together in Egypt. His work in Cairo was done. Instead of staying cooped up for a few more weeks waiting for the quarantine in Jerusalem to lift, he decided to make the two-month detour to Petra. Robert wrote in his journal on *29th January 1838*:

"I HAVE AGREED TO GO TO SYRIA WITH MR. PELL, BY WAY OF MOUNT SINAI, PETRA, HEBRON, AND JERUSALEM. MR. PELL PROMISES TO BE READY IN EIGHT DAYS."

While John Pell outfitted himself, Roberts finished painting a panorama of Cairo. On 6th February 1839, his final day in Cairo, Roberts wrote:

"ALL DAY OCCUPIED IN BUYING PROVISIONS FOR OUR JOURNEY THROUGH THE DESERT."

BAB ZUWEILA

Sharia Khayamiya
Old Cairo

SUQ
AL-KHAYYAMIAN

~~~~~~

Suq al-Khayyamian is the best place to buy provisions for an adventure in the desert. The tent-makers market sprawls outside the city walls, south of Bab Zuweila. The market sprung up in the mid-1600s to provide Hajj pilgrims with the provisions they needed for the spiritual journey – leather saddles, water bags, ropes, and tents to navigate the Arabian sands safely and comfortably. Roberts elaborates in a letter to his daughter Catherine before he sets out for Sinai, Petra and Syria.

"I HAVE PROVIDED EVERYTHING REQUISITE FOR MY JOURNEY. A TENT (A VERY GAY ONE, I ASSURE YOU), SKINS FOR CARRYING WATER, PEWTER DISHES, PROVISIONS OF ALL SORTS, NOT FORGETTING A BRACE OF TURKISH PISTOLS, AND A WARM COVERING FOR NIGHT. IMAGINE ME MOUNTED ON MY CAMEL, MY BLACK SERVANT ON ANOTHER, AND TWO MEN WITH MY TENT AND LUGGAGE; THE OTHER TWO GENTLEMEN SIMILARLY FURNISHED AND ACCOUTRED, SURROUNDED BY A HOST OF THE CHILDREN OF THE DESERT—THE WILD ARABS; AND YOU WILL HAVE AN IDEA OF WHAT AN EASTERN MONARCH I AM."

On my final day in Cairo, I am at the Khayyamian too. I follow the narrow Bayn al-Qasrayn as it meanders towards the southern walls of old Cairo, lined with intricately decorated buildings from bygone eras and modern-day shop fronts. I lean into the sweaty crowd to forge a path. Goods of all kinds are being hawked. Knock-off Nike tennis shoes and handmade slippers, lacy underwear and black full-length *burkhas,* NY baseball hats and colorful silk scarves.

The aroma of falafel being fried stalls my progress. John finds us aluminum chairs to sit in amidst the melee in the shadow of the twin minarets of Bab-e-Zuweila. A smorgasbord of Egyptian street food lands on our table. John is pleased with my willingness to eat in the street. I dig into fresh Arabic flat bread, fava beans cooked in cumin seeds, crisped eggplant doused in chili sauce, pickled radish and carrots and freshly chopped onions – all served and eaten family-style.

Nearby, men are selling traditional carpets, their shops leaning against the walls of al Mu'ayyad Mosque.

"Carpetmaking and selling runs in their family. Some of these families have been selling carpets for three hundred years. The great-great grandfather of this young man probably sold carpets while David Roberts sketched," John says, "And two hundred years from now, his great-great grandson might be selling carpets when another artist comes here traveling in the footsteps of Sunil Shinde."

bab Zuweilay, old Cairo

THE EASTERN DESERT

~~~~~~~

On a crisp December morning, we are gathered outside Bab El Nasr. John, his head wrapped in a woolen scarf, waits in the 4X4 parked outside the old walls of Cairo. Showqi blows thick blue smoke rings, his head tilted against a clear blue sky. He casually leans his tall, muscular body into a tall, muscular 4x4, his ripped forearms bare in the desert breeze. His stillness, every movement measured and economical, broadcasts a commanding presence that the twinkle in his eyes cannot disguise. He looks like a guy who can handle himself. I resist a strong urge to take a photo with him to send it to my family with a caption: this is Captain Showqi, who will be driving me. I'm in safe hands.

I cradle my sketchbook in my left arm, my pencil races frantically, putting finishing touches to the sketch. My thumb and index finger poking through the snipped-off cheap gloves are as stiff as the pencil they hold. Old Cairo is waking up. The muezzin's call to prayer rings through the empty streets. The early morning sun skims the top of the rectangular towers of the Gate of Victory. Teenagers wait at the bus-stop, one boy slinking behind the shelter to take one last drag of the cigarette before boarding the bus. A woman covered head to toe in a *burkha* shushes her baby while speaking on the phone and walking at a clip. Delivery vans, loaded with goods, honk and rattle, hurrying though the ancient gates to stock empty shelves.

The square towers of the Victory Gate, one of the three surviving gates from the original eleventh century construction, have stood here braving winds that bring sand from the desert and rampant changes of modernization.

Not far from where I stand, on 7th February 1838 Roberts' caravan gathered in an empty courtyard between an old cemetery and a ruined mosque. Roberts had assembled a motley crew: two Europeans, an Arab translator, three Arab servants, fifteen Bedouin guides and bodyguards, and twenty-one camels.

Hanafee Ismail Effendi, whom Roberts met in the courtyard of Sultan Hassan, agreed to join them as their interpreter. Roberts realized how precious Hanafee could be on the trip. Not only was Hanafee fluent in English and Arabic, but he was also equally familiar with the Muslim customs of the desert as he was with the social etiquettes of the Scottish Highlands. If Roberts hadn't found Hanafee, he would have had to invent him.

Also riding with Roberts and Pell was John Kinnear, 39, a banker from Edinburgh who was in Egypt on a business trip en route to Beirut. He met Roberts just the previous week and, fascinated by the adventure, decided to join their detour through Sinai and Petra on a whim. John Kinnear's decision was aided by John Pell's presence, who came across as, "a weather-hardened European." The banker had faced a severe setback in his business and an adventure was exactly the distraction he was looking for. Kinnear kept a detailed journal of the journey. His account helps fill the holes in Roberts' written account and provides us a precious behind-the-scenes look at Roberts' glorious paintings.

A retinue of fifteen Bedouins of the Beni Said (pronounced *Sa-yeed*) tribe accompanied them as their guides and bodyguards. The strapping nomads of the desert wore colorful desert regalia and carried long matchlocks, giving the caravan a processional appearance that Kinnear and Roberts enjoyed and commented about in their journals. Roberts and John Kinnear's personal assistants, Salem and Sayd (also pronounced *Sa-yeed*), rode along with a baggage train of twenty-one camels laden with tents, mattresses, water-skins, and personal luggage.

Late in the afternoon the picturesque caravan headed east, followed by a noisy gaggle of children until they reached the edge of town. Elders clicked their tongues and shook their heads, unable to comprehend the futility of healthy and prosperous European men heading into the open desert in search of ruins, leaving behind a city that had everything, including ruins.

By comparison, our departure goes unnoticed. Captain Showqi fires up the 4x4. The ventilation fan floods the cockpit with dust, a wordless blessing of the desert and an auspicious start to our sandy sojourn. We are traveling light; Our backpacks by our feet, a duffel bag each packed in the boot along with a carton of bottled water, two 5-gallon army surplus cans filled with petrol and a bag full of ripe oranges.

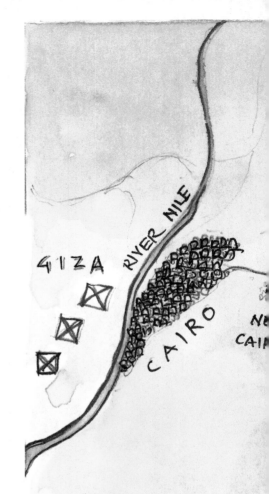

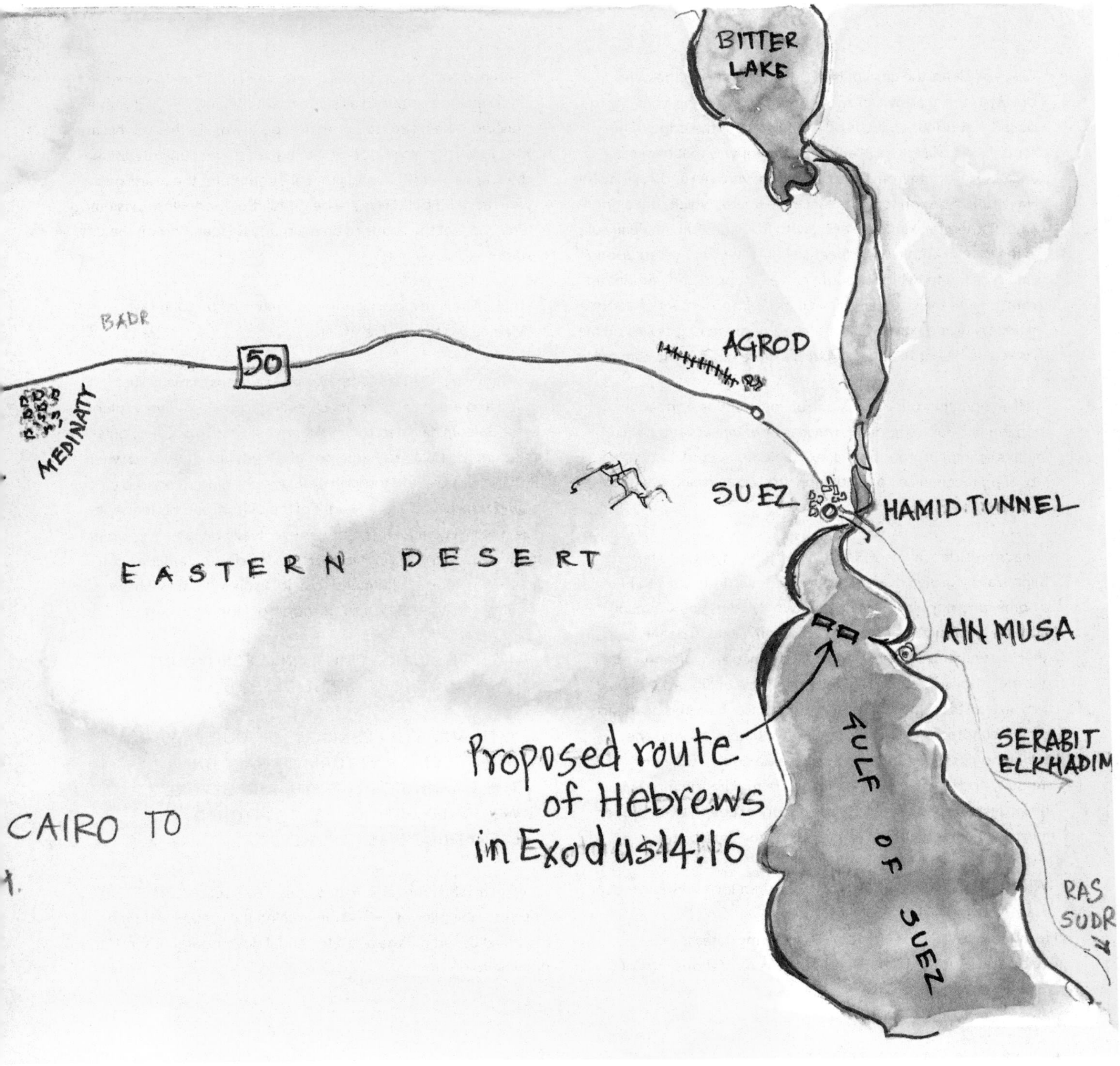

BITTER
LAKE

BADR

50

MEDINATY

AGROD

SUEZ

HAMID TUNNEL

EASTERN DESERT

AIN MUSA

Proposed route
of Hebrews
in Exodus 14:16

SERABIT
ELKHADIM

GULF OF SUEZ

CAIRO TO

RAS
SUDR

Our 4x4 clears the city limits of Cairo and pierces the ochre desert as the shadows grow shorter. The transition from city to desert is sudden – Cairo is built almost up to the edge of the sand. Route 50M is a six-lane asphalt highway that traces the ancient Hajj route from Cairo to Mecca, via Sinai and Aqaba. The Hajj route is laid on top of the Incense Route, which, once upon a time, carried frankincense and myrrh from the Arabian Peninsula to the Roman Empire. The Incense Route itself is layered upon the Spice Route, which brought cloves, pepper and cardamom from India to the Greco-Roman cities. This movement of goods of necessity and comfort have etched permanent grooves on the surface of the earth, and our 4x4 is a mere bead in the channel.

Half an hour into our drive, signs of construction appear on the horizon. Pick-ups and dump trucks, water tankers and concrete-mixers scamper through sleek exoskeletons, scurry beneath hovering mechanized arms of monstrous cranes and scaffolds several stories tall.

"That's President al-Sisi's New Cairo," John says. Cairo has haphazardly grown over the last eleven-hundred years to be a home for a population of twenty-two million. A new capital is being constructed at the cost of forty-five billion dollars to keep up with the modern demands of space and infrastructure of a megapolis. The new city will be the size of Singapore, with forty-five districts, two-thousand schools, six-hundred hospitals, twelve-hundred mosques, forty-thousand hotel rooms, one million homes, and a spanking new parliament. ("But none of the antiquity and history!") The numbers are mind boggling. This is the largest construction site in the history of Egypt, even bigger than the pharaonic construction sites on the Giza plateau.

"What's the catch, John?" I ask. He does not look very excited.

He laughs nervously, "New Cairo accommodates about five million residents. That means hundreds of thousands of Cairenes will end up with a three-hour commute to work for people who can afford a residence in the new city. If it is ever finished." He points to another large township that is whizzing past us on the other side of the highway. The construction has been abandoned. In parts that are complete, the roads and wide and the buildings are beautiful. But the township is empty. One can feel the sands of time already descending on the city, starting to devour it.

"That's Madinaty, Hosni Mubarak's new Cairo." John says. "Madinaty is the *old* New Cairo."

The highway to Suez is littered with skeletons of many such failed and emerging satellite cities and townships. Every ruler since Saladin has tried to build for himself his own Cairo, only to return to el-Qahira. Skeletons of camels lined this road when Roberts was passing through here. A sick, injured, or tired camel would buckle under the weight of the pilgrim and his luggage, never to get up again. The bones eventually became a pebble in the cairn, pointing in the direction of a destination they could not reach. Roberts continued to write in his journal as if he was sending a telegraph on a short supply of farthings:

"7TH FEBRUARY: LEFT CAIRO FOR MOUNT SINAI AND SLEPT IN THE DESERT.

"8TH AND 9TH FEBRUARY: ON OUR WAY. OVERTAKEN BY A STORM OF RAIN ON THE EVENING OF THE 9TH, AND BEFORE WE COULD GET OUR TENTS PITCHED EVERYTHING WAS IN A MESS."

Thankfully John Kinnear's diary comes to our rescue. He describes the piles of camel bones lining the road, the sighting of his first desert mirage and a torrential downpour that sends the party helter-skelter:

"IN A MINUTE THE STORM BURST UPON US IN THE MOST TREMENDOUS RAIN, THUNDER AND LIGHTNING, I EVER WITNESSED. EVERYTHING WAS IN CONFUSION. IT BLEW A GALE OF WIND, AND, THE TENTS NOT HALF SECURED, WERE FLAPPING ABOUT AS IF THEY WOULD HAVE BEEN CARRIED AWAY ALTOGETHER. TO ADD TO THE COMFORT OF OUR SITUATION, WE HAD ALL THE WORK TO DO; FOR THE ARABS SEEMED SO TAKEN BY SURPRISE, AND SUFFERED SO MUCH FROM THE COLD, THAT THEY WERE NEARLY USELESS TO US. AFTER HOLDING ON BY THE WET CANVAS TILL OUR HANDS WERE BENUMBED, AND WE WERE THOROUGHLY DRENCHED, THE TENT WAS AT LAST SECURED; AND WHEN WE HAD LIGHTED A CHARCOAL FIRE TO DRY AND WARM OURSELVES, THE BEDAWEENS CAME CREEPING IN BESIDE US, SHIVERING AND RATTLING THEIR TEETH AS IF THEY HAD HAD THE PLAGUE."

Where Robert's party battled the natural elements, an hour outside Cairo, we see plumes of dust clouds marking a fracas in the desert. A buff-colored Abram tank is grinding up a dry wash, its engines growling in low gear, the long barrel of the gun pointed up at the sky. Half a dozen armored vehicles surround the tank, pushing it against the dry bank. The gang of saber-tooth tigers has nailed the lonely mammoth in this round of their war game.

The desert stretches out as a far as the eye can see. As a blue slice of the Red Sea comes into sight, strands of industrial-grade barbed wire strung several feet high enclose the desert on our left. Inside the barbed wire is a rock and adobe defensive wall built by the Ottoman. Occasionally, a Mamluk-era watchtower peeps over the barricade. Several generations of military commanders have been guarding this area. What is in there? A fresh-water spring? Perhaps a gully wide enough to hide a battalion? An opening to an underground cave system? Time and again, new battles are fought on old battlefields with new weapons for age-old reasons. In a terrain as harsh and flat as this, a tiny tactical advantage can change the outcome of the battle. Roberts had passed by the Adjeroud fortress on the third day after leaving Cairo by Suez. That fort had to be inside the military compound. Could we find out? Had we not passed a gate?

"It's a bad idea," Showqi says, his jaw taut. "But you are the boss, Insh'Allah." He turns the 4x4 around, leaving the highway and joining a service road before slowing the car to a crawl. He lowers all the windows and asks me to put my hands where they are visible. He estimates at least three binoculars are trained on us right now. We drive past a MiG-21 that has seen action in the Six-Day War, propped up on a metal spike. Two Humvees with turret-mounted machine guns keep it company along with battle-worn jeeps covered in desert camouflage, halftracks and a dozen rockets of various sizes. We stop two hundred meters from the gate, which is already swinging open. A soldier in desert camouflage approaches us. Tall, square jaw, shiny Ray Bans and a dull-metal machine gun slung across his chest.

Salaam-alaikum. Yes, there is a small fort in the compound. A few ruined walls are all that is left. There is nothing to see. No, I have not heard of David Roberts. Yes, Napoleon camped here in 1799. No, permission is not possible. No possibility of a visit. No, you cannot speak to a supervisor. Have a nice day.

As we drive away, a very relieved Showqi is laughing, "Mister Sunil! You are not in a shopping mall! You could be shot for asking him for his supervisor!"

BEIRUT

CAIRO SUEZ

SUEZ

〰〰〰

We stop at a roadside stall for an early lunch. The owner of the stall speaks seven languages, none of which I understand, so I leave John to order us a feast. We pull up plastic chairs around aluminum tables. The dishes arrive at the table as soon as they are ready, served on battered aluminum plates to be shared family-style. We wolf down leavened bread smeared with fava bean purée, fried eggplant doused in chili sauce, cut onions marinated in lemon juice, pickled carrot and radish, cut cucumbers tossed with cilantro, freshly fried wedges of potato sprinkled with salt and red pepper powder. Afterwards I lie down in the sun, my back warm against the concrete, until my tongue no longer burns from all the spice.

We check into a hotel that is walking distance from Port Tawfik. The young lady at the reception wears a headscarf that only exposes her face between her eyebrows and her lower lip. She asks John questions in Arabic. She then turns to me and speaks in fluent English. *Why are you here? Where are you going? How long are you staying? Why are you here again? She reminds us that the Suez Canal is a military establishment. Photography is strictly prohibited. You will go to jail for many years,* she says. I assure her that I have no intention of taking any photographs. But is it okay to sketch? The query catches her off guard. I show her my sketchbook. She flips through it, her long delicate fingers tracing the pencil marks as if reading braille. She admits that she has never been asked that question before. She promises to find out.

I take a rickety elevator to the fifth floor. The red carpet is tattered and stained. The room is tiny and dank. The sink in the bathroom is yellow with grime. The tap splutters for several minutes, threatening but never delivering. All of this is forgiven once I discover a tiny balcony with an enormous view of the Gulf of Suez shimmering under the December sun. Turquoise water flows into the Suez Canal under the shadow of ochre bluffs. The mountain-side sports three white lines across the face, like the forehead of a Hindu sage on the bank of the Ganges. A gigantic tanker is preparing to enter the passageway, its rust-colored deck loaded with containers painted in bright primary colors. The deck creaks as the ship lumbers towards the Mediterranean, an octogenarian complaining under the weight of a grocery bag.

That evening, Showqi, John, and I head to the city market in the oldest part of Suez. Night descends quickly on the desert town. One minute it's light, the next it's pitch dark. The

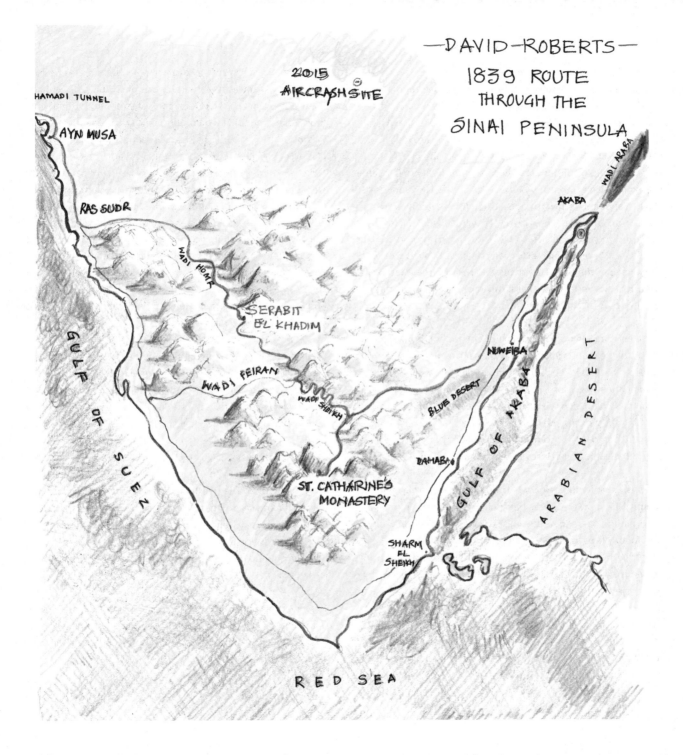

temperature plummets with the ball of sun. The two layers I am wearing are already insufficient. Most of the squat, sand-colored buildings are in a state of disrepair. The concrete is cracked, and the paint is peeling, but the construction looks recent. John provides a satisfactory explanation. Suez was destroyed in the war of 1967. Everything around us has been built since. Naked bulbs dangling on unprotected copper wires flicker to life. Street side stalls sell macaroni and pasta, spices stuffed in gunny bags, chicken and rabbits in wire cages. Dried fruits and dates are lined up on yesterday's newspaper. A stall sells shots of freshly squeezed sugarcane juice laced with lemon. In one corner of the market a cast iron pot harvests charcoal ember. Locals pick up glowing coals the size of coconuts with pairs of tongs and place them in bowls under their chairs – an age-old, cheap but highly effective personal heating system.

All of this I can see from my perch in a coffee shop right in the middle of the thoroughfare. The shop is full of men in long robes clutching thick blankets, sucking on gurgling flasks of shishas, keeping their eyes glued to a television mounted high on a wall. Mohamed Salah is on the pitch, his legs a blur when the football is at his foot, piercing the mid-field with ease. I could snip a hair off every beard in the room and go unnoticed, so engrossed are they in the game. Salah is revered in this part of the world.

"Suez is a layover town. It is what you Americans call flyover country," John says, "Cruise ships pull into the port at night. At first light, the passengers are whisked away in air-conditioned vans for day trips to the Giza plateau and Islamic Cairo or St. Catherine's. They are back on the ship for dinner and sail before dessert is served." I look around. I am the only tourist in the bazaar that night.

The Suez Roberts saw in February 1839 was a sleepy little town run by a clutch of famous characters from Cairo. This was thirty years before the famous canal would be complete. Thomas Waghorn, an officer of the Royal Navy and an entrepreneur, laid down a route between Alexandria and Suez, connecting the Mediterranean to the Red Sea. A steamer from Bombay (now called Mumbai) would bring mail and passengers to Suez. Waghorn's staff would relay the passengers on horse-drawn carriages to Cairo, staying overnight at Waghorn's inns. In Cairo, a paddle steamer would pick them up to float down the Nile to a barge on the Mahmoudieh Canal, which would take them to the port of Alexandria on the Mediterranean where another steamer would have them on their way to London. Mr. Hill, a Cairene socialite and hotelier, ran an inn at Suez, which was frequented by English army officers and traders, where Roberts' party found warm food, cold London Porter, and soft divans to sleep on. By morning they were up and away, hurrying into the desert and leaving behind the last vestiges of civilization for many days to come.

Breakfast is served on the top floor of the hotel. A panoramic window faces the canal. A white mega-yacht with a bright yellow helicopter on its roof and a smaller yacht in tow is making its way towards the Red Sea. I pile my plate with the last continental breakfast I will have for the next several days: hash browns, two pieces of toast, a cup of yogurt, and a small, moist pile of scrambled eggs. I work the grinders over the eggs. Two turns of salt and many turns of pepper to satiate my perpetual craving for spice. The gentleman loading his plate behind me leans over and says, "There you go my boy, the British parted the desert for that black pepper," he nods towards the Suez Canal, "It tells you a thing or two about British food doesn't it? Men digging up the desert to get spices to their tables quicker." He laughs heartily at his joke.

The canal was built by a Frenchman, not an Englishman, and the primary cargo on the ships that crossed the canal was not spice. But I do not correct the gentleman. Why let facts get in the way of a good joke?

SINAI

~~~~~~

We worm under the Suez Canal via the Hamid tunnel, crossing from Africa to Asia. The entrance to the tunnel is secured by an airport-style scanner scaled to the size of a truck. The road soon ends in a T-junction on the Asian side of the tunnel. Arrows point directions to Arish and Sharm-el-Sheik. Arish, situated in northern Sinai, had been in the news a month before I departed from Seattle. In November 2017, a Sufi mosque 40 kilometers from Arish was attacked by jihadi militants. Two hundred and thirty-five locals attending Friday prayers were killed. The modus operandi of the attack had ISIS' fingerprints all over it. This was the first time that ISIS had targeted Egyptian civilians on Egyptian soil. The attack sent the Arab world into shock. The Egyptian Armed Forces quickly set up a posse that cornered the jihadis in the mountains outside Bir al-Abed, before Egyptian fighter jets swooped down and pulverized them. Fortunately, the US mainstream Western media barely covered the attack, which saved me the effort of explaining my safety in Sinai to my family. We followed the other arrow pointed to Sharm el Sheik in the south.

We pass through checkpoints every 20 to 30 minutes. Zigzagging road barriers are used to slow the vehicles. A low wall of sandbags behind the barriers discourages a rogue automobile from hurtling through. And just in case an attempt is made, a pair of Humvees with turret-mounted machine guns manned by gas masks wearing commandoes waits patiently. An Egyptian commando frisks our 4x4; he peers under the seats, pokes the cushions, opens the bags, unzips every compartment of our backpacks, and looks under the car with a mirror mounted on a stick. Throughout the process, his intelligent brown eyes and an easy smile keeps us engaged.

In under three minutes, he has covered every inch of the 4x4 without missing a beat. I wonder if I should ask him if he spotted my favorite yellow Lamy Safari. The ink pen has been missing since yesterday.

Many of the soldiers are very young, some mere teenagers. Dressed in desert fatigues they tote squeaky-clean automatic weapons with the safeties off. The soldiers take a keen interest in where we are going, how we are getting there, how far we propose to go, how long we intend to stay. John writes down these details on chits of papers several times in a day. For the first couple of times, Showqi introduces me as *al-Amriki* – an American. He realizes that my brown skin and unmistakable Middle Eastern looks cause Egyptian brows to furrow deep, and require long, winding explanations. He eventually settles for *al-Hindi – an Indian,* which lands better. Everywhere in the world, Indians are irrevocably associated with Bollywood, the Indian film industry, but nowhere more so than in the Middle East. The association gets me a nod and a smile every time. As well as questions about their favorite actors and actresses: "Is Katrina Kaif still unmarried?"

"Did you notice how they send the soldiers with easy smiles to talk to people?" I share my observation with John. "The glum looking ones are always standing in the back."

"The ones standing in the back are their best shooters," John deadpans, bringing me back to earth.

We are driving through the landscape of the Exodus. In the Old Testament, the Israelites followed the charismatic Moses in search of the land promised to them by God. From Giza, the Israelites crossed the Red Sea, traveled through the desert, and arrived at what is now believed to be Mount Sinai, or Jebel Musa. There, God dictated the rules and covenants to Moses, who transcribed them onto stone tablets.

In 1838, a few months before Roberts' arrival, an American named Edward Robinson undertook a journey from Cairo to Beirut. He traveled with another biblical scholar named Eli Smith and they identified over two hundred places in the Holy Land named in the Bible using their collective knowledge of the scriptures and Arabic place names. Robinson published *Biblical Researches in Palestine* in 1841 based on their findings. It became the founding survey that spawned the biblical archaeology genre. Over the next century, thousands would follow in Robinson and Smith's footsteps, spade in one hand and Bible in the other.

~~~~~~

Ain Musa is considered the marker of the place the Israelites reached after their Red Sea adventure. They encountered brackish water that Moses is said to have made potable by a strike of his staff. The water at Ain Musa was brackish when Roberts and his convoy reached it on 12th February 1839 and is still brackish, as we find out when we briefly halt to stretch our legs. Seven of the original twelve springs still exist as shored up holes in the desert covered with a flotsam of plastic bottles and empty bags of Ruffles potato chips. I wonder why Moses' miracle did not improve the condition of the water permanently.

Not far from Ain Musa, Roberts' convoy split away from the coast and headed into the mountains along Wadi Homr. For the next four days they passed through "narrow sandy valleys, between rugged precipitous crags of calcareous rock, mixed with beds of gravel and indurated sand."

"THE CRAGS ROSE SOMETIMES
PERPENDICULARLY, LIKE ENORMOUS WALLS,
THEIR SUMMITS RIVEN AND SHATTERED INTO
THE MOST WILD AND FANTASTIC FORMS;
OCCASIONALLY THE VALLEYS OPENED OUT

Egypt

sea

Ain Musa, Sinai

WIDER, AND HIGH ISOLATED MASSES OF
ROCK ROSE ABRUPTLY FROM THE SAND,
CURIOUSLY TURRETED AND EMBATTLED,
AND HAVING THEIR NAKED SIDES WORN AND
UNDERMINED BY THE DRIFTING SAND, AS IF
THEY HAD BEEN SUBJECTED TO THE ACTION
OF A TORRENT."

Roberts was in high spirits. He described the view alternately
as sublime and desolate. Open desert travel often invokes
philosophy when one is forced to simultaneously face the
harsh terrain and the devils within oneself. Roberts sketched
as often as he could, sometime starting on foot an hour before
the caravan to get himself situated and finishing by the time the
caravan arrived.

On 16th February, Roberts and John Kinnear parted with their
caravan and along with their favorite Beni Said guide climbed
Jebel Gerabe to reach the ruins of Serabit el-Khadim. This
side-adventure was deliciously captured by both travelers in
wonderful detail, John Kinnear in his journal and Roberts in
his sketchbook. The two contemporaneous artifacts serve as
a wonderful insight into the mood of the friends at the time
and the flavor of the adventure that suited their spirit. After
completing "a precipitous climb" – they had to sometimes
crawl on all fours – they "stumbled across" ruins – upright
stones amidst centuries-old rubble. Overjoyed, they carefully
examined the ruins and traced the plan and dimensions of
the building. They measured the courtyards, and concluded,
grandiosely and scholarly, that the building must have been
a temple. They cleared the sand from the hieroglyphs on the
pillars and copied them into their journals. Kinnear went so far
as claim to recognize one or two cartouches from the obelisks
in Luxor.

In short, the two travelers spent several hours enacting great desert travelers who stumble upon "undiscovered" ruins, mapping and interpreting them under intense time pressure.

As a matter of fact, the ruins had been discovered in 1761 by Reinhold Niebuhr and had already been visited by ardent travelers and antiquarians like Burkhardt, Henniker, Laborde, and Linant. As the sun started to set, Roberts and John Kinnear descended the mountain and rendezvoused with their caravan, where their tents had been pitched for the night and, in true colonial style, a hot stew been put on the stove.

So tickled was I by Roberts' side trip to Serabit el-Khadim that I wanted to go, too. John promised "to look into it." Several days later, John got back to me with a thousand apologies and the news that the area around the ruins I was interested was out of bounds for recreational access. This was just after the blasts in Arish.

As we pass the town of Abu Zemina, I wistfully watch an asphalt road fork away to the east, marked by a little rusty sign that points to Serabit-el-Khadim. We whiz past it like an express train past a minor railway station, headed south and towards St. Catherine, where we will meet again with Roberts' caravan.

We drive past sea resorts situated along the Gulf of Suez named after exotic faraway lands: La Playa, La Hacienda, Moon Beach. Rows and rows of empty cookie-cutter buildings sit along the turquoise waters of the Suez across a teeny tiny strip of a beach. I am reminded of a Paul Theroux line in his book *The Pillars of Hercules*: "Nothing is sorrier than a resort out of season."

Past the tiny town of Ras Abu Rudesis, Showqi pulls over behind an armored army truck. He gets out of the car and lights up a cigarette. Offshore oil rigs loom on the horizon. Bedu boys come up to the windows peddling frosty Coke cans and hot

falafel wrapped in the daily news. Within half an hour six or seven vehicles pull up behind us. Bookended by a military jeep at the rear, we head into the mountains towards St. Catherine.

My very own caravan!

The two military vehicles, like parents shepherding their children at Disneyland, keep the civilian vehicles in a tight cluster, staying within eye contact of each other. We can no longer slow down or stop at will and are safer from a threat that neither Showqi nor John can articulate.

We climb up the bone-dry riverbed of Wadi Feiran, which is wide enough to fit a commercial airport runway. The Wadi quickly narrows and turns mountainous, lined on both sides by two-thousand-meter-tall granite behemoths. For the scientific minded, we are driving up a million-year-old riverbed that was, once upon a time, fed by snow melt rushing to meet the Red Sea. For the theologians, we are traveling along the six-thousand-year-old geography of the Old Testament – Exodus 17. Forty-five minutes into the drive, we see the first date palms and tamarisks of the oasis of Feiran, which abounds with ruins of churches and monasteries from the fourth and fifth centuries. This place has more stories than a village barber shop.

The gut-wrenching sound of a hard object hitting the windscreen startles us. A spiderweb of cracks appears in the windshield just behind the rear-view mirror. While Showqi moans, his normally twinkling eyes clouded with pain at the thought of the expense of fixing the glass, John and I heartlessly ignore him and joke about narrowly having survived a sniper ambush in the pass. I silently prayed it was a joke.

The road turns south after the pass and joins an artery coming from Nuwiba, bringing more traffic with it. We pass the tomb of Sheikh Nabi Saleh, the prophet revered by the Bedouin. We are released from the caravan once we are in the square of St. Catherine's village, and we head to our sleeping arrangement for the night. I am put up in a free-standing stone bungalow, which has clean white bedsheets, an attached bathroom, and a view of orange-golden mountains. I decide to skip dinner and turn in early. As the heater blasts hot air, I creep under the sheets and fall asleep immediately.

The monastery of St. Catherine, sinai, EGYPT

ST. CATHERINE

‿‿‿‿‿

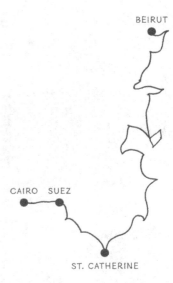

BEIRUT

CAIRO SUEZ

ST. CATHERINE

We eat a hearty breakfast in the communal kitchen, listening to the cook whistling the tune of an old Hindi song. Judging by the liberal use of chilis in the omelet, the music is clearly not the only Indian influence present. Strengthened by a cup of strong coffee, I step out into the cold morning. The wind slaps me across the face. Showqi wipes frost off the windscreen with his little finger and licks it with glee. We drive to the monastery a few miles away. The parking lot is empty except for an army jeep and a gleaming black Mercedes that looks out of place in the otherwise austere setting. I hurry past the shops with barrel vaulted roofs, still shut at this time of the morning, eager to get my first sighting of the monastery. The monastery is so picturesque in Roberts' paintings that I delayed researching it as much as I could, afraid the real edifice would not hold the same splendor. Assured by several recent photos on the internet that Roberts had not imagined the fortification walls, I am still experiencing an irrational fear that the online images are somehow not faithful to the real structure. Am I about to be disappointed?

The walls of the monastery soar high and mighty as they have for the last fifteen centuries. The morning light has scrambled over the towering Jebel Musa and bathes the monastery in a stunning glow. I slow down, now that I have the monastery in my field of view, to inhale the fragrant desert air, which tingles with the scent of oranges and lemons emanating from the monastery garden. The plaza in front of the monastery is coming to life. A young shepherd leads a camel train into the mountains – more animals in his custody than years in his age, the beasts scuffing up dust clouds with their hooves. A Bedouin boils habak leaves in a tin kettle on a fire the size a hand. An octogenarian reaches into a jute sack and pulls out rocks etched with the stories of the desert – quartz geodes, agates, sandstone with fossilized plants and dried starfish, and arranges them on a checkered cloth like a grandmaster fussing with his chess pieces.

I am standing outside the longest continuously inhabited Christian monastery in the world. The church that gives the monastery its name was built in the sixth century and the impregnable fortifications incorporates Moses' burning bush.

The monastery of St Catherine, Sinai, Egypt.

High on the wall facing the square I spot a covered wooden balcony about forty feet off the ground that prominently features in John Kinnear's journal entry on 18th February. Roberts and his troupe had crossed the mountain and reached a plain called Wadi er-Raha near the monastery. It was late in the day and the granite mountains were already bathed in moonlight when the weary passengers trudged towards the monastery. The monks observed their approach from atop the walls with trepidation as had monks of the monastery since its inception. Its remote location made it an easy target for brigands, insurgents, and lawless tribes of the desert. Once Roberts' caravan stopped outside the walls, the monks opened a trapdoor in the overhanging balcony and lowered a rope carrying firewood and a lamp. In one stroke, the offering served as a humanitarian gift for the guests and a security apparatus for the monks to help them see in the pitch dark forty feet below. The friendly but cautious monks were protected by the immaculate defenses of the Byzantine military architecture, but no wall is tall enough once the door is open. If they detected any foul play, they would slash the rope and the monastery would once again become an impregnable fortress. Roberts accepted the gifts from the monks and sent up with the rope the *firman* and letters of introduction he was carrying. After the documentation had been suitably verified, the rope was lowered once again.

John Kinnear wrote in his journal:

"THE ASCENT IS SOMEWHAT NERVOUS, I ASSURE YOU; FOR THE WHOLE APPARATUS CONSISTS OF A ROPE WITH A LOOP AT THE END OF IT—RATHER OMINOUS—VERY LIKE BEING 'KILTED UP IN A TOW'—YOUR WHOLE SAFETY DEPENDS ON YOUR HOLDING THE ROPE FIRMLY WITH YOUR HANDS, AND YOU FIND CONSTANT EMPLOYMENT FOR YOUR FEET, IN KEEPING YOURSELF FROM COMING IN COLLISION WITH THE ROUGH PROJECTIONS OF THE WALL. THEN THE OLD MONKS WALK SO SLOWLY ROUND THEIR WINDLASS ABOVE, THAT YOU THINK YOU ARE TO BE LEFT ALL NIGHT DANGLING IN THE AIR; AND, WHEN YOU ARE FAIRLY WOUND UP, YOU FIND YOURSELF HANGING TWO OR THREE FEET FROM THE WINDOW, WITHOUT THE POSSIBILITY OF GETTING IN, TILL THE MONKS GET HOLD OF THE ROPE AND LAND YOU LIKE A BALE OF GOODS."

All the while, his friends who remained below guffawed and offered boisterous advice, oblivious to the fact that they too would go through the same ordeal. The rope pulley was the only way into the monastery and eventually one by one the travelers were pulled up onto the balcony. Once ensconced in the safety of the walls, and after a long, satisfying pull at the cold, sweet water drawn from the monastery's well, John Pell was able to use his patchy Greek to secure them accommodation for a few days. They were offered a meagre meal of rice, dates and a tot of strong *arak* before retiring to the dormitory rooms.

Our entrance lacks such drama. Almost directly below the wooden balcony, a door has been hewn into the walls for the modern visitor entrance to the monastery. We stoop beneath the nine-foot-thick walls, a sharp transition from the cold open desert to the warm confinement of the monastery. Inside, a jumble of buildings from across the centuries cram against each other jostling for space, sunlight and ventilation like the flora and fauna of tropical jungles.

Only a very small portion of the original Byzantine village is accessible today to visitors. A left turn at the entrance takes you to the Burning Bush, the focus of the Sinai pilgrimage for centuries. It's the very spot where God is said to have conferred prophethood on a reluctant Moses. You retrace your footsteps past the entrance, take a left at the Fountain of Moses, where Moses is said to have met his future missus, and pass a beautifully carved sixth-century cedar door, which leads into an atmospheric sixth-century church. After you have gorged on a mosaic of the Transfiguration and venerated the remains of St. Catherine, you exit the building, take a left, climb a staircase, stoop under an arch and follow a narrow passageway that delivers you outside the walls through a modern exit. It's a circuit that can be completed in less than one thousand steps.

This is not how it was in Roberts' time. I reflect as I find a place to sit as far back in the church as I can and pull Roberts' drawings of St. Catherine out of my rucksack. Roberts had free access to the monastery, and he made the most of it. In his four-day stay, he gathered in this sketchbook enough material to produce nine drawings, which were published between 1842 and 1849. His compositions include three scenes of the monastery from the outside, in which he shows the fortification walls and the village as it can be seen from an elevation. Two more sketches were made inside the monastery. In the first, he captured the nave of the Church of Transfiguration and in the second, he is deeper inside the monastery, in corridors that are out of bounds for the present-day visitor. On the day he climbed Mount Sinai, he sketched the stone steps snaking up the mountain to the gate of repentance, the chapel originally built by Emperor Justinian to commemorate the spot where Moses is said to have received the commandments from God, which is framed by the rugged mountainous landscape in high sun, and the Chapel of Elijah, illuminated dramatically by a lamp that is tilted at a rakish angle.

Roberts was astonishingly productive. He consistently put pencil to paper despite fatigue, discomfort, sickness, adverse weather, hunger, constant thirst and an inevitable painter's block.

"Don't forget that Roberts had a retinue of servants who cooked and cared for him and took care of his camels and carried his bags and baggage and pitched his tent every night." John was trying to console me. "His bodyguards did all his grunt work. He had more time to get things right."

I stayed in hotels, slept in a warm bed every night and had at my disposal an SUV that zipped along at 100km/h while he lumbered 15 hours a day on camelback. On the one hand his slow speed gave him more time to get it right, but he was also away from his family longer. He exchanged only two or three letters with his daughter during his trip whereas I was able to send and receive texts to my wife and daughters every day. And I still worried and thought of them all the time.

Roberts' prolific production was never at the expense of his hallmark quality. His sketches have oomph. His eye for detail, evident in every sketch, is unsurpassable. The architectural details he painted in his study of the sixth century church of Transfiguration – the nuances of the Greek-Coptic monastic dress, the arrangement of the water jars in the monastery, the design of the clay pipes, the intricacies of the firing mechanism of the Bedu matchlocks – nothing escaped his attention. He copied every detail quickly and perfectly.

"But he is accurate only when he wants to be," says John, pulling out of the sheaf of printouts a print titled *The Monastery of St. Catherine*. In the lithograph, Roberts has painted a wide-angle view of the monastery and its surroundings from an elevated angle. The monastery is depicted with a high degree of accuracy but is placed against a backdrop of massively exaggerated mountains. The mountains are made to look steeper and taller, towering above the monastery like a spire, resembling hands joined in prayer up towards the sky. John has made this observation before. Standing in front of Sultan Hassan in Cairo, he pointed out how the size of the entry portal of the mosque had been exaggerated in Robert's painting.

David Roberts was too accomplished a topographical artist for these discrepancies to be an error. If it ended up in his painting, then Roberts meant for it to be there. Perhaps his training as a stage painter kicked in automatically to add drama to an already dramatic scene. Maybe he took to heart the famous adage: *Don't paint what you see, paint what you feel.* Maybe from his spot in front of the monastery, in a high state of excitement as a traveler and a pilgrim, the mountain believed to be the one Moses climbed to meet God did indeed feel taller and steeper. Who knows? "This sliding scale of accuracy in detail in the foreground and imaginary backgrounds may well be considered theme for Roberts' representations," writes Uzi Baram, an archaeologist whose expertise includes Ottoman archaeology and historical archaeology.[2]

Camphor burns in a censer placed near the altar. The interior is lit up dramatically with diffused light. The church is incredibly atmospheric. Twelve monolithic granite columns, a profusely decorated sixth-century mosaic, innumerable gold-plated silver lamps hanging from a gold-plated green ceiling and an exquisitely decorated iconostasis. It is a church that can make even an atheist feel a pang of piousness.

[2] Baram, Uzi. "Images of the Holy Land: The David Roberts Paintings as Artifacts of 1830s Palestine." *Historical Archaeology*, vol. 41, no. 1, 2007, pp. 106–117.

St. Catherine's Monastery, Sinai

A middle-aged woman walks past me gingerly, her fingers raised to her mouth, her eyes frantically trying to take in everything in the room. "There's so much history here that I'm getting a headache," she says. I throw my pencil down in exasperation, as I am myself bogged down by the plethora of religious paraphernalia in the church. That is when I notice Yahia standing behind me, observing me struggled with my penmanship. He gesticulates for my sketchbook and flips through it, starting at the last page, a reminder that I am in a country where the script is read right to left and a book is opened from what is the back cover in the west. He flips through it with a grave expression on his face, giving each page its due time.

"No smoking!" He wags his finger at a sketch that shows a Bedouin lighting up a cigarette.

"Why drawing? No camera?" He asks me, every verb in the sentence acted out as if we are playing a game of charades. I tell him about my project. When the name David Roberts fails to register with him, I show him Roberts' sketches of St. Catherine. Wordlessly he peruses them, giving each sketch the time it deserves, taking in every detail. When he comes to the sketch of the Church of Transfiguration, he crosses himself. When he is looking at the sketch that Roberts made deep inside the monastery, he taps his fingers and asks, "Do you want to see this?"

~~~~~~

Back outside, a Bedouin makes us tea. We sit cross-legged as he transfers boiling water from a chipped enamel pot to a pair of chipped enamel mugs. He smooshes *habak* leaves with his thick, nicotine-stained fingers and offers us the mugs. I sit in the sun slurping the tea.

st. catherine village, Sinai

"I have been coming to St. Catherine for twenty-five years," says John. "Never have I been invited to visit the interiors of the monastery!" He is incredulous about Yahia's offer. Yahia has asked us to return in the afternoon. He is going to get permission from his superiors for us to visit the interiors of the monastery, where entry is forbidden for visitors. I feel like a deep undercover cop who has been invited to a secret gang den.

With two hours to kill, we loiter around the St. Catherine bazaar, which caters to the pilgrims. Showqi picks a yellow checkered *keffiyeh* from a metal hook and wraps it around my head, Sinai Bedouin style.

"Insh'Allah, you look like a Bedouin! The *keffiyeh* will protect you from the sun. From the wind. From the cold." He picks another one from the hook and goes on to become a *keffiyeh* salesman. He wraps it around his fist "It is a bandage." He ties two knots. "It can be a bag. A wrap. You can use it to filter water. It is a desert survival kit." He said, "And don't forget this." He places a coil of rope called agal on top of the head wrap. "That's a ladder. A hand cuff and…" he pretends to wrap a garotte around his neck and mimics tightening, tilting his head dramatically, tongue dangling out, eyes crossed. "A lethal weapon, Insh'Allah. If you know how to use it."

We buy falafel, wrapped in the morning news, and wash it down with *chai*. I find a warm spot under the sun and lie down waiting for Yahia to call us. At 2 o'clock he is waiting for us under the big arch of the monastery's exit.

"No permission today." He says, shaking his head. "Come back tomorrow."

~~~~~

That night we stop at a Bedouin camp in the village of St. Catherine. A big smokeless fire blazes in the center of the tent. I sit on cushions laid on the floor, my back against a divan covered with red and blue Bedouin rugs. A black cat is curled against me. A Bedu offers me a flat case. Inside, neatly hand-rolled cigarettes sticks are lined on one side, and a faded color photograph of his family tucked inside the cover – the means to die and the reason to live all neatly packed together in a beaten-up tin box.

A low table in the center of the tent is laden with food. Lentil soup. Chicken kabobs. A shank of lamb leg cooked so slowly that the meat is falling off the bone. Shawarma. *Ful* with warm Bedu bread. I empty my umpteenth sweetened Bedu *chai* out of a shot glass. An Egyptian family is also enjoying the Bedouin hospitality. The head-scarfed mother pulls on a hand-rolled joint, holding it between her index finger and thumb, and releases a thin stream of blue smoke through her delicate nostrils. She passes the joint to her son. A mother and son passing a joint back and forth would be a scandalous scene even in liberal parts of the Unites States.

The son, Farouk, winks at me, reading my thoughts and offers me the joint, which I politely decline. "Are you sure? The Bedu have the best hashish," he says. I tell him I am sure. I am coming up to my first anniversary of quitting my twenty-four-year-old tobacco smoking habit and I am happy to stay away.

Farouk's effortless, accent-free English, his cultivated casual mannerisms, his gentrified, logo-less clothes – all indicate a very subtle affluence.

"Did you drive here in the black S-class that is in the monastery parking lot?" I ask him. The presence of the ostentatious car is still bothering me.

"No, no. Not mine," he laughs, "I noticed it too. In Egypt, you don't own an expensive Mercedes until you can afford to give away three." He is not referring to giving away wealth to charity, rather a system common in developing countries in which the superrich share wealth with powerful people so they can collectively be safe.

"What brings you here?" Farouk asks me, "I don't see many Indians at St. Catherine."

I tell him why I am here. He asks to see my sketchbook and flips to the back cover to open it. He stops himself, laughs and starts from the front page. He pauses at a sketch I had made near the citadel of an Arab pulling on a sheesha in a shop that I had titled *A Typical Coffee Shop*.

"Edward Said just turned in his grave," he says, shaking his head.

I do a double take when I hear Farouk's offhand comment, which was clearly made in jest, forgotten by him as soon as it was uttered. Farouk is referring to a professor at Columbia University who published an authoritative work titled *Orientalism*. The central idea of Said's theory is this: Europeans invented the term Oriental to describe a world completely different from their own, hiding their disdain for a foreign land and its rules under a thin veneer of curiosity and inclusiveness, and as a means to advance their imperial ambitions to colonize the Middle East. Said ensured the word Orientalism was no longer considered an artform and had no romanticism attached to it; rather, it should be seen as an unequal power equation between two civilizations that had followed completely different arcs in the last twelve centuries, the Europeans pulling ahead only because of "guns, germs, steel" – and unadulterated ambition.

st. Catherine

I sketched the coffee shop in Cairo because the scene had struck a chord. I was intending to capture a corner of Cairo, where people could slow down for a few minutes in the afternoon to read the newspaper while the rest of the world hurried along. Right in front of me was the Cairo I had imagined, and I wanted to capture it in my sketchbook: men sucking on the gurgling *sheeshas*, sipping countless cups of sweet tea, sitting under a canopy made of turquoise beads.

But this was exactly the central theme of Said's *Orientalism* – how Westerners used the quaint, the picturesque, to show how the Middle East was backward, exotically alien. In a moment of epiphany, I remembered a time when I was with some of my American customers in Bangalore. We were standing in front of a spanking new mall that sold Prada purses and $15 protein shakes. Young software engineers thronged the malls, sporting expensive wireless headphones and Apple watches, sipping their macchiatos in Wi-fi enabled cafes. But one cow on the road would get the American visitors excited. Their phones would come out of their pockets instantly, photos would be snapped with gay abandon and uploaded immediately. They would be happy to take an image of India back to America that conformed with their idea of India. In that one moment, it suddenly all came together for me.

~~~~~~~~~

We walk back to our bungalow under a massive starlit sky. The temperature has plummeted, but my full stomach warms me.

I wonder: is my following in Roberts' footsteps also a part of my inadvertent Orientalism? Roberts has been accused of being an Orientalist. Uzi Baram, an anthropologist who teaches archaeology at New College in Florida, succinctly makes the case. "From Said's critique of Orientalism, it is clear that Roberts created picturesque landscapes that embodied British concerns and imagery. Landscapes that were translated for the Western gaze. Roberts did not simply capture the landscapes of Palestine: similar to the other Orientalists, he fashioned an image of the Holy Land rather than representing all that he saw."[3]

Roberts traveled to Egypt and the Holy Land with the express intention of returning with a portfolio. It was a business endeavor with a future commercial value. The market in the West was clamoring for images of the land of the Bible, of the very places where Jesus and the saints had walked. Roberts, like every good artist, carefully chose what was included in his compositions. An artist chooses a specific angle that shows the Taj Mahal under a rising moon to tell a specific story. A journalist standing ten feet away might include a pile of trash in the frame and tell a different story. Would the two photos, juxtaposed, discredit the artist for choosing the aesthetically pleasing view, which might be purchased by a tourism company?

Was Robert's Orientalism as inadvertent as mine? I make a mental note to reach out to Professor Uzi Baram once I return to the US.

On the way back to our bungalow, John stops at the village grocer.

"Do you want to grab a snack in case you get hungry at night?" he asks. "You did not eat much."

It is a tiny, two-aisle store. Every square inch is packed with products from Egypt, Oman, Russia and Israel, side by side. I pick up a packet of the largest dates I have ever seen, remembering that David Roberts had eaten a dinner of rice and dates on his first night in the dormitory of St. Catherine.

I go to bed that night with one question in my head: will I get to see the library of St. Catherine's Monastery?

The monastery's library has a large collection of the oldest books of the Christian world. The collection at St. Catherine is considered second only to the Vatican. A great heist was perpetrated on its premises in the nineteenth century. Granted, the *objet du désir* of the crimes was a book, the thief a bespectacled scholar, and the heist pulled off over a 15-year time span – not exactly the story that would inspire a sequel of Mission Impossible, but it caught my attention. Keen to pay a visit to the library, I asked John about it.

He replied, "Where do you get these ideas? Why can't we go to a beach or something?"

John Kinnear wrote in his journal in 1839:

"THE LIBRARY CONTAINS A SMALL NUMBER OF PRINTED BOOKS, AND GREEK AND ARABIC MSS; BUT NONE, I BELIEVE, OF ANY GREAT ANTIQUITY. THEY APPEAR TO BE IN SAD CONFUSION, AND THE GOOD SUPERIOR SEEMED TO BE VERY INNOCENT OF ANY KNOWLEDGE OF THEIR CONTENTS. HE PUT INTO MY HANDS, WITH AN AIR OF GREAT IMPORTANCE, A VERY THIN OCTAVO, WHICH HE APPEARED TO ATTACH CONSIDERABLE VALUE TO. IT WAS AN ANNUAL REPORT OF THE LONDON BIBLE SOCIETY!"[4]

[3] Baram, Uzi. "Images of the Holy Land: The David Roberts Paintings as Artifacts of 1830s Palestine." *Historical Archaeology, vol. 41, no. 1, 2007, pp. 106–117.*
[4] *Cairo, Petra, and Damascus in 1839: With Remarks on the Government of Mehemet Ali and on the Present Prospects of Syria, by John Gardiner Kinnear*

Monastery of St. Catherine, Sinai

John Kinnear could not have been more wrong. I have often wondered if it was an elaborate ploy by the monks to feign ignorance about the documents on their shelves. For the monastery has one of the richest collection of documents and icons from the early days of Christianity. The veneration of icons gained popularity in the sixth and seventh centuries in the Byzantine empire. The cult of the icons created a powerful industry that led to unhealthy competition, unfair practices, and unabashed corruption. The industry spiraled out of control. The pendulum had swung to it farthest point. Then it reversed and swung back rapidly. The hatred of the icon industry and the growing popularity of Islam sparked a movement to return to the traditions of the Old Testament. Iconoclasm was born in the mid-seventh century. Icons and images in churches and homes were ripped out and smashed to pieces. Icon worshippers were persecuted.

The Monastery of St. Catherine was too geographically remote for the ripple of change to reach it. Furthermore, the tight control by the Orthodox Greek Church ensured it was immune to iconoclasm. The monastery was able to preserve the icons it had on its premises, and today it owns the most enviable collection of icons in the world. The oldest known icons and ancient documents of Christianity are thus beautifully preserved in the library of the monastery. One such document from the monastery shook the Christian world, thanks to the efforts of a devout scholar called Constantin von Tischendorf.

Tischendorf was a man on a mission. He was trying to find the oldest Bible he could lay his hands to repeal the vicious attacks of scholars on the Hebrew Bible. Since it was written, discrepancies had crept into the text of the Bible as a result of the holy book being copied and translated by multiple scribes and scholars over hundreds of years. The words were modified, a little here and a little there, sometimes by error, at other times to correct a previous error. Disillusioned by the corruption of the original words that came from the mouth of God, Tischendorf was looking for the oldest manuscript he could find. His thesis was: The older the Bible, the more faithfully it would convey the actual words God spoke. The monastery's reputation as the repository of the oldest known books in the world brought Tischendorf to St. Catherine in 1844, five years after Roberts. Just like Roberts, Tischendorf was welcomed and offered shelter and food. During his stay, Tischendorf chanced upon a basket stuffed with papers ready for the fireplace. He happened to recognize biblical text on the papers and frantically rescued them – at least, that's Tischendorf's story of the discovery of Codex Sinaiticus, which he stuck to as long as he was alive. The monk realized the value of the pages, but Tischendorf managed to take them with him, and the oldest Bible in the world saw the light of day.

Not satisfied with the scraps that he had rescued, Tischendorf returned to the monastery in 1853. By this time, the monks had carefully hidden the manuscript in the monastery and yet, once again by sheer chance, Tischendorf discovered a small fragment of the Bible, which was being used as a bookmark. The fragment had only 11 lines of script, but it was enough to make Tischendorf want to come back a third time. Return he did in 1859, this time financed by the Russian Tsar.

He found nothing during his stay at the monastery until the very last night there, when Tischendorf happened to take an evening walk with a monk. The monk invited Tischendorf back to his cell where he was reading a manuscript by candlelight.

Suddenly Tischendorf was holding in his hands a manuscript made of prepared animal skin with text written using a form of upper-case letters without word divisions known as Biblical majuscule. This was the manuscript he had been searching all his life. The handwritten Bible was the oldest he had ever seen and by extension, the oldest Bible in the world. Tischendorf realized that the Bible had more pages than he had suspected. He could not bear the thought of leaving the Bible lying wrapped in an old cloth in the austere dormitory of a monastery in the middle of nowhere, and he used his considerable powers of persuasion to carry the book to Cairo under the pretext of copying it. From there Tischendorf used his even more considerable political clout to install a new archbishop who in turn allowed him to take the Bible to Russia.

Tischendorf wouldn't be the first European to borrow an artifact from Egypt and never return it. The Stalin government, who claimed the Bible had been presented to them by the monastery, sold the Bible to the UK in a bizarre 1933 transaction. The Bible is currently displayed in the British Museum in London. The Codex Sinaiticus, as the manuscript came to be known, is the oldest surviving Bible, written around 340 CE. It contains parts of the Old Testament and the entire New Testament. The discovery of the Bible made Tischendorf instantly famous and the monks of the monastery permanently hate and distrust Western scholars. The doors of the library have been permanently shut to the Western world ever since.

Fortified by the sweet dates of the night before and a spicy masala omelet with hot coffee in the morning, I return to the monastery at sunrise. I am keen to sketch the monastery from an angle that requires a hard scramble up the shoulder of the mountain. I attack the rocks with gusto, the climb working on my body like a masseur. I have another twenty feet to go when I hear a command hissed at me from somewhere ahead of me. The sound lands on me like a whiplash.

"Stop!" John's voice coming from behind me is urgent. He is out of breath as he struggles to bring himself alongside me. He need not have bothered. I am frozen in my tracks already. "This is how far we are going today," he manages, his chest heaving.

Between breaths, John tells me that I have accidentally stumbled upon a sniper nest. An Egyptian commando suitably camouflaged is crouching somewhere nearby with a powerful rifle fitted with scope. I surreptitiously look around without moving my head. Despite being so close and knowing the sniper is with earshot, I cannot spot him. He probably had me in his crosshair for a few minutes as I was climbing.

"Is this normal security?" I ask John.

John shrugs his shoulders, "I never climb here," he says. Two monastery security guards were killed in an attack in April 2017. John thinks the increased security could be a result of that incident.

From this vantage point, the monastery looks like a 3D souvenir model sold in the bazaar. The monastery is spread over an area roughly equal to a modern city block, jam packed with courtyards and balconies and buildings that jostle and butt into each other. The Church of the Transfiguration, the oldest building in the compound, was built in the sixth century, while the campanile presented by the Russian Tsars in 1871 is more recent (and hence absent from Roberts' sketch). From up here some of the decisions that Emperor Justinian's architect made become apparent. For example, the church is aligned on an east-west axis. Had the architect built the compound walls parallel to it, one corner of the compound would jut out into the mountain while another would dangle over the deepest part of the wadi, putting itself in the path of inevitable flash floods. The architect let the church stay aligned to the cardinal directions but simultaneously rotated the compound so that it was aligned to the geographical location. The two alignments of Monastery of St. Catherine are a wonderful compromise of function over form, a syzygy of faith and defense. Everything in the monastery has at least two functions. Defense and one other thing.

As we scramble down to the courtyard, a door under an arched doorway at the back of the monastery opens and closes. A man in a dark suit emerges, accompanied by a monk in dark robe. "Isn't that the library?" I ask John, fully knowing that it is. Why is there activity around the library? My curiosity is aroused.

The monastery has a rhythm. The day starts at 2 am. The monks wake up in the wee hours to offer their prayers and vespers. By 2:30, pilgrims gather outside the monastery to start their trek up Jebel Musa / Mount Sinai for the sunrise hike, which takes about three hours. After sunrise, the pilgrims start their trek down and reach the monastery by 8. The doors of the monastery open at 9. Visitation is until noon. The monastery shuts its doors to allow the monks to eat their only meal of the day and rest until 1:30 pm. Afterwards the monks complete their chores until 4:00 pm and attend service until sundown. The monks then continue meditation and reading in their private dormitories on their own time.

We wait in the courtyard for the gates of the monastery to open. Bedouins are setting up their goods for sale. A monk in a dark robe sweeps the courtyard with a long-handled broom. The

smell of burning cedar wood permeates the valley. A delicious silence hangs in the air. This isn't just another a popular tourist site waiting for the gates to open. There is a holiness about the scene, a certain authenticity attributed to a place that has more pilgrims than tourists. It is a time capsule in which the way of life has not changed much in the last fifteen centuries. The scene would have been no different when Roberts saw it.

I am in my favorite seat at the back of the church soon after the gates are thrown open. A delegation of Greek Orthodox priests is visiting from Mount Athos near Thessaloniki. The casket containing the mummified head and the hand of St. Catherine has been brought out and is under Yahia's supervision. I line up behind the pilgrims to pay my respects. The line inches forward and each person kissing the casket is sprinkled with holy water.

Yahia's eyes lit up when he sees me. "I am glad you are back," he whispers, "Meet me here at 1:30." Once again, John and I spent two nervous hours outside the monastery.

"Will they let us inside the library?" I ask John again.

At 1:30 Yahia comes to fetch us. His smile telegraphs his success in getting us permission.

"Let's go before the superior changes his mind," John translates Yahia's Arabic for me. *Yalla!*

A short staircase up the west porch, across a white-washed terrace, up a dodgy wooden staircase set in the north wall and, just like that, I have a vantage point across the land that the monastery stands on. When Emperor Justinian fortified the compound with the state-of-the-art methods of the sixth century, survival was top of mind, and he was not going to leave it to God. Within the two hundred years following the death of Christ, the devout started gathering around the Holy Land, to touch the earth walked by the prophets. They were looking to settle in the surrounding desert to live the spartan life of the ascetics. The community was ravaged repeatedly by the elements and the warring tribes of the desert, but it survived. Empress Helena, Emperor Constantine's mother, visited the site of the monastery in the fourth century and built the first church near the "Burning Bush," in which the early monastic community could congregate. Justinian rebuilt the church in the sixth century and the building still stands tall and proud today. For a moment I am jealous of Justinian. To have built something so wonderful and then something even more grand: the Hagia Sofia in Istanbul (then Constantinople).

Yahia opens a door and we find ourselves standing on the wooden balcony hanging forty feet above the monastery courtyard. The heavy metal door that John Kinnear mentions in his journal has been replaced by a lightweight wooden trap door, which Yahia opens for a few vertigo-inducing seconds. The massive pulley that dangles above the trap door and a rope as thick as my forearm betrays the force required to haul visitors up to safety.

We pass by the Fountain of Moses. The freshwater spring is the main source of hydration for the monastery. Yahia points out that the fortress has been constructed so that water can also be accessed from outside the fortifications. This would prevent thirsty bandits from sacking the convent for its water, one more detail that contribute to the longevity of the monastery.

Yahia points out another: a press used since ancient times to crush olives for their oil.

"The electricity of ancient times," Yahia explains, "We grow our own olives. We make our own oil. No matter what happens anywhere in the world, the monastery is an independent unit, geared to survive. We are soon getting our very own solar plant for electricity."

Yahia brings us to the minaret, which towers above a building that used to be a guesthouse for the pilgrims. After the wave of Islam swept across Arabia in the seventh century, the priests of the convent petitioned Prophet Mohammed for protection. It is said that Mohammed visited the monastery in 625CE. After visiting the Burning Bush and Mount Sinai, so enamored was Mohammed with the place where "God's feet touched twice," he personally signed an order of protection – an *astiname*. According to the document, a photocopy of which is displayed in the monastery store, Muslims are not allowed to plunder St. Catherine and are not to spoil the church in any way. They are also not allowed to impose taxes on Christian monks and are not allowed to marry Christian women without their consent. Christians cannot be forced to carry arms and Muslims are obliged to protect them at all times. The *astiname* was nothing less than a peace accord between the Muslims and the Christians – except when it was not. Hence, just in case, the guesthouse was converted into a mosque and a minaret was constructed over it, visible from outside the fortification.

I press my face against a dust-streaked window through which I discern a dark room. Somewhere in there is the oldest known surviving wooden minbar in the Muslim world. The door of the mosque is locked.

"You cannot go in there." John anticipates my question as I turn around to him, my plea stuck in my throat.

Yahia leads me towards the back of the compound, past the monastic dormitories and corridors that hang over courtyards and points out the spot that Roberts skillfully captured in his sketch – the spartan hidden world of the monks where they pray, toil, eat and sleep. I am in the middle of their day. They are finishing their lunch and probably getting ready for the 2 pm prayers. I can sense our private tour ending.

"Yahia, do you go to the library?"

"Often," he says. The monks have free access to it. They go there to pick up reading material every week. I ask him if I could visit. I had to ask. The answer to an unasked question is always No. Yahia opens his eyes wide until his pupil swim in the whites of his eyes. He shakes his head vigorously and smiles. I do not push it.

Tischendorf's shadow still falls on the monastery of St. Catherine.

Yahia lets us stay for as long as we want, allowing me to make a few sketches. When I am done, we exit through the archway, past a light eyed Bedu of the Gebeliya tribe sitting cross-legged on a handspun rug. Emperor Justinian brought the light-haired mountain people from Macedonia in the sixth century to guard the monastery. They were still guarding the monastery when Roberts departed on 22nd February 1839. They are still here today.

Ossuary @ St. Catherine

The mountains are frozen when we leave the St. Catherine's village the next morning. A spreading fuchsia blot in the eastern sky signals a clear day ahead of us. A thin sheet of ice blankets the ground, which Showqi stomps, cracking and crunching it with the zest of a five-year-old. He has been cooped up at the monastery the last four days and is ready to head out into the desert.

We are headed to the easternmost tip of Egypt, to the town of Taba, which borders Israel. We cross the peninsula, skirting the grey granite mountains of the Sinai, passing under outcroppings of orange sandstone bluffs and a jumble of craggy interlocking ochre wadis that would drive the Minotaur crazy. As the desert opens, so does Showqi. He retired from the Egyptian army as a one-star captain. He had been posted in the Libyan desert at the start of his career and in the Sinai for the rest of it. He knows his way around both the deserts, in light and in dark, and in every season of the year. He talks about the grueling training they had to undergo in the arduous terrain – forced marches, camouflage, reconnaissance, weapons, navigation by stars and living off the land.

His shares with me his most memorable night in the armed forces:

In the 1970s, the relationship between Colonel Muammar Ghaddafi and Anwar Sadat had reached a nadir. Egypt had unsuccessfully fought in the so-called Yom Kippur War of 1973. Ghaddafi's dreams of leading a united Arab front against Israel had been crushed by Egypt's softened stance after the war. Matters boiled over in 1977 and the two neighbors clashed in the Libyan desert. With tensions high, shots were fired, and insults were exchanged publicly. In a fit of rage after a particularly insulting tirade from Ghaddafi, Sadat ordered a mission into Libyan territory. Egyptian commandoes flew in helicopters that ducked under Libya's Soviet-manufactured radars, soldiers rappelled into a secure compound in Benghazi and delivered a handwritten note to Ghaddafi's bedroom. The mission was a show of strength to demonstrate to Ghaddafi that he could be reached anytime Egypt wanted. Showqi was a commando on that sortie in the summer of '77.

I listen with increasing fascination. As a teenager, I had often dreamed of joining the Indian army as a commissioned officer with a possible career in military intelligence. It was not meant to be.

We stop for tea at a Bedu house in Wadi Arada. Sheik Ferigg, the patriarch of the house and Showqi know each other from their days in the army. The two share laughs, stories and cigarettes sitting in the adobe courtyard of the rural house. Sheikh Ferigg's family gathers around us: His wife, two daughters-in-law and a dozen kids, ranging from two months to twelve years old, look at me as if I alighted from a flying saucer. I put my polaroid camera to good use. They are fascinated to see their pictures appear on paper, probably the first time kids of the digital age are seeing themselves in an analog image. Soon each child wants a solo photo and I happily oblige, following them to their favorite spot in the backyard, letting them pose shyly.

In the courtyard, the elders sit cross-legged while the youngest daughter-in-law shows me a coin-purse made of beads. I could have bought one just like it in a souvenir shop on the Giza plateau, but receiving it from the veiled Bedouin woman makes me feel like a family heirloom is changing hands. After I have paid her, she pushes another one in my direction.

"A gift for your kids," John translates.

Back under the desert sun, the 4x4 glides along the scribble of a road. I spot a girl in a green hijab, 10 or 11 years old, leading a herd of sheep into the open desert. Her steps are quick and determined, as if she has fought the world. She heads to a little

St Catherine Bazaar, Sinai. Egypt

stream behind an outcropping of rocks in the distance, the only one in the area that has a guaranteed seep at this time of the year, Showqi tells me. I watch, fascinated, as the heat eddies stretch and deform her tiny figure, smooshing her into the horizon; one minute she is there, the next she is gone.

The Persian-blue expanse of the Bay of Aqaba appears on our right. A twelfth century fortress guards the mouth of the bay where four lands come together in a tight fist. Roberts' relief at the sight of the blue after several days in the rugged desert could not have been different from my own.

On 23rd February, Roberts wrote a delightfully detailed entry in his journal:

> "...WALKED FOR TWO HOURS, THEN SPREAD
> OUR CARPETS AND BREAKFASTED, ON BREAD
> BAKED BY THE MONKS, COLD MEAT, BUTTER
> FROM CAIRO, DATES, OLIVES, AND WATER
> DILUTED WITH A LITTLE BRANDY TO TAKE OFF
> THE BITTER TASTE. AFTER RESTING ABOUT
> AN HOUR, SMOKING A PIPE OF THE FINEST
> TURKISH TOBACCO, WE START AS USUAL
> AFTER THE CARAVAN..."

But the best material is once again found in John Kinnear's writing. He writes about seeing in the distance a light blue mist rising over the deep blue water of the sea, only to realize as they got closer that the vapor is actually fine sand. They had to walk through this cloud of white sand for two hours; the storm was so intense they could not see more than ten yards.

Sand in every nook and cranny of their body – "I felt it grinding in my teeth the whole evening" – was not their biggest problem that day. They had completely run out of water and had to dispatch a Bedouin ahead in the sandstorm with empty camel

PRINCIPAL COURT OF THE CONVENT OF ST. CATHERINE
BY DAVID ROBERTS, R.A.

skins in search of water for the group. He returned empty-handed, adding to the misery. Samuel Coleridge's lines "Water, water everywhere, not any drop to drink" composed just 40 years before, would have correctly summarized their misery.

Roberts eventually made it to Aqaba. The hurdles in the journey seemed to be of even more epic proportions once they had been successfully overcome.

I am starting to see my hurdles in the form of barbed wire fences as we drive north. An army post barricades the road ahead of us. Aqaba is a mere twenty-six kilometers from where we are. If Showqi could keep driving, we would be there in forty minutes. Unfortunately, there are two international boundaries in between – Egypt touches Israel and Israel touches Jordan at Eilat. Showqi's 4x4 turns back at Taba, and heads for Cairo. A different drive, driver and companion wait for me on the other side.

El Khazneh, Petra

JORDAN

~~~~

"I have often thrown my pencil away in despair of ever
being able to convey any idea of this extraordinary place."
— DAVID ROBERTS, 8TH MARCH 1839, PETRA.

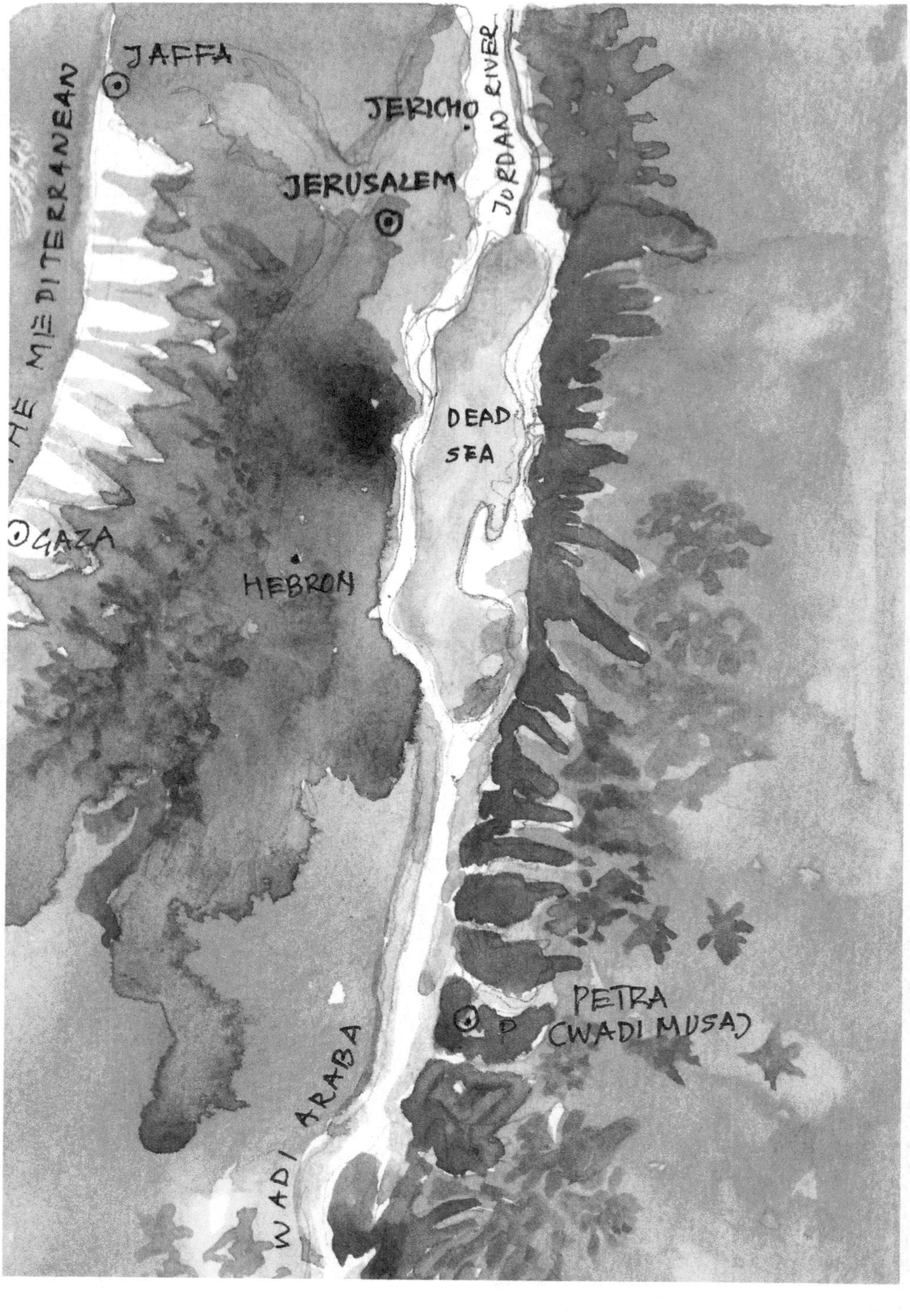

JAFFA
THE MEDITERRANEAN
JERICHO
JORDAN RIVER
JERUSALEM
DEAD SEA
GAZA
HEBRON
PETRA
(WADI MUSA)
WADI ARABA

AQABA

~~~~~

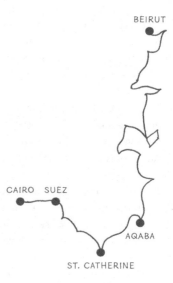

No two international borders so close to each other could be more different.

The border between Egypt and Israel is the result of a flick of a pen. The line could have been drawn a few millimeters here or there, hundreds of acres of arid land changing nationality, the landscape on either side of the barbed wire otherwise indistinguishable – a usual feature of a manmade border. The line of ink got Israel a wedge-shaped landmass with a tiny but strategic toehold on the Gulf of Aqaba and a seat at a very important political table. On the other hand, Israel is demarcated with Jordan along Wadi Araba, a valley created by monumental tectonic forces that tore Africa from Asia hundreds of millions of years ago. Jordan sits on the Arabian plate. Israel is on the Sinai microplate. The two countries float in magma older than some stars in the sky and the two plates steadily drift away from each other every day.

Diverse geographies induce different climatic conditions that force different ways of living, different cultures and sometimes different people across the divide. The people on either side of Wadi Araba speak Arabic, pray to Allah, and have Bedouin blood running through their veins, yet they could not be more different. The people of Jordan are, on the whole, more educated, more liberal, and better off economically. They are lighter skinned and light eyed. They stand taller, hold their shoulders back confidently, and speak more softly than their counterparts in Sinai. It is believed that the Bedouins east of the Wadi Araba inherited these physical traits from the Circassians who migrated thousands of miles into the Levant thousands of years ago. They decided to stop short of entering the Sinai Peninsula for reasons that are no longer known or understood.

John and Showqi are by now back in Cairo and I am in Aqaba with Ananth, whom I have known for over a decade. I reached out to Ananth as soon as I started planning the David Roberts adventure. Despite having a toddler at home, a fledgling startup, and an Indian passport that requires the navigation of red-tape visa processing, Ananth promised to meet me in Jordan ("… and Lebanon, if I can swing the visa," he said.)

Ananth and I were colleagues across thirteen time-zones in the flat world of globalization. Work trips would take me to Bangalore three times a year. After long grueling days in the office, fulfilling quirky Western demands through a maze of quirkier Eastern hacks, Ananth would use his intimate knowledge of the "Garden City" to find the best watering holes for the visitors in the evening.

One learns to tolerate most colleagues at work. Some are fun to meet over beers at the end of the day, a few you might invite home for dinner. A tiny fraction, if any, make good travel companions. Ananth was a member of that very small, handpicked club.

So, here we are, at the southernmost tip of Jordan on a bright sunny day, the shimmering emerald-green water of the Red Sea lapping at our feet where three deserts smash together – the Arabian, the Negev and the Sinai – a spot so strategic that King Solomon docked his naval fleet to guard the gold ships from Ophir. The present-day countries of Saudi Arabia, Jordan, Israel, and Egypt converge here and, with the Gulf of Aqaba, clench together like a fist.

This is the site of the famous Battle of Aqaba in World War I, in which the forces of the Arab Revolt won a tactical victory over the Ottoman army. The Arabs were advised by a misfit British officer and the battle was depicted in an epic Hollywood blockbuster, with the lead played by a charismatic, misfit British actor. The battle and the movie immortalized them both, T.E. Lawrence and Peter O'Toole respectively, each being called "Lawrence of Arabia" for the rest of their lives.

The site of the Battle of Aqaba is the tiniest fortress I have seen – the size of a small cathedral, decorated in the Mamluk style with crenellated turrets and an elaborate shield carved over the main entrance. For centuries, the fort guarded the only known fresh water well in the region. Later it became a khan for Hajj travelers to Mecca. The Crusader structure was rebuilt by Sultan Ghuri in the early sixteenth century and was also used by trading ships as a storage bay.

Between 27th February and 1st March 1839, David Roberts set up a camp somewhere between the fort and the bay. This was as far east as the Beni Said tribe would guide him. Roberts' caravan was to be handed over to another Bedouin tribe, the Alloween of Wadi Musa. While they waited for the Alloween to arrive, Roberts passed the time swimming in the gulf and fending off the advances of the Governor of Aqaba, who was known to be untrustworthy.

The leader of the Alloween, Sheikh Hussein, was well-known amongst the European travelers in the Levant. Maurice Linant, whose sketches of Petra had inspired Roberts, had traveled with Sheikh Hussein to Wadi Musa and graciously sent an elaborate letter of introduction along with Roberts. But the Alloween were late to arrive. Was the three-day delay in the Sheikh's arrival a power play to keep the Europeans helplessly trapped under the desert sun? After all, a price had not been negotiated with the Sheikh. Every little bit of leverage matters in a negotiation. Finally, when the two parties settled down to negotiate the arrangement, Sheikh Hussein's opening gambit was exorbitant. Roberts threatened to return to Cairo rather than accept. After much back and forth, haggling, posturing and drama, with Roberts amused initially and irritated increasingly as the day progressed, they finally came to an agreement. For a sum of £45, or 4500 piastres, the Alloween would take Roberts to Wadi Musa, where he could stay for as long as he wanted and then safely conduct him to Hebron in Palestine.

Once the deal was sealed, the parties sat down for a celebratory dinner. A goat was procured from the fort, along with some fish from the gulf. Rice was cooked with plenty of butter and onions and served with *mismish* – apricots – from Damascus. Coffee was guzzled and plenty of Turkish tobacco was smoked. The feast ended a long stressful day. Roberts said goodbye to the Bedouin of Beni Said, whom he had grown very fond of, and started his onward journey on the Kings Highway toward Wadi Araba.

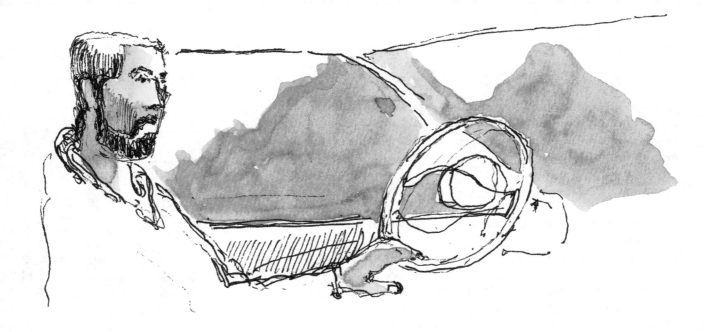

The news has spread that a party is looking for a ride to Wadi Musa. Ananth and I are surrounded by a group of ragtag taxi drivers.

"45 Jordan dollars to go to Wadi Musa," says a young driver with a set of pearly white teeth.

"25 Jordan dollars," I counter.

"No negotiating, mister. Prices are fixed," he says, surprised with my lack of knowledge of how things work around here.

"No negotiating" is the starting point of all negotiations. "I can show you prices on the internet," I wave my phone, which does not have a signal, a bluff that usually works.

"I can show you the prices on this board," the taxi driver counters. I follow the indignant driver around the corner of the building and stand in front of a five-foot tall board, which has a pricelist painted in oil, the numbers agreeing with the driver's offer.

Once the price is settled, the pearly white teeth reappear, and we warm up to Zaid quickly. In the Arab-Bedouin tradition, he welcomes us to Jordan, hand on his heart and head bowed, he offers Jordan to us as our second home and informs us that we are now in Zaid's hospitality. His smile gets wider when we tell him to stop for a quick bite, but only if he takes us where he eats regularly. He is hungry himself, he says, and drives us to a hole-in-the-wall that is clearly popular with the taxi-drivers. He orders a feast – *mansaf*, falafel, hummus, *fattet*. We eat Arabic-style, twisting pieces of pita bread and using them to scoop food from the bowls placed in the center.

Ananth notices Zaid stealing glances at a blue-eyed girl seated at a nearby table.

"My mom is trying to get me married," Zaid fake-moans, when Ananth ribs him about it. "I am only twenty-five. I am a free bird, Insh'Allah. I come and go as I please," he declares, unable to take his eyes away from the blue eyes across the room. He refuses to let us pay.

"You are my guests," he says thumping his chest with an open palm.

The four-lane Route 47 attacks the desert with gusto, like a workaholic at his desk on a Monday morning. As our car cleaves the desert of Wadi Rum, so did Roberts, traveling up Wadi Araba with his new caravan of twenty-three camels and dromedaries belonging to the Alloween tribe. Roberts noted with some disappointment that the Alloween were not as colorfully dressed as the Beni Said. Roberts had liberally used the Beni Said as models for his compositions. The lack of decoration did not stop Roberts from sketching the Alloween tending to the camels and setting up camp on the leeward side of a rock in a stunning composition. John Kinnear's journal noted that the meal that evening consisted of Arab bread, Dutch cheese and the remains of some mutton. On top of the rocky outcropping is a watchtower built by the Nabateans, an ancient signaling circuit along the ancient trade route. Roberts dated the sketch 5th February 1839 – a mistake, as he was still in Cairo on that date. He probably meant to write 5th March.

Zaid keeps us entertained through the two-hour drive. He talks about the declining tourists to Petra. (This was his first trip in six days.) He talks about his love for Bollywood. (Would he meet Deepika Padukone if he traveled to Mumbai?) He talks about the Syrian war. (Jordan is safe. No *Daesh*. No *tha-thai-thai!* he says, his index finger and thumb imitating the L shape of a recoiling firearm.) But mostly he talks about his village, his friends who are returning from the city because of unemployment and his paranoid mom, who wants him to be married before his hormones lead him astray.

Petra

A friend introduced me to an outfitter in Amman who specializes in personalized trips. I sent him an email while I was in Cairo. He called me back promptly. "Sunil, I want to make sure I understood your email correctly. You want to ride a camel from Aqaba to Petra?"

I admitted that I did. He heard me out patiently, his breathing as heavy as his accent. He was familiar with David Roberts' work. In fact, he had a Roberts Petra lithograph on the homepage of his website.

"Have you ridden a camel before?"

I hadn't.

"A horse?"

Negative.

"A bicycle?"

"Yes, I have!"

"For five consecutive days, riding all day?"

Negative.

The line was silent for a few seconds; perhaps he hoped I would use the time to reconsider my idea. I powered through the silence. I have come far enough in life powering through such silences.

"It can be expensive," he said.

"How expensive?"

He quoted a ridiculously high number.

"No problem" I said, deciding to call his bluff.

He promised he would call me back.

He called back three days later. The journey would take six days. I would need two men and five camels. He was confident he could find the men, but he was not so sure he could find suitable camels. The camel owners he had talked to did not remember their camels ever having made such a long and arduous journey. Instead, why don't I ride the camel for 3 hours in Wadi Rum? Would that work?

Ananth's dates had not been finalized. That left me with no time to tighten the logistics of hiring a camel. I had by then also better defined my David Roberts adventure. I dropped the idea.

WADI MUSA

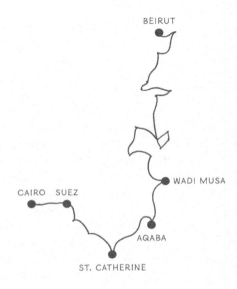

BEIRUT

WADI MUSA

CAIRO SUEZ

AQABA

ST. CATHERINE

"Since the Arab Spring ..." I quickly tune out the melancholy-looking man at the reception who is photocopying our passports. Our hotel is kitty corner from the Petra visitor center. Even though it is empty, we have been put up in a wing removed from the main building. The room allotted to us seems to be the handiwork of an artist who took time out of his busy schedule building prison cells to concoct, in the middle of the most picturesque ochre wilderness, a room with no windows.

A first-century Nabatean cave has been converted into a restaurant. Ananth and I are seated in an ancient niche in the ancient wall of the cave. The restaurant is virtually empty. Half a dozen tourists are sprinkled on tables around the cave, back from a day amidst the ruins of Petra. A Bedouin wearing a handspun robe yodels a plea to his lover in Arabic, strumming a vintage *oud*. Ananth dips warm *shrek* in a lentil soup laced with crushed green chilies on our request and savors it, eyes closed, isolating in his mind the ingredients of the silky thin Bedouin bread. "This is Arabic *rumali* roti." He concludes, referring to popular north-Indian bread, a large unleavened circle of dough cooked on an iron pot turned upside down on burning charcoals.

Ananth had stated three goals for his adventure in the Near East. Eating every possible variety of freshly made Arab bread tops the list.

Sufficiently fortified, we set out into the night. I am immediately numbed by the frigid desert wind that mercilessly penetrates the layers I am wearing. We walk through a slot canyon, the *Siq*, which leads towards the ruins of Petra in total darkness, keeping our torches switched off, navigating entirely by the strip of brilliantly illuminated inky-blue sky above. Eventually, we turn a bend and are greeted by the sight of the tastefully illuminated Khazneh – the Treasury. Reams have been written by travelers who have walked through this Siq and turned around the corner to come face-to-face with the most famous canyon architecture in the world. Not one of them describes the famous Khazneh at night.

The courtyard in front of the Khazneh is covered by several rows of battery-operated tealights wrapped in translucent paper bags. Bedouin rugs are laid out in neat lines on the ground. Steaming hot sweet tea is being served. I take up a spot as far back in the shadows as possible. A couple dozen people eventually turn up in the bitter January night. At the appointed time, a Bedouin wrapped in a thick blanket takes his spot in the middle of the courtyard and plays a soulful tune on his flute. The Petra sound and light show matches its reputation of being a trite tourist trap, like sound and light shows all over the world. Halfway through the performance, I slip to the back of the canyon where I pretend to mingle with photographers nursing cameras on tripods. Then, hiding my condensed breath in a gloved hand, I quietly melt into the darkness of the canyon. Not daring to switch on my headlamp, I tip-toe, my right arm extended forward, fingers brushing against the rock wall until my eyes have acclimatized to the darkness. The canyon veers left and the Khazneh is visible no more. Walking past an area suitably named Street of Facades, a couple of hundred feet further, my shin painfully finds a jutting rock that I rest my butt on.

The wind moans. It bends along the canyon, lit up by the star-studded night. Under the pleasant starlight, Petra stands still, as it has for twenty-three centuries. Bells tinkle in the darkness; a camel somewhere close by senses my presence. Naked electric bulbs illuminate the cavernous entrances of hundreds of caves pecked into the mountainside like the glowing eyes of a pack of predators waiting by a waterhole. The air is smoky. Meat barbeques on open fires in open-air kitchens on ridges hugging the mountainside. Bedouins live in these rock shelters, which have been passed down for generations.

How different could this scene have been in 1839? Roberts approached Petra from the south, following a sheep track over the mountains. On 6th March he pitched his tent in open space besides the stream that gurgled down the canyon. But only after he paid a sum of 300 piastres to the Fellaheen Bedouins of Wadi Musa did they made it clear that the Alloween guides, who had guided Roberts from Aqaba, had no jurisdiction inside the canyon. Roberts' camp lay within sight of the royal tombs,

just past the Roman colonnade, a spot not far away from where I sit rubbing my bruised shin. Over the next six days, Roberts would do some of the best work of his life. His lithographs of Petra have a timeless quality, accurately capturing the shimmering desert light on beautiful pink-orange sandstone cliffs. While Burkhardt discovered Petra in 1812, it wasn't really until the 1840s that the West discovered it through Roberts' sketches, so stunning are his compositions.

JL Burkhardt's story deserves a mention. The explorer-traveler was the first European to lay eyes on the ruins of Petra since the Crusades. Burkhardt was on his way from Syria to Central Africa in search of the source of River Niger. He eschewed the well-known, safer route through the Holy Land. Instead, he took the lawless, bandit-infested, lesser-explored desert on the east of the River Jordan because that is just how Burckhardt did things. He was born into a wealthy Swiss family and had ended up with the African Association, which was looking to explore the heart of Africa. The race to discover and conquer the "Dark Continent" was just beginning to heat up. Burkhardt trained for his mission the way the Karate Kid trained for his title match: he practiced walking barefoot several miles every day, slept in the open on simmering hot and bitterly cold days, acclimatized to surviving on raw vegetables and learned to find and conserve potable water. He took crash courses in Arabic, astronomy, chemistry, medicine, and minerology before he moved to Syria. He lived there for a further three years, perfecting various local dialects of Arabic and learning the nuances of local Bedouin customs. He had immersed himself in the task with so much vigor that towards the end he was indistinguishable as a person of European origin. He was no longer in disguise; he had become Ibrahim ibn Abdullah, the alias he assumed in Syria.

In May 1812, Burkhardt started from Aleppo in Syria and traveled south through Damascus, Ajloun, Jerash, Amman, Madaba, and Kerak – towns and cities that are tightly woven into the tapestry

street of facades, Petra

of the Middle East history, but largely unexplored. In the course of his travels, Burkhardt picked up rumors about the ruins of a lost city situated on an ancient trade route where Prophet Harun[5] was believed to have been buried. He stopped at the village of Wadi Musa, which consisted of three hundred houses enclosed in a wall that had three entrances. In exchange for a pair of old horseshoes, he convinced a Lauthene Bedouin to guide him to the tomb of Harun in order to sacrifice a goat. He had the foresight to bring with him a goat all the way from Shobak, a crusader-era castle town twenty miles away, because that is how Burkhardt did things – meticulous planning and even more meticulous execution.

J. L. BURCHARDT

Burkhardt's Bedouin guide led him along the flowing stream into the *Siq,* at the end of which he encountered the jaw-dropping sight of al-Khazneh. Still following his guide down the meandering valley, he ran smack into the old, ruined city, "half as old as time," his expert eyes experiencing, deciphering, and recording the astonishing sights simultaneously. He knew the indifference Arabs had towards ruins – unlivable old buildings were everywhere and worthless in the day-to-day life-and-death situations of thirst, hunger and survival. Burkhardt understood that he needed to assume an attitude of nonchalance towards the ruins yet slow down the guide enough to peek into some without arousing suspicion. Trudging behind his guide while the ruins screamed to be explored, measured, and sketched on that hot summer day of August 1812 was easily the most challenging day of his life – and the most fulfilling.

In the time it took him to walk from one end of the city to the other, with small diversions to peep inside the buildings carved into the rock, Burkhardt carefully tracked everything he saw. Later that night, after he slaughtered the goat to the Prophet Harun, exhausted by the exertion and excitement, his clothes still drenched in the goat's blood, he huddled beside a tiny fire

and recorded his observations in his journal with extraordinary detail and passion. The journal, his most prized possession, was then carefully hidden in his voluminous turban. He was afraid that the discovery of his writing would lead to its confiscation and destruction, before he was put to death. In the small hours of the next morning, Burkhardt walked to the Siq on his way back, but the darkness cruelly stole his last chance to see the city one more time.

Burkhardt spent less than twenty-four hours in Petra, but his name is linked to it forever. He continued to Cairo, where he waited for a suitable caravan to Niger and Timbuctoo, which never came. Instead, he traveled up the River Nile where he discovered the temple of Abu Simbel. He reached as far as Shendy in Sudan before heading towards the east coast of Africa to catch a boat to Jeddah. There, Burkhardt spent three

[5] Prophet Haroun is the brother of Moses, known to Christians as Prophet Aaron.

months disguised as a panhandler in Mecca to avoid attracting any attention, before retuning back to Cairo, where he died of dysentery in 1817. He was just 33.[6]

In 1819, several old manuscripts and books that Burkhardt collected on his expedition were shipped back to Cambridge University. His leather-bound and weather-beaten journal that contained the handwritten pages describing his breathtaking twenty-four hours in Petra had outlived the author. They now reside in the archives of the Royal Geographical Society in London. Burkhardt never again laid eyes on Petra, but his description led Captains Irby and Mangles to visit the ruins in 1818. Linant followed in 1828 and Roberts followed Linant in 1839. Now here I am, thrilled and privileged, walking in the footsteps of David Roberts, 179 years later.

I pull out of my bag a printout of the fourteen pages Burkhardt wrote the night of 22nd August 1812. In the dim glow of the headlamp cupped in my gloved hand, I read through my favorite parts.

For somebody under enormous time pressure, Burkhardt was an extraordinary observer with a near-photographic memory and was able to quickly put two and two together. For example, he correctly guesses how the location of the Khazneh was chosen:

"... THE SITUATION AND BEAUTY OF WHICH ARE CALCULATED TO MAKE AN EXTRAORDINARY IMPRESSION UPON THE TRAVELER, AFTER HAVING TRAVERSED FOR NEARLY HALF AN HOUR SUCH A GLOOMY AND ALMOST SUBTERRANEOUS PASSAGE."

He goes on to call al-Khazneh "the most elegant remains of antiquity existing in Syria." After estimating the dimensions of the interiors of Khazneh and describing the architecture in great details, he astutely concludes that the building, considered a royal residence, was in fact "...the sepulchre of a prince." Walking through the area that is now called the Street of Facades, he comments that "...these fronts resemble those of several of the tombs of Palmyra," and that "...there are no two sepulchres in Wady Mousa perfectly alike."

Passing by the Roman theatre, an architectural style that he must have recognized instantaneously, he notes, "... theatre cut entirely out of the rock, with all its benches. It may be capable of containing about three thousand spectators," an estimate accurate even today. Walking further down the canyon he writes:

"THE FINEST SEPULCHRES IN WADY MOUSA ARE IN THE EASTERN CLIFF, IN FRONT OF THIS OPEN SPACE, WHERE I COUNTED UPWARDS OF FIFTY, CLOSE TO EACH OTHER. HIGH UP IN THE CLIFF, I PARTICULARLY OBSERVED ONE LARGE SEPULCHRE, ADORNED WITH CORINTHIAN PILASTERS."

Burkhardt's exasperated Bedouin guide finally uttered the scary words, "I see now that you are an infidel, who has some particular business amongst the ruins of the city." At that point, Burkhardt had no choice but to abandon any more exploration to assuage his guide's suspicions and proceed to the tomb of Haroun to sacrifice the goat.

---

[6] Osman Effendi, whose house David Robert's had rented in Cairo, was with Burkhardt until the end, through the latter's fatal illness. He directed the Muslim funeral for the renowned explorer, laying him in a grave in the Bab al-Nasr cemetery with his own hands. Thompson, Jason. "Osman Effendi: A Scottish Convert to Islam in Early Nineteenth-Century Egypt." *Journal of World History*, vol. 5, no. 1, 1994, pp. 99–123.

"IT IS VERY UNFORTUNATE FOR EUROPEAN
TRAVELLERS THAT THE IDEA OF TREASURES
BEING HIDDEN IN ANCIENT EDIFICES IS SO
STRONGLY ROOTED IN THE MINDS OF THE
ARABS AND TURKS; NOR ARE THEY SATISFIED
WITH WATCHING ALL THE STRANGER'S
STEPS; THEY BELIEVE THAT IT IS SUFFICIENT
FOR A TRUE MAGICIAN TO HAVE SEEN AND
OBSERVED THE SPOT WHERE TREASURES
ARE HIDDEN … IN ORDER TO BE ABLE
AFTERWARDS, AT HIS EASE, TO COMMAND
THE GUARDIAN OF THE TREASURE TO SET
THE WHOLE BEFORE HIM. IF THE TRAVELLER
TAKES THE DIMENSIONS OF A BUILDING OR
A COLUMN, THEY ARE PERSUADED THAT IT
IS A MAGICAL PROCEEDING. EVEN THE MOST
LIBERAL MINDED TURKS OF SYRIA REASON
IN THE SAME MANNER, AND THE MORE
TRAVELLERS THEY SEE, THE STRONGER IS
THEIR CONVICTION THAT THEIR OBJECT IS TO
SEARCH FOR TREASURES."

In his heart of hearts, Burkhardt knew he had made an
amazing discovery. Being the scientist that he was, he stated
his observations and provided a recommendation, but in the
absence of proof, he left the conclusions to the experts. He
chose to end his entry for the day humbly:

"OF THIS AT LEAST I AM PERSUADED, FROM
ALL THE INFORMATION I PROCURED, THAT
THERE IS NO OTHER RUIN BETWEEN THE
EXTREMITIES OF THE DEAD SEA AND RED
SEA, OF SUFFICIENT IMPORTANCE TO
ANSWER TO THAT CITY. WHETHER OR NOT
I HAVE DISCOVERED THE REMAINS OF THE
CAPITAL OF ARABIA PETRÆA, I LEAVE TO THE
DECISION OF GREEK SCHOLARS."

EL SIQ, PETRA

An electronic beep brings me out of my reverie. The screen of my phone lights up.

"We are almost done here, *Indian* Jones," pings a text message from Ananth. I fold the papers and stuff them in my pocket. I must head back to the Khazneh before my absence is noticed.

~~~~~

At first light, we walk through the serpentine slot canyon once again, as we would many times over the next several days. The sound of our shoes scraping the ancient pavement echoes in the confined space. We are the only visitors at the gate at this hour; the guard at the entrance is ensconced in a thick woolen blanket, struggling to keep his eyes open. Halfway down the *Siq*, we are met by a dog; his wagging tail needs no translation. He leads the way to the end of the canyon, turning frequently to ensure we are following him. The rose-pink façade of the Khazneh is glowing orange in the predawn light. The compression of the *Siq* and the spectacular opening in front of the classical frontage does not fail to take my breath away, even though I am expecting it. The dramatic reveal looks like the work of a master magician.

The coffee and souvenir shops in the courtyard of the Khazneh are still closed. Ananth and I settle down for a splendid morning, grateful for the tourist slowdown that allows a once-in-a-lifetime crowd-free experience of Petra. The sunrays finally tilt down onto the ancient columns, the pungent smell of burning wood permeates the canyon, the stalls open and mint tea makes its way to a table where I sit and sketch.

A man wearing a camel-hair trench coat and sporting a patch of beard is posing for me. After I finish, I offer him my sketchbook and with rare humility, add, "I am not good at drawing people."

'Issah, I am not good at drawing people'
'I can see that'

Issa

"I can see that" he quickly retorts. This is how we meet the charming Issa.

"You made me look fat," he accuses me, with a twinkle in his eyes.

"I can fix that," I offer with a wink, "For every dollar you give me, I can reduce a pound."

He asks if we need a guide. We decline.

By the time we have finished our third cup of sweet mint tea, a dozen people mill in the courtyard – still more locals than visitors. Bedouins in black, with pointed beards and kohl lined eyes; camels in technicolor regalia; kids selling postcards and trinkets. I amuse the kids by pointing my polaroid at them, the whirring motor spitting out a white square. Their eyes grow agog when the white paper changes into their likeliness after I pretend to cast a spell on it, my fingers wiggling, cackling like a wizard. They scamper off, returning to their friends, wanting to show each other the magician with the magic paper. Amidst toothy giggles and laughter, I take plenty of pictures. They want to keep their pictures. Their hands stretch in front of my face.

"What do I get?" I ask.

I am offered a wide-eyed, innocent look, but I have two daughters at home. That look no longer works on me. A young girl offers a bracelet for her photo, but I refuse again.

She adds a camel-tooth ring and I finally accept the deal.

"You bargain like a Bedouin," Issa tells me. He has been hovering around us, "keeping an eye," in his words.

THE HIGH PLACE OF SLACRIFICE, PETRA

We agree to let him take us to a spot that has a bird's eye view of the Khazneh. Getting there requires a hard scramble, the kind that at the halfway mark makes me question my decision. *What were you thinking?* Thigh muscles screaming, heart doing handsprings in the ribcage, I eventually make it. Nearby fresh coffee is brewing under a thatched shelter. At this angle, the Khazneh looks even more majestic, the people in the courtyard mere dots from this distance. It all comes together for me here and now – morning light on the pink sandstone, two-thousand-year-old architecture, and a cup of fresh coffee after a hard hike. I can hear the architect of the Khazneh agreeing with me. This is where he sat to plan and detail the monument. Later, from this very spot, he must have guided the workers, shouting one moment and sitting back to enjoy his handiwork the next.

We are at that point on the mountain where the climb up is cheaper than the climb down. So, up we go. All around us, nooks and crannies, invisible from the canyon floor, have been claimed and occupied, human beings crawling into every available habitable space. The shelters are of all sizes and levels of permanency. A corrugated sheet pushed into the mountainside, supported by two wooden beams. A second home? A two-brick high wall with a canvas roof and a dish antenna. A man-cave? A stove and a pot hidden behind rocks. A hiker's bivouac? A blanket snuck behind a rock. Lover's rendezvous?

The only way to move forward at this point is to drop down to all fours, my face pressing against the rock. I would rather lose face than risk a limb. Soon, we crest the mountain that towers above the Khazneh. This is the High Place of Sacrifice, an ancient altar with channels for draining blood – hence the name. A heady place to take heads off.

We stop at a coffee shop run by Issa's wife. After several cups of sweet mint tea and the purchase of a carved rock amulet, we part ways with Issa, but not before he tells us where to eat. "Issa will make the reservations," he says, "Be there in an hour. You don't want to keep Umm Abdulla waiting."

We cross the mountain and descend to a spot that has an aerial view of the valley. The white houses of Wadi Musa shimmer in the distance, dancing in the dust wave. Ananth lies down on a bare rock, his head supported by his palms, fingers intertwined under his head, his face tilted up to the sun. He has been following a cricket match between India and England on his mobile phone and the repeated clucking of his tongue betrays India's dismal performance. A bleating sheep nibbles on blades of grass pushing through cracks. I find a spot where Roberts composed a memorable composition titled *Entrance to Petra*. From this spot, facing east and south, Roberts sketched the stream meandering from the Khazneh, looking over the Roman amphitheater carved out of the natural rock bowl.

As I sketch, I try to remember everything I have read about ancient trade routes. The West was a massive market for myrrh and frankincense between classical Greece and the fall of the Roman empire. The aromatic resins were applied as antiseptics, dissolved in perfumes, burned for rituals, embalming the dead, flavoring the wine, deodorizing armpits, and on and on. Five thousand tons of the good stuff traveled from the Arabian Peninsula up a spidery web of trade routes to Mediterranean ports every year. One such lucrative route passed through Nabatean territory, before it crossed the mountains of Avram and the desert of Negev culminating at the port of Gaza. The route was dotted

with caravanserais, watchtowers and forts – structures connected by geography and flowing water that offered traders safety and comfort in exchange for toll. Petra was a major stop on the route.

Sunbeaten travelers would arrive close to sunset – aching, sick, and thirsty. They would enter the *Siq, cool even on the hottest day and warm on a cold day. The Siq led to the* Khazneh – mysterious, beautifully lit, architecture rising out of the desert magically – a sign of prosperity, strength, safety, and luxury.

The travelers would continue deeper into the city, following the Street of Facades where just enough stone has been carved to create an impression of mighty architecture from around the known world: Roman columns, Greek capitals, Egyptian obelisks, Assyrian steps. The weary traders pitched tents. Cold water. Hot food. Music and dance. Carnal pleasures. A night's rest before it was time to move on. The travelers would be up at first light and gone before the sun's rays reached the bottom of the canyon.

A prosperous little strip in the middle of a parched desert, designed for an overnight stay or two, decorated with architecture from all around the world. Does that not sound like a megapolis in the United States associated with the moniker of lost wages?

Was Petra the Las Vegas of the incense route?

"The Khazneh is not a tomb or treasury or a temple then? It's a billboard?" Ananth laughs.

Welcome to Petra. Rooms Available. Free HBO. Burkhardt would probably stab me through the heart with his pencil for such a preposterous interpretation.

From my elevated vantage point, the two levels of habitation in Petra are clearly visible: the 'business' district at street level with Roman/Egyptian/Mesopotamian style architecture, and

THE ROMAN THEATRE, PETRA JORDAN.

ENTRANCE TO PETRA BY DAVID ROBERTS, R.A.
10TH MARCH 1839

the Arab-style homes wedged into tiny caves on narrow ledges about 25-30 feet above the street.

A Bedu kid, not more than ten years old, runs up the hillside and stands behind me. His shadow falls on my sketchbook.

"David Roberts, food is ready," he sniffles, undoubtedly coached by Issa to say the exact words, accompanied, uncoached, with the universal sign of a pursed fist pecking at puckered lips. His other hand holds up his shorts that are threatening to slide off his hips at a moment's notice. "Umm Abdulla is waiting for you."

Hundreds of natural caves dot the mountains in Petra, many of which are inhabited by the Bedouin. The caves have belonged to their families for several generations – in a few cases, several centuries. I look around. The great-great-great grandfathers of some of these

families watched, perplexed and bemused, as David Roberts scribbled in his sketchbook. Worried that the *effendi* was looking for the famed treasure of Petra, the discovery of which would bring more of his kind of men into their private territory, the Bedouin decided to shake things up. Roberts was threatened, intimidated, held to ransom, and vandalized while he struggled with his own demons:

"I HAVE OFTEN THROWN MY PENCIL AWAY IN DESPAIR OF EVER BEING ABLE TO CONVEY ANY IDEA OF THIS EXTRAORDINARY PLACE."

Umm Abdulla's cave sits recessed into the mountainside, twenty feet above the canyon floor, with a panoramic view of the first-century royal tombs that are carved into the face of Jebel al-Kubtha. The approximately three-hundred-square-foot cave is secured with a metal door. Half of the cave is a kitchen with a wood-burning stove and an open pantry, neatly lined with cans of condiments. Plastic crates full of tomatoes, potatoes and green vegetables sit on the counter. The smell of freshly baked bread welcomes us. Umm Abdullah wears a *chador,* the smiling oval of her face uncovered, and applies *ghee* to a row of freshly kneaded balls of dough ready to go into the oven. The floor of the rest of the cave is covered with reed mats. Cotton cushions are set against the cold rock wall that I lean against, sipping mint tea, waiting to be offered the menu for lunch. Several Bedouin stoop through the entrance, greet Umm Abdulla, pick up polythene bags packed for them, put money on the counter, thank her, and leave, surprised to see us in their secret lunch spot.

Our lunch arrives – looks like Issa has pre-ordered it for us. Spinach and potato, spiced with *za'atar* and tahini, stuffed inside round, flat bread that has been baked in the adobe oven. The food is served with a tangy green mint, cilantro and chili sauce. We dig into the hot lunch with gusto, sitting cross-legged on the Bedouin mats, tearing the bread into strips with our bare hands still smeared with Nabatean dust.

~wwww~

I receive a cryptic text from John, my guide in Cairo and Sinai. *Did you read about the library in St. Catherine?*

I wait for several hours to get enough coverage on my phone to search online. In the meantime, tornadoes whirled in my head: *had the library been robbed? Who was the grey suit emerging from the library? Why was a sniper situated in the mountains? Who drove the gleaming black Mercedes I saw in the parking lot?* I had sensed that something was going on in the library of St. Catherine. *What was it? What did I miss?*

I must have a wry smile on my face when I finally read the news in the comfort of our hotel: after three years of extensive restoration work, and just 48 hours after my departure from St. Catherine, the library had been thrown open to the public. The inauguration ceremony was attended by the Egyptian Minister of Antiquities, Khaled Anany, along with a group of Egyptian officials and foreign ambassadors.

If there was a good reason for the inauguration ceremony to have been conducted with a level of secrecy befitting an Illuminati ritual, it escaped me. I had obsessed about the room full of untold treasures for several weeks. I could have been anywhere in the world in December 2017, but I was within a hundred feet of that room for four full days. Then the library had been opened to visitation and I had missed the event. I feel cheated for having lost the chance to visit it before it becomes an item on a million bucket lists. *Close your eyes and breathe*, I tell myself. Sometimes it's the only thing left to do.

Buried in the press release, an innocuous sentence attributed to a monk working at the monastery's library catches my attention. "The most valuable manuscript in the library is the Codex

Sinaiticus, dating back to the fourth century. This is the most precious manuscript in the world."

The scintillating statement makes it appear as if the Codex *is still in the library*. Once my heart is no longer beating wildly, I realize that this is a reference to the twelve complete leaves of parchment found by the monks of St. Catherine's Monastery in May 1975 during restoration work. Yes, a part of the Codex Sinaiticus is still at the monastery.

~~~~~~

The terrain of Petra is ideal for hard scrambles.

From a distance the cliff looks smooth like a wave, unconquerable and inhospitable until you get close and it offers a variety of ways to traverse – hand and toeholds, sheep trails, steps new and old. It is a hard terrain. It needs to be conquered with sweat and time. There are no shortcuts. The rocks are beautiful in shape, texture and color – orange, pink, red, and blue. The decision by ancient architects to carve, rather than build, seems obvious.

Ananth and I hike innumerable trails leading to many inaccessible ruins. Hiking is the second of the three goals Ananth had for the trip. One afternoon when there isn't a cloud in the sky and the sun is beating down mercilessly, we go looking for a slot canyon I had read about. Looking for the mouth of the side-canyon, we find ourselves away from the tourist trail, down Wadi Mudhlim, passing by the Sextius Florentinus tomb. Scurrying away from a fierce looking dog that does not like our presence, Ananth spots the first turn into a side-canyon that is marked as Sidd Maajn on my hand-drawn map. The canyon meanders deep inside the belly of the Jebel al-Kubtha, the mountain whose north face is carved with the royal tombs. About twenty minutes in, I call out to Ananth, who is walking several feet ahead of me, shattering the delicious silence we are soaking in. We must have already passed

the entrance to the slot, I tell him. We turn around and walk back until we are almost at the entrance of the side canyon, then turn back. After a few failed attempts at locating the entrance to the slot canyon, we find a spot to sit down, pull out our water bottles and guzzle cold water. I mentally kick myself for failing to write better directions in my journal.

Just as I reach the conclusion that we might need to turn all the way back and head to the *Siq*, a local comes lumbering around the corner, his feet shod in heavy-duty mismatched hiking shoes, carrying a tattered multi-day backpack. I put on my best nonchalant-as-an-owl look, but my sheepish grin gives my foolishness away. He winks as he passes us – clearly, we are not the first set of travelers he has rescued in this labyrinth. We scramble after our savior, who ducks into the slot canyon, which was less than twenty feet away from us. The opening is hidden under a dark patch of a shadow that we would have missed even if we were standing next to it. Once inside the canyon, the view changes again. *It must be the change in light*, I tell myself. After all, we had taken a ninety-degree turn.

It isn't just the light. The slot canyon is quieter, if it's possible to have grades of silence. The sandstone feels colder and smoother to touch but has faint indentations like the grooves of a screw, which pull me deeper into the canyon. I can smell water, a subcutaneous sensor in my nostril sensing humidity in this bone-dry place. I let our impromptu guide and Ananth walk ahead, the scraping of their feet fading until I cannot hear them anymore. I stand in the middle of the slot, my hands spread out, palms flat against each side of the canyon wall. I am barely breathing. I am experiencing a familiar sensation, but I cannot put a finger on it.

Two feet above the normal line of sight is a niche carved into the rock thousands of years ago by the Nabateans. A deity was enshrined in that niche once upon a time, now faded and eroded. Was this a place of prayer? Am I feeling spiritual, as if inside the innermost sanctum of an ancient temple? Or was this a place of sacrifice – ritual slaying to satiate a demon? Is my subconscious picking up the atrocities of a long time ago? Or is this just plain old claustrophobia? Am I experiencing the exact fear Nabateans felt in this exact spot? Was the carved niche an antidote for that fear?

Petra

I wait until my heart is no longer doing handsprings before continuing down the canyon. The slot narrows until I must take my backpack off and turn sideways to go further. It exits where a Nabatean dam diverts rainwater into a channel. A country so devoid of water has, in fact, been formed by water. A few inches of rain falling a few miles away can cause deadly flash floods in the canyons. A seemingly small drizzle can push dangerous volumes of water high and fast in these tight spaces. Was it the fear of a flash flood I felt back in the narrow confines of the slot canyon? Dry landscapes are deadly. They kill the weak. And they kill the ignorant.

~~~~~

Issa's pickup truck is idling in the empty parking lot, belching clouds of diesel smoke. He is inside, a cigarette dangling at a dramatic angle between his lips, smoke curling up lazily.

"You keep Arab time!" he says. I am running fifteen minutes late. Issa looks groggy. He had to wake up before sunrise to meet us for the early morning jaunt. I ignore him for the next few minutes as he mutters under his breath: *Issa needs his beauty sleep. An early morning Bedouin is not a happy Bedouin. An early Bedouin catches the cold.*

The village is still waking up when Issa's pickup rattles through the narrow streets of Wadi Musa. He stops outside the village bakery, its shutter still half closed like Issa's eyes. He disappears into the shop and emerges, fifteen minutes later, with a bag of freshly baked bread. Now awake and happier, Issa stops and chats with people he sees on the street, breaking a piece of bread and offering it, the offer always accepted with a smile and a shokran followed by a few minutes of chit-chat.

"Stories are village currency," he says, noisily munching on the bread.

It takes us a good part of an hour to emerge from the village. We are not in a hurry. We are moving at Arab time. The pickup truck rumbles toward Little Petra, where we stop for a spot of mint tea and for Issa to shake more hands and distribute more bread.

Ananth is quickly on his case.

"Are you trying to win an election or are you starting a commune?"

"I am trying to find a wife."

"Didn't we meet your wife yesterday?"

"Yes, that's wife number 1."

"You want wife number 2?"

"You are about to meet wife number 2. I am looking for wife number 3."

The pickup truck leaves the road and bumps along a dirt track, crisscrossing sandstone and dry washes. We are following an ancient Nabatean sheep trail, which is used as an alternate entrance to Petra. We ditch the truck at the bottom of a sandstone dome. A scramble over the slick rock brings us to steps that zigzag up the face of a near vertical cliff. The view changes with every meter of elevation we gain. Millions of years ago, the earth, unable to contain the bottled-up heat and pressure inside its core, spilled its guts, innards strewn everywhere like the floor of a butcher's shop. The razor-sharp lava rock then accumulated layers and layers of sand over thousands of years, compacting and hardening it. Earthquakes have shaken the substrate, creating deep fissures that water and wind then chiseled and sandpapered, shaping and smoothing. The colors and textures of this natural artwork are proudly on display all around us.

At the top of the mountain, Issa's wife (number 2) pours us mint tea. She is curious about my sketchbook and flips through the pages before she shows us a brass and copper ring inlaid with colorful quartz, which I buy. We follow a cairned path with a sickeningly sheer exposure on one side. We pass an excavated Bronze-Age dwelling older than everything else around it except for the rock it is built on. A final massive cairn in the distance turns out to be the capstone of Ad Deir, the Nabatean monastery we are headed to.

The spot at top of the mountain has everything that makes me happy, which somehow Mark Adams managed to accurately convert into a handy formula in his book *Turn Right at Machu Pichu: (R+S) x E – Ruins plus Solitude multiplied by Exertion.* The monastery carved in stone, like everything else in Petra, is better preserved than the Khazneh, less crowded because of the strenuous access. Even David Roberts' painting of Ad Deir is more enchanting than that of the Khazneh. Roberts masterfully knocks off a shoulder of the mountain behind the monastery to reveal the royal tombs in the distance, giving the scene gorgeous depth, clearly showing his skills as a landscape painter. He used his sketch of the Khazneh as the cover of his Petra volume, but I am sure he must have been tempted to use the painting of Ad Deir.

We are now at the other end of Petra, the ancient city bookended between the Khazneh and Ad Deir. From the treasury to the monastery – contemplating that for a title for an as yet-unwritten book on philosophy – we buy sweet mint tea from a shopkeeper who is stretched out under the early morning sun. We descend eight hundred Nabatean steps to the bottom of the hill where they merge with Roberts' path out of Wadi Musa.

Roberts was satisfied with his work in Petra. He knew he was leaving with sketches that were far superior to Linant's. After almost two centuries, his paintings of the city, bathed

AD DIER, PETRA

EL DEIR PETRA BY DAVID ROBERTS, R.A. 8TH MARCH 1839

in translucent early morning sunlight, still achieve the goal of modern travel books – to make the reader get up and go. On 11th March, Roberts left Petra with a heavy heart. There is a passionate paragraph in his journal, the only time in the journey Roberts laments leaving a place:

> "I REPEATEDLY TURNED BACK TO LOOK ON THE DESERTED CITY, SO SAD A MEMORIAL OF DIVINE JUDGMENT. IN ITS STRENGTH IT MUST HAVE SCORNED ALL HUMAN MEANS OF DESTRUCTION, FOR, IN COMPARISON, ALL WALLS BUILT BY MAN WERE INSIGNIFICANT."

TRIUMPHAL ARCH ACROSS THE RAVINE LEADING TO PETRA BY
DAVID ROBERTS, R.A. MARCH 1839

WADI ARABA

~~~~~~

Khaled picks us from the hotel. He is tasked with driving us out of Petra following Wadi Araba. *Khaled is my cousin. Best driver in Petra*, Issa texted me the night before. I bid goodbye to Issa. *Come back again, my friend, he texts me back. I will invite you to the wedding.*

Khaled arrives on time, speaks good English, and owns an odorless sedan. He is surprised how light Ananth and I are traveling. He gestures at our backpacks, "You should buy more presents," he implores. Once on the road, we insist that Khaled play us his favorite playlist.

"I thought you would like English songs," he says, gleefully replacing Taylor Swift with music whose tempo evokes a scene of endless sand dunes over a starlit sky, a flickering campfire, a roasting leg of lamb, and a stringed instrument being plucked by a vagabond who welcomes the rising sun without knowing what the new day will bring. We settle down for the ride.

Khaled drives us first west and then north on the spanking new King's Highway through Wadi Araba. The modern highway ends in Madaba, 280 kilometers north of Petra. In ancient times, the road continued further north all the way to Damascus and further into the fertile crescent, a route that connected the port of Aqaba to the Euphrates. The road even finds a mention in the Old Testament as the path that Moses was not permitted to let the Israelites use. After Islam swept through the Near East, the highway became known as Darb al-Hajj, the route that the devout used to reach Mecca.

Tires screech. Khaled leaves rubber on a turn and takes another corner an uncomfortably high speed. Bracing myself, I ask him to take it easy. He eases his foot off the accelerator for a minute or two until the next open strip of tar challenges him. This repeats a few times and I let him know that.

"Issa said you wanted the best driver in Petra," he says, disappointed by disappointing me. I tell him that the best driver is the one who drives the safest, not the fastest. His disappointment turns into disenchantment.

"Anybody can drive safe. You don't need Khaled for that!"

I see a camel tied up at the side of the road. I want to take a photo to send to the outfitter in Amman who had trouble finding me a camel. Instead, I ask Khaled: what does it mean to see a camel tied to a tree beside the road?

Khaled chuckles.

"It means there is a Bedu shitting nearby."

Encountering scenes and experiences typical of the time and recorded splendidly by John Kinnear for posterity (and the commercial value they guaranteed) – a jackal feasting on a carcass of a camel, buying milk from a "savage" Bedouin tribe – Roberts' caravan had descended into Wadi Araba a few miles south of the Dead Sea and headed toward Hebron in Palestine. Once again, Roberts had seemingly effortlessly crossed a natural border that today has hardened to separate two nations and two people. Jordan to the east, Israel to the west.

There are three spots on the Israel/Jordan border where one can cross legally: in the south, along the Red Sea, at Eilat/Aqaba – a border that my daughter and I had crossed on foot back in 2015; in the north, near the Israeli town of Beith Shean,

across the River Jordan; and, finally, the popular King Hussein/Allenby Bridge in the middle, closest to Jerusalem, which skirts the northern tip of the Dead Sea. My American passport ensured an easy and seamless passage, a visa stamped on arrival with a smile and a wink.

Not so for Ananth who carries an Indian passport.

Even for a short visit to Israel an Indian citizen needs to apply for a short-term visitor visa 6-8 weeks in advance. The complicated application needs a sheaf of supporting documents like income tax returns, bank statements, return air tickets, hotel accommodation confirmations, proof of insurance and, extraordinarily, a no-objection certificate from their employer. Furthermore, a passport stamped with an Israeli visa faces an automatic rejection by Lebanese immigration (our destination after Israel). Ananth had to choose between Israel and Lebanon for this adventure.

A fighter jet cuts a gash in the western sky, the morning sun reflecting off its gleaming metal. Within a few seconds, a second aircraft follows in the thermo-wake. They bob up and down, cutting a graceful arc in the sky before flying away from us, the two dots merging into one.

"They belong to another country." Khaled says, his lips a thin straight line, not willing to name the neighbor to the west. The fighters were by now at the edge of Negev desert somewhere near Hebron, where Roberts was headed.

"I'll see you in Lebanon," Ananth says.

I am left needing "to pull an Indian yogi trick," to levitate and follow in Robert's footsteps, across the mountain of Judaea and through the Negev Desert to Hebron.

Spice Market, Jerusalem.

PALESTINE AND ISRAEL

~~~

"The court was quite a bazaar, filled with merchants and pilgrims
selling and buying crosses, rosaries and staffs."

— DAVID ROBERTS, 29TH MARCH 1839, JERUSALEM.

Cave of Patriarchs, Hebron.

HEBRON

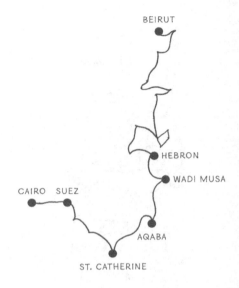

"Palestine looks so peaceful!" says my wife, Monica, lover of all things peaceful, who has joined me in my quest to track David Roberts' footsteps in Israel and Palestine.

We have a panoramic view of Hebron from the terrace of the apartment block. A short squall has freshened the city, washing away the dust from the air, the petrichor invigorating. Buff white and grey buildings gleam in the sun, a rainbow bending over the horizon. The apartment building is located near the western border of Israeli-controlled Hebron and has an unobstructed view of the city. On our left is the mound of Tel Rumeida, where excavations in the last fifty years have uncovered biblical walls ("Old Testament, mind you," Sagi, our Israeli guide in Hebron, tells us). The silhouette of the old city of Hebron is visible to our right. The fortress-like walls of the Tomb of the Patriarchs are a focal point of the city and tower over the neighborhood. Not far away are the Jewish and the Muslim cemeteries, which have been in use for many centuries.

From this distance, the scene is so idyllic that I don't have the heart to break the spell that's been cast on Monica. Hebron is about to do that to her anyway, just like it did it to David Roberts, who sighted the city on the fourth day after leaving Petra. He noted in his journal on 16th March 1839:

> "ON TURNING ROUND THE SIDE OF A HILL, HEBRON FIRST BURSTS
> UPON YOU. THE SITUATION IS BEAUTIFUL, AND THE HOUSES,
> GLEAMING BRIGHTLY IN THE NOONDAY SUN, REMINDED ME OF
> ENGLAND. THE CHILDREN, WHO CAME OUT TO MEET US, WERE
> HEALTHY AND PRETTY, THEIR BLOOMING COUNTENANCES VERY
> UNLIKE THE SQUALID CHILDREN OF EGYPT."

Roberts' romantic vision did not last for long, however, as he soon discovered the narrow, dark, unclean alleys and the sparse bazaars. He accepted an invite to have breakfast with the only Christian family in a town of four thousand people and realized that that they were on unfriendly turf on account of their religion.

Sagi, our guide in Hebron, is a wiry millennial in his late twenties with a shock of copper-colored curly hair cascading to his shoulders. He has a drooping moustache that would make a sailor jealous, above which is a straight, thin nose and bright, intelligent eyes. With a sweeping gesture of his left hand, he covers a swath of the western horizon and says, "All of that is under control of Palestine and is called H1. We are in H2."

We drive down a hillside, crossing two military checkpoints on our way to visit the Tomb of the Patriarchs. We pass by a street lined with bright green shutters and rusted awnings. The shutters are down, shut and locked, and have four-foot-tall blue six-pointed stars spray-painted on them. Al-Shuhada Street used to be a busy Palestinian thoroughfare, but it was closed by Israel in 1994 following widespread unrest in Hebron.

"This street is off-limits for Palestinians in order to maintain law and peace," Sagi says. "Just like there are streets in Hebron that are off limits for Israelis. And mind you, Palestinians who live on al-Shuhada are free to come and go as they please."

Sagi provides an oversimplified picture of one of the most complex issues plaguing the Israeli–Palestinian conflict.

We stop at a cantilevered crash beam barricading the road. I roll down the window and a *tzahal*[7] commando stoops to my eye level, the smell of oil that makes his Uzi gleam wafting into my face, his finger taut beside the trigger.

"Are you Muslim?" his eyes expertly sweep the interior of our rental. I hear Monica's sharp intake of breath. She is sitting in the back of the car, while Sagi sits shotgun, a Middle Eastern configuration.

Earlier in the day, Monica and I made our way into the Judean Mountains, following a ribbon of a road lined with vineyards and orange groves, before approaching Hebron, the oldest Palestinian city of them all. Inside the city, we drove though clusters of prefab concrete buildings where kids played soccer barefoot on concrete roads.

[7] In Hebrew *tzahal* is an acronym for Tzava Haganah Le'Yisrael. They are known as Israel Defense Forces (IDF) in English

"No, I am a Hindu," I tell him. The commando's eyes don't miss a thing. Sagi's leather messenger bag in his lap, my khaki backpack in the back seat next to Monica's Osprey daypack.

"Hindu?" He rolls the word in his mouth as if uttering it for the first time.

"I am from India," I add.

His eyes light up, "You mean like Shah Rukh Khan?"

"No, Shah Rukh Khan is a Muslim."

Sagi steps in. Hebrew flows back and forth. Two adults speaking about you in a foreign language in a foreign land is like a couple of masked doctors deliberating over your ECG while you lie naked on a steel table. The commando looks over the interior of the car one more time before giving the door three thumps. The gate lifts. We pull into an empty parking lot and Sagi springs out to hold the door open for Monica.

"The only reason they asked you about your religion is because Muslims have a separate entrance to the mosque. All Muslims use that entrance," Sagi explains. "*We* are a secular country. We welcome people of all religions." Sagi represents a stereotypical Israeli youngster – a young, clean, well educated, army-polished, proud patriot who has drunk the Israeli Kool Aid. He carries the Jewish ethos proudly, wrapping the collective memory of thousands of years of pain and suffering in modern packaging.

The Tomb of the Patriarchs, also called the Cave of Machpelah, is built like a fortress. Before there was Jerusalem, there was Hebron. Hebron is mentioned several times in the Old Testament, laying claim to being one of the oldest continuously-inhabited cities in the world – most certainly the oldest in Palestine. The site has been recognized as the place of burial of

the patriarchs (Abraham, Isaac, Jacob) since time immemorial. King Herod built a compound around it in the first century BCE, about the same time as building the cyclopean walls of the Second Temple in Jerusalem and the fortress of Masada in the Negev Desert.

"We are at the oldest holy site in the Holy Land," Sagi says. "Holy sites remain holy. Holy places are built on top of holy places." Sagi says as we walk towards the Herodian-era walls.

"Explain it to me like I'm a kindergartner," Monica challenges him.

Sagi dives into the narrative of the Old Testament. Abraham is revered as the patriarch of the Jewish people. After his wife Sarah died, Abraham bought a cave to bury her, permanently laying Jewish roots in Palestine and marking the first Jewish acquisition of land in Israel. Later Abraham was buried in the cave, as was his son, Isaac, and his wife, and their son, Jacob, and his wife.

I follow Sagi and Monica up the stairs of the Tomb of the Patriarchs. Monica listens intently as Sagi talks; her head tilted over her left shoulder. A beam of sunlight, providing light but not heat, illuminates the edifice, and a stiff breeze working its way through the narrow alleys of the ancient city sweeps away the words Sagi is uttering.

King Herod sealed the cave and built a compound around the site that the Jewish people had already considered holy for twelve hundred years. The Byzantines converted the compound into a church. The Muslims turned the church into a mosque. The Crusaders converted the mosque back into a church. Mamluks converted the church back into a mosque in the thirteenth century and barred Jews and Christians from entering the holy ground.

As we enter the stone structure, colder inside than outside, Sagi repeats: Holy sites remain holy. Holy places are built on top of holy places...

"Sounds wholly complicated!" says Monica, never one to mince words.

Archaeologists have never found the original entrance to the compound that Herod commissioned. Was it built without an entrance? Did Herod foresee the issues the site was going to pose in the coming centuries? Was he quarantining it? Keeping the chaos inside? Or keeping the chaos outside?

On Jewish land lie Christian walls, converted to a Muslim holy place, now controlled by the Jewish state. This is a microcosm of one of the central issues that plagues not only Palestine and Israel, but also the Middle East at large – an intractable mesh of religion, geography, history, and politics.

Sagi leads us to a portico that has been built, repaired, and added to by kings, conquerors, and commanders from a wide swathe of eras: Byzantine, Crusader, Mamluk, Ottoman, British, and contemporary Israel. Four cenotaphs surround a central courtyard. The side we stand on is a synagogue; the other side a mosque. The two are separated by transparent bullet proof glass. Ten days every year, Muslims get entry to the premises of the synagogue and Jews get access to the Ibrahimi mosque.

"That's a ticking time bomb," says Monica.

Back outside, I find a spot in the sun to stretch and sketch. Sagi goes off to explore the possibility of a much-touted Hebron experience – lunch in an Arab house on al-Shuhada Street.

Hebron is also known as al-Khalili; the word in both Hebrew and Arabic means "friend," referring to the Patriarch of the Jews, Abraham who is the friend of God. On first contact, nothing about this city seems friendly or about friends or friendship anymore. This is a peaceful day in Hebron. There are no protests, no barbed wire blockades, no tear gas, no stones being hurled. Yet the situation is tense. The prejudices are well set. The battle lines are drawn. It is a keg of gunpowder in a roomful of tinder in a barn full of hay on a swelteringly hot day. One tiny spark is all it needs.

While Hebron is ground zero of the Arab-Israeli conflict, scholars consider 1929 to be year zero. A community of six hundred orthodox Jews lived amid twenty thousand Arabs, largely to stay close to the tombs of their forefathers. They climbed to the seventh step on the stairs along the southwest walls, from where Isaac's cenotaph was visible from a hole in the wall – as far as the Jews could go under the law in place since the Mamluk era. On this fateful day in August 1929, a series of rumors and misinformation created a domino effect of events that culminated in Jews dying at the hands of Arabs and Arabs at the hands of Jews. Jewish houses were pillaged, synagogues desecrated, graves vandalized, Torah scrolls burned, and women raped. The surviving Jews, fearing for their lives, escaped from Hebron and, for the first time in thousands of years, were completely uprooted from their forefathers.

When the Israeli army invaded Hebron in the Six Day War of 1967, the Jewish people were giddy with joy at the serendipitous reunion with their patriarchs after seven hundred years. They entered the compound of the Tomb of the Patriarchs and offered prayers to their ancestors. Over the next few months, eight hundred Jews moved into Hebron and settled permanently. In retaliation, a hand grenade was lobbed at the Jewish worshippers, injuring fifty. Retaliating the retaliation, a Jew entered the mosque with an assault rifle and mowed down twenty-nine worshippers during Ramadan prayer. Barricades were erected by the Israeli army. Movement by Palestinians was restricted. Bans, protests, curfews, emotions, situations, tensions, explosions, confrontation, retaliation, revenge, reprisal, politics, massacre, intifada. It is an unending cycle, and the blood-soaked ground is never allowed to dry. The hatred and grief are being passed down through generations.

As I sketch, I realize that a gentleman is sitting next to me nibbling on an apple plucked from his backpack. He must have overheard part of my discourse with Monica as I sketched the south corner of the tomb. A group of orthodox Jews in long black robes and long white beards stop at a spot. This is where the stairs with the sacred seventh step used to be, now dismantled. The eldest of the group leans against the wall, while others bring out books from their packs. The eldest starts sobbing, clawed hands reaching up against the stones, his body shaking in anguish.

I sit still, spellbound by the spectacle unfolding in front of me, when the man leans over me and whispers, his New York accent twanging, "They have found a wall to grind their foreheads and wail."

~~~~~~

David Roberts never managed to enter the Tomb of the Patriarchs. In 1839, only Muslims could enter the compound, but that did not prevent him from making an accurate depiction of the city from a nearby hill, close to the terrace on which we had stood earlier in the morning.

Monica asks me, "Didn't Roberts have a *firman* from Muhammed Ali to enter any mosque of his choice?"

"Well, the *firman* allowed him entry to any of the four hundred mosques in Cairo. Not only was Hebron too far from Cairo to enforce the *firman*, but Muhammed Ali was not a popular Pasha

at the time. In the middle of a plague in which half a dozen people were dying every day, the Pasha was conscripting citizens for a war with the Ottoman Empire."

Sagi can't find us a suitable host for a Palestinian lunch. Instead, I asked him to take us to his favorite hole in the wall – where he would eat if he wasn't with us. We stop at a falafel stall in Kiryat Arba, which is popular with members of the *tzahal*. The commandoes stand in a line, their machine guns slung carelessly over their shoulders and clanging into one another as they pass falafel wrapped in Arab bread to their teammates behind.

In Hebron, David Roberts discovered Jerusalem was still in quarantine even after his detour through Sinai and Petra. He paid Sheikh Hussein the 3,000 piastres that was due to the Alloween and bid him goodbye. Then, before they got quarantined in Hebron or lost their beasts of burden to conscription, they hastily detoured once more towards the port of Gaza.

After lunch, we follow Roberts' path west-northwest over the Judaean Mountains into verdant valleys. We pass through thick clusters of olive trees and lush meadows laced with red and yellow flowers, stretching as far as the eye can see. The desert landscape of Wadi Araba, a little over two hundred miles away, seems like it is on a different planet. We arrive at the Beit Guvrin – Maresha National Park and pull over at the archaeological mound of Tel Maresha, a town built during the time of the Crusaders, itself built on top of a much older settlement. The bedrock in this region is plentiful in calcium carbonate, which has been harvested for the chalk, leaving behind splendid caves. Sagi takes us through a series of caves that were converted thousands of years before into an olive oil factory, several beautifully painted burial chambers, and a spacious amphitheater. One large cave was once a first century BCE columbarium dovecot, tiny niches carved into the walls for keeping the pigeons. The pigeons were used as sacrificial offerings at the Second Temple of Jerusalem, a day and half's walk from Beit Guvrin.

For a couple of hours, I am Huckleberry Finn, crawling in and out of the caves, my hands and clothes covered in chalk.

Outside the Maresha National Park, we stop at the archaeological remains of Bet Guvrin, which David Roberts visited on 19th March 1839.

It was a typical day in Roberts' life in the Near East. He woke up early in the morning, with plans to head toward Gaza, only to be thwarted by the camel-drivers mutiny. They refused to proceed any further until they were paid in full. Roberts had paid them half their fee in Hebron and the other half was not due until they reached Gaza, as was the usual practice of the time. The mutiny was eventually quashed when Roberts and the other Europeans stayed firm. Once the camel-drivers realized the only way to get the rest of the money was to reach Gaza quickly, they loaded the camels and hurried. Roberts stopped at the ruins of Bet Guvrin after riding for 6–7 miles. He mentions the ruins in his journal as, "…the remains of a castle, and Roman ruins, consisting of a number of marble columns…" After a break they rode again until sunset and stopped in a village, still two and a half hours shy of Gaza. They rode a total of ten hours that day. In the short time he had at Bet Guvrin, Roberts made a sketch titled *Beth Gebrin* in which he depicts three massive, vaulted arches that are still prominently visible today. From a roadside stop, the arches look precisely as Roberts painted them on that day in March. His visual accuracy in depicting the trivial detail of a nondescript ruin is astounding. His discipline in terms of putting pencil to paper every single day, irrespective of weather, fatigue, mood, or his own physical state, is exemplary.

From here, David Roberts continued west to the port of Gaza. That journey is merely an hour's drive, but it may as well be a three-day hike. The border between Israel and Gaza is so contentious that Monica, not one to routinely shirk from adventures, swats down the idea of getting any closer. This is as far west as we will go today.

Sagi feeds Jerusalem into the popular Israeli GPS app, Waze.

"Google bought Waze for a billion dollars." His pride in the Israeli startup is obvious.

"Didn't Waze get the IDF in trouble recently?" I tease him, trying to conflict Sagi the soldier with Sagi the Waze fanboy. I remind him of the incident: in March 2016, an IDF truck was driving on a road, following step-by-step directions provided by Waze. The driver thought they were inside the Israeli border but turned out to be wrong. The truck was stoned and set on fire. A few hours of mayhem ensued before the two Israeli soldiers inside were retrieved unharmed. One Palestinian lost his life. Sagi sticks his tongue out at me.

We drive towards Jerusalem along Highway 60 – the Way of Patriarchs, a road that was frequented by all three patriarchs: Abraham, Isaac, and Jacob.

"Because roads are built on top of roads." I modify Sagi's favorite line: *Holy sites are built on top of holy sites.*

Instead of taking the bait, Sagi tells us the biblical story of a youthful David slaying the Philistine giant Goliath with his slingshot. "…Probably happened not far from where we are now…"

I listen to the story, which Sagi tells with passion and conviction. The Philistines were a giant race, if not a race of giants. The ancient sea people settled on the coastal plains of the Levant. They were great warriors with large armies and the latest warfare technology, which gave them political clout in the region. The Jewish people, meanwhile, were a fledgling mountain tribe fighting for survival.

David is now Goliath.

GAZA TO JAFFA TO RAMALLAH

~~~~~~

BEIRUT

JAFFA

HEBRON

WADI MUSA

CAIRO SUEZ

AQABA

ST. CATHERINE

David Roberts reached Gaza on 20th March 1839. He found the port, once a lifeline between Syria and Egypt, in a dilapidated state, "... it's ancient grandeur entirely gone," he wrote in his journal. Despite his inability to find any worthy ruins, his sketch captures some shattered marble columns as if Samson had just escaped the Gates of Gaza – a tip of the hat to the story of the Hebrew muscleman whose superstrength waxed and waned on the back of his haircut. In the sketch Roberts captures Ismail Pasha's army marching in the background. The army was part of the military build-up that would lead to the Oriental Crisis of 1840. Despite the "wretchedness of the place," Roberts made Gaza look fresh and welcoming.

He continued through Ashkelon and Jaffa, where he bid farewell to John Kinnear. Kinnear was originally on his way to Beirut but had detoured through Sinai and Petra on an impulse after stumbling across John Pell and David Roberts. Roberts and Kinnear had grown fond of each other on the trip. When Kinnear published his memoir of the journey in 1840, he dedicated the tome to Roberts, with a paragraph that captures their chemistry:

"MY DEAR ROBERTS, THE INTERESTING SCENES THROUGH WHICH
WE PASSED LAST YEAR MUST BECOME BETTER KNOWN IN THIS
COUNTRY FROM THE ADMIRABLE PRODUCTIONS OF YOUR PENCIL,
SO FULL OF TRUTH, SO REDOLENT OF THE VERY ATMOSPHERE OF
EGYPT AND ARABIA, THAN ANY WRITTEN DESCRIPTION CAN MAKE
THEM. BUT HOWEVER LITTLE OTHERS MAY FEEL INTERESTED IN
READING THE FOLLOWING PAGES (OF JOHN KINNEAR'S BOOK),
I MAY HOPE THAT YOU WILL FIND HERE AND THERE SOME FEW
WORDS OF CONVERSATION WITH OUR OLD FRIEND SHEICH HUSSEIN,
OR SOME LITTLE INCIDENT, UNHEEDED BY OTHER READERS,
WHICH SHALL RECALL TO YOUR MIND SCENES THAT COULD NOT
BE MADE THE SUBJECT OF YOUR ART, AND WERE TOO DRAMATIC,
PERHAPS, FOR ORDINARY PROSE DESCRIPTION. MEMORY WILL
FILL UP THESE MEAGRE OUTLINES, SUPPLY ALL THE ACCESSORIES
OF THE PICTURE, AND IMPART TO IT THE COLOURING OF NATURE.
IN INSCRIBING THIS LITTLE VOLUME TO YOU, THE COMPANION OF

GAZA BY DAVID ROBERTS, R.A. 21ST MARCH 1839

"SINCE CHILDHOOD I HAVE NOT FELT SUCH
A PERFECT ENJOYMENT OF THE BEAUTIES
OF NATURE AND THIS EXHILARATION OF
SPIRITS CAN ONLY BE FELT BY THOSE WHO
HAVE PASSED THOUGH THE DESERT TO THIS
BEAUTIFUL COUNTRY."

Roberts' poetic state of mind reflected his increasing
excitement as he came closer to the fabled city of Jerusalem. On
March 28th they were finally camped outside the Zion Gate. He
wrote in his journal:

"NIGHT FOUND US ENCAMPED OUTSIDE THE
CITY OF SION. ALL IS PERFECTLY SILENT SAVE
THE BAYING OF A DOG AND THE HOOTING OF
AN OWL PERCHED ON THE BATTLEMENTS, A
FITTING EMBLEM OF ITS DESOLATION."

Roberts couldn't wait for Jerusalem to open its gates.

MY WANDERINGS, I OFFER BUT A SLIGHT
EXPRESSION OF MY SINCERE REGARD OF
MY VALUE FOR YOUR FRIENDSHIP, AND MY
ADMIRATION OF YOUR TALENTS.

JOHN G. KINNEAR. GLASGOW, OCTOBER 1ST
1840."

Roberts' sketches in Jaffa prominently feature the Jewish
pilgrims in broad brimmed hats, but he was unable to find the
antiquities he sought. As he drew closer to Jerusalem, Roberts'
quest for biblical scenes intensified. He continued towards
Jerusalem in the company of the indomitable John Pell, Ismail
Effendi, their servants and eight horses. From Jaffa, the little
caravan turned eastward, crossing the plain of Sharon and
passing through Ramallah before reaching Jerusalem. He was in
good spirits. Roberts wrote in his journal:

JERUSALEM

〜〜〜

We drop Sagi at his home on our way back from Bet Guvrin. It is well past sunset by the time the great walls of Jerusalem are in our sights. Despite the cold, I cannot help but feel a warm tingle of excitement upon entering these fabled walls. All the feet that have touched streets of this city! If only these walls could speak!

Naked lamps hang from the awnings of closed shops throwing yellow pools of light on empty streets. The odd passerby, clutching a winter coat at the throat, hurries towards shelter and heat. A smell of crackling logs of wood hangs in the air, bonfires lit up at street corners, locals gathering around them, sharing their tobacco and worries.

Our hotel is situated on the south side of the Old City, just inside the ramparts, between the Zion Gate and the Dung Gate. The two-hundred-year-old building used to be the office of the Chief Rabbi of Israel once upon a time. It is now a clean and a charming boutique hotel with walking access to all the historic sites in Jerusalem. Monica instantly falls in love with our beautiful room with its marble floors, vaulted roof, and arched windows that offer a view of the domes of the four synagogues.

It is cold, clammy and wet, the kind of day that makes you groan first thing in the morning. We are in the middle of a bitter Jerusalem winter. I wake up in the morning, my body aching like I am Batman. I am determined to make the most of the week in front of us. Monica is ready before I am, yet more presentable. We set out before Jerusalem wakes up, walking past the Zion Gate (outside of which David Roberts camped on 29 March), through the Armenian quarters and to the main square inside Jaffa Gate. A tiny slit of a door between the visitor center and the historic The New Imperial Hotel leads to a café that I visit every time I am in the Old City of Jerusalem. We buy a big piece of warm bread smothered with olive oil and za'atar to go with our coffee. Realizing I do not have enough shekels to cover our bill, I ask the big guy behind the counter if I can pay in dollars.

"One thousand dollars for an American," he says, teeth gleaming amidst a jumble of facial hair, eyes crinkly. "But the Indian can come back tomorrow and pay." I am pleasantly surprised by his generous offer, which I accept, promising to return the next day with the right denomination.

Zion Gate, Jerusalem

David Street is waking up. Shutters are being pushed up. Icons and crosses are being hung from the awnings. Incense sticks are being lit. Frankincense and myrrh are being poured on charcoal embers. Cut pomegranates are being fed into juicers. Jerusalem is starting to display its paraphernalia for its visitors, exactly as it has for twenty-five centuries. We duck through an ageless archway, leaving David Street and heading towards Mursitan, deeper into the Christian Quarter.

The Rotunda, Church of Holy Sepulchre, Jerusalem

CHURCH OF THE HOLY SEPULCHRE

~~~~~~

Monica and I pass through a market that is still shut in the morning cold. The smaller street has none of the hubbub of the main thoroughfare. It's like crossing from one level of a video game to another. We turn a corner, with the eighth century Mosque of Omar on our right and arrive in the tiny courtyard of the Church of the Holy Sepulchre. We find a spot to sit with our backs against a timeworn wall; Monica is tucked on my leeward side as a cold breeze that blows across the courtyard of the most important church of them all. I feel a tingle of excitement with my feet on the hallowed ground that a long list of famous travelers have touched through the centuries. I am also aware of an unreasonable pang of guilt for not having to go through their ordeals to reach it.

Monica pulls the scarf down from her face and asks, "Isn't this where Jesus is buried?"

Her lips are blue. She is freezing. I put my arm around her, hoping the act of sharing my body warmth is not perceived as a disrespectful public display of affection.

Monica's question is rhetorical. The tone of her voice betrays the real question: *is this it?*

The unassuming L-shaped structure, with its tiny courtyard and plain façade, would go unnoticed for its architecture in any medieval village in Europe. Roberts himself lamented the lack of atmosphere that he expected in a structure with so much antiquity and gravitas. I shake free a Roberts sketch from my backpack and hold it up for comparison. The twelfth century façade of the church is depicted accurately but only after he cheated masterfully. With deft strokes of his pencil, he emptied the crowded quarters around the church, giving it much-deserved breathing room. Nearby, he placed a terrace at a convenient height where he posed some locals in colorful garb; he even planted a palm tree. His artistic decisions were an attempt to create the level of atmosphere that you would expect from a church of such historical and religious significance. His 'corrections' for the future audience of his book were done in good faith, I defend him in an imaginary debate.

Older churches existed on this spot, constructed in the fourth and eighth centuries BCE, but each was destroyed almost completely within a couple of hundred years of its construction. The building visible today was built during the Crusades in the twelfth century, and it was almost lost to fire a few times. Going back to Monica's question about the actual site as it relates to the final events in the life of Jesus, I defer to Edward Robinson. Known for his accurate archaeological observations in Palestine and considered the father of biblical archaeology, Robinson was in Jerusalem almost exactly a year before David Roberts and writes:

> "THAT THE EARLY CHRISTIANS AT JERUSALEM MUST HAVE HAD A KNOWLEDGE OF THE PLACES WHERE THE LORD WAS CRUCIFIED AND BURIED, THERE CAN BE NO DOUBT; THAT THEY ERECTED THEIR CHURCHES ON PLACES CONSECRATED BY MIRACLES, AND ESPECIALLY ON CALVARY AND OVER OUR LORD'S SEPULCHRE, IS A MORE QUESTIONABLE POSITION."

"Look, the ladder!" Monica exclaims.

Mosque of Omar

Church of Holy Sepulchre, Jerusalem

ENTRANCE TO THE HOLY SEPULCHER
BY DAVID ROBERTS, R.A. APRIL 1839

of the church. They overzealously guarded their territories, so much so that they were in a constant state of conflict with each other, often over very trivial things. Called to arbitrate on these matters too frequently, an irate Ottoman Sultan circulated a *firman*, which enforced that no change, however minor, could be affected in the church until all the sects agreed to it, giving birth to the famous Status Quo of 1757. Since that *firman*, every matter that could not be settled amicably had to be left in its existing state. The window of the second floor of the church was being repaired the day the *firman* was circulated. A workman had left his ladder propped against the wall overnight. It is still there. The ladder is the most visible, easy to understand, and sometimes laughable impact of the Status Quo.

There are other less funny consequences of the *firman*. For example, the inner sanctum of the church does not have an emergency fire exit. All six Christian sects would like to have one, just not in their part of the church. The fire hazard with a church that is typically teeming with thousands of pilgrims is enormous, as was proven in the Holy Fire catastrophe of 1834 when a couple of hundred people died in a stampede. The negotiations are still ongoing.

Having sufficiently warmed up, she is comparing the lithograph I am holding up with the scene in front of us. In the lithograph, a ladder is visible, propped against a window on the second floor of the church. Monica's comment is the result of her glancing up and discovering a ladder still propped against that exact same window.

"The ladder is still there!"

Monica is having her first David Roberts moment.

"The ladder was already in there for *eighty-two years* when David Roberts saw it," I add to her amazement. I tell her the story:

Various Christian sects have occupied the Holy Church of Sepulchre since the Crusades. The sects occupied different parts

(I used to wonder how historical buildings were left so vulnerable to fire despite modern fire-fighting equipment and city codes, especially after Notre Dame in Paris was engulfed in flames in 2019, and realized that history is doomed to repeat itself, sometimes purely to prove that it repeats itself.)

Inside the church, a thin but steady stream of pilgrims trickles in from all over the world. I settle on a wooden bench under the rotunda, from where I can see the pilgrims enter the tomb of Jesus housed inside a marble Edicule built thirty years before Roberts visited. Monica leaves me to my sketchbook, which I use alternately as a disguise, an excuse, and a shield against questions, queries, and stares. An hour later, as I am finishing

The Edicule, Church of Holy Sepulchre

my sketch, Monica returns, her face agog with excitement. Breathlessly she tells me that she had been wandering in the church, letting the shafts of lights and smells of frankincense guide her through the maze of chapels and naves, stairs, and corridors. She found a chapel all to herself where she sat in peace until a guide brought a group of tourists. On her way out, she overheard, to her astonishment, the guide referring to the chapel as the Calvary. The site of the crucifixion abounds with hundreds of devotees every day. And for a whole twenty minutes, Monica had the Calvary all to herself.

Monica has bagged her own Jerusalem moment.

Walking towards the Souq el-Dabbagha, a waft of happiness – the smell of freshly baked bread – hooks us, and we let it reel us in. A man dressed in a traditional *khaffiyey* and shrouded in ennui sits in a chair with loaves of freshly baked bread neatly arranged for sale beside him. In a moment of epiphany, I understand how the word loaf applies to both a molded mass of bread and the act of doing nothing.

Salivating, I am figuring out what to choose from the variety on display, when the bread-seller springs to life and asks, "Are you from Mumbai?" Rather proud of my ability to blend seamlessly in a crowd in the Middle East, I feel like the spy whose cover is blown at the port of entry.

"Are you from Mumbai?" he asks again.

After I acknowledge my connection to the city, he sits up and leans forward to offer me a piece of bread. Then, in a hushed voice, he utters the name of a Bollywood actress, who is in Jerusalem with her boyfriend. The bread-seller waits, hoping to encourage me to participate in the gossip. The only thing I know about the actress is that she was born to a famous Bollywood actor who played villainous roles in the '80s and '90s. I was brought up in an academically focused family where discussion of extracurricular topics was frowned upon, to put it mildly, and especially if they were connected to the entertainment business. He is disappointed that I have no views on the private lives of Bollywood actors.

The freshly baked bread laced with sesame seeds, on the other hand, is chew-worthy.

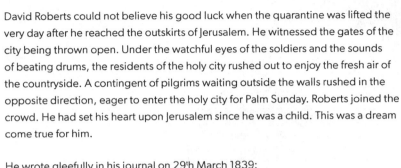

David Roberts could not believe his good luck when the quarantine was lifted the very day after he reached the outskirts of Jerusalem. He witnessed the gates of the city being thrown open. Under the watchful eyes of the soldiers and the sounds of beating drums, the residents of the holy city rushed out to enjoy the fresh air of the countryside. A contingent of pilgrims waiting outside the walls rushed in the opposite direction, eager to enter the holy city for Palm Sunday. Roberts joined the crowd. He had set his heart upon Jerusalem since he was a child. This was a dream come true for him.

He wrote gleefully in his journal on 29th March 1839:

"IT IS BETTER TO BE BORN LUCKY THAN RICH."

Roberts secured living quarters with a Christian family, a critical logistical detail since the boarding rooms were quickly gobbled up by the pilgrims pouring into Jerusalem. Without wasting any more time, he set out to explore the city. He surveyed Jerusalem from the top of the walls, orienting himself to the various important sites in the city. The detailed map published by Fredrick Catherwood in 1835, the most accurate map of the city available at the time, was probably his travel companion, but Roberts did not record these details in his journal. He went on a whirlwind tour of the city, visiting all the key sites of Jerusalem in rapid succession, in case they had to leave the city in a hurry. The next two days, 30th and 31st March, Roberts worked extra-long hours and made many high-quality sketches of all the sites, cramming his sketchbooks with the sights and colors of Jerusalem, recorded in situ from direct observation.[8]

[8] The need to draw "on the spot, from direct observation" was probably first felt by Roberts in 1829 when he was making his first historical painting *The Departure of the Israelites from Egypt.* The painting was well received, though not very accurate: there were way too many pyramids on the horizon, the buildings in the foreground looked distinctly European and the colossal statues of the pharaohs knelt in the most non-Egyptian way. Roberts was using illustrations made by other artists as reference material, an experience he must have found extremely disorienting.

Sabil of Qaitbey

Temple Mount, Jerusalem

TEMPLE MOUNT

~~~~~~

After Saladin's Mamluks assumed power in the late thirteenth century, Christians and Jews were no longer allowed on Temple Mount (as with the Tomb of the Machpelah in Hebron). In the sixteenth century, the Ottoman annexed Syria and Palestine from the Mamluks. Suleiman the Magnificent fortified Jerusalem and, once again, the holy city experienced the golden days of its glory – but only while Suleiman lived. After his death, Jerusalem once again lost its prominence, deteriorated rapidly, and fell into decay. Christians and Jews continued to be barred from visiting the Mount Moriah, the Haram al-Sharif, and the Temple Mount, even more so in the first half of the nineteenth century. When interest in the Holy Land had reached a peak, Jerusalem was just a minor province of the Ottoman Empire.

The first known Western account of the Temple Mount is based on the exploration by a Spaniard, a spy in Napoleon's army, who spent several days on the sacred ground in disguise in 1807. His published account created a stir that led to further tightening of security. Without a special *firman*, which could only be acquired via highly placed connections in the Ottoman bureaucracy, there were only a handful of ways to get past the Turkish guards: a clever disguise, a suitable bribe, or a risky mad dash. One such daring operation was performed by Frederick Catherwood in 1834. The sketcher-explorer-traveler, today famous for his lithographs of Mayan ruins in Central America, was helping Muhammed Ali Pasha survey mosques in Cairo. Catherwood dressed himself as an Egyptian army officer and used the *firman* to gain entry to the Temple Mount. For several weeks, Catherwood measured and sketched and surveyed the Haram al-Sharif at leisure, under the pretext of surveying deteriorating structures that were ripe for repair. He

left in a hurry only when his cover was at risk of being blown by an accidental visit by the Governor of Jerusalem, who had no idea Catherwood was involved in such an enterprise. Catherwood walked away with the first detailed survey of the Temple Mount and several beautifully rendered sketches of the Dome of the Rock, the first of its kind ever made.

The incident led to further tightening of the security protocol, to the extent that Edward Robinson, who walked into Jerusalem with the most immaculate set of introductions in 1838 having identified key biblical sites in Palestine, was unable to find a sponsor who could grant him access to the Temple Mount. Neither could Roberts. Whether it was his usual brevity, or his bruised ego, Roberts journal has a terse line, "...a Mahometan mosque that no Christian is allowed to enter." He does not even call it by its name. But his sketchbook tells a different story. Page after page is filled with sketches of the Temple Mount. The Dome of the Rock and Al Aksa mosque feature in no less than six lithographs, as if Roberts was unable to take his eyes away from it.

Had Roberts arrived in Jerusalem a year later, things might have been different.

Late in 1839, a few months after Roberts left, a wave of modernization, called *Tanzimat*, swept through the Ottoman Empire. It was a desperate attempt by the Ottoman Empire to stay relevant during the rise of the colonial empires. During the early years of the *Tanzimat*, the first Ottoman banknotes were published, post offices were opened, and non-uniform taxes repealed. The reforms continued for the next thirty years, under which many other major changes were affected: slavery was abolished, homosexuality was decriminalized, selective military conscription was discontinued. The most important change was to extend the protection of life and property, irrespective of religion. This secularization abolished any rules that prevented

The dome of the Rock, Jerusalem

people from gaining access to holy sites based on their religion. Had Roberts arrived a year later, he could have freely sketched on the Temple Mount. But had he arrived forty years later, he would have seen that the *Tanzimat* only succeeded in providing the Ottoman regime a temporary respite, only delaying the inevitable stranglehold of the European colonies in the East. By 1922, the Ottoman Empire was no more.

~~~~~~

Monica and I join the end of the line at the Mughrabi Gate, the only gate non-Muslims can use to enter Haram al-Sharif. Men and women stand in separate lines that snake into airport-style metal detectors located in a barrack manned by the Jordanian Army. My turn comes and I push my backpack through the x-ray machine. A soldier waves a magnetic wand over my torso, front, and back until it beeps to his satisfaction.

He asks me, "What is your religion?"

Satisfied with my answer – Hindu – he rifles through my backpack and finds a copy of David Roberts' biography, which he flips through and sets aside. He pulls out my water bottle and holds it up to the sun. He pulls out my watercolors, shakes them, and smells the case. He finally removes my sketchbook. He puts the backpack down and flips through the pages, pausing at a sketch or two.

"Artist." Various parts of his face work in synchronization – bushy eyebrows come together and lips pucker – to convert that single word into a complete sentence, the craning of his neck delicately adding a question mark at the end.

I respond in the affirmative, a response I reserve for when I am asked the question in Asia: a place where I am being asked about my ability to create. If I were in the Western hemisphere, I would answer in the negative, because making art is not my vocation.

Monica, a first generation American born to Hindu parents of Indian origin, has never had to answer the question about her religion. Thinking quickly on her feet, she follows my example but probably only because she sees me passing through security without any further questions.

"The soldiers are ensuring visitors are not carrying any non-Islamic scriptures to the Temple Mount," I tell Monica as we walk up the wooden bridge, the Western Wall visible through the gaps in the vertical slats. "No one wants a fanatic carrying a Bible or a Torah on the Temple Mount."

I gave my daughter Rhea the same explanation after we passed through the security check back during our father-daughter adventure in 2015. That visit, Rhea had keenly watched a female soldier fuss with her little lady-backpack, pulling out her copy of *Pride and Prejudice*. It was a sweltering hot day. The soldier then shuffled through Rhea's tiny journal, which was fastened by an elastic band. Outside she leaned into me and asked, *sotto voce*, "Papi, what about eBooks stored on mobile phones? What about iPods with audio books on them?"

I was glad she had the presence of mind to wait until we were well out of the earshot of the soldiers. At the end of the Mughrabi Bridge, a soldier had glared at Rhea and asked her to cover up. Rhea hesitated: She had prepared for this well in advance. A colorful cotton *dupatta* – a cotton scarf, covered her head, shoulders and arms. She was uncertain what she was expected to do, as was the soldier, who could only manage to hiss, "Cover up more!" In the heat, she donned a sweatshirt. Only then were we allowed to enter the Temple Mount.

No prompt from an ill-tempered soldier is needed at the Temple Mount today – the biting cold ensures that we are draped in several layers. Monica and I are pulled towards the dull gleam of the Dome of the Rock, passing by the al-Aqsa mosque. We climb the steps of the platform towards the blue-green octagonal building, passing beneath delicately carved white arches. At the top of the platform, we wordlessly split in different directions, walking at our own pace. I had picked my spot a few weeks in advance. Monica lets her instincts and the vibe of the place guide her.

King Solomon, King David, Herod the Great, Jesus Christ, Anthony and Cleopatra, Prophet Mohammed, Caliph Omar, Sultan Saladin, Sultan al-Mam'un, Suleiman the Magnificent, Napoleon Bonaparte – this is just a fraction of historical luminaries who have stepped foot on the Temple Mount. Sorely and surprisingly missing from this illustrious list is Alexander the Great, who after the siege of Tyre in the 334 BCE was in Gaza, less than fifty miles from Jerusalem. Yet not one of his famous biographers – not Arrian, not Plutarch, puts Alexander in Jerusalem. Known to pay his respect to every local God, this appears to be an inexplicable lapse in the Alexander saga and that of the Second Temple, which would been standing on Temple Mount when Alexander passed by like a meteor.

A minority report does exist, however, written by one Josephus Flavius. The first century Jewish historian, who is a witness to the demolition of the second Temple of Jerusalem, writes a detailed account of Alexander's visit to Jerusalem. Despite an

accurate depiction of the personality traits of the various actors in Josephus' story, thereby demonstrating a tremendous grasp of the geopolitics of the time, the story is considered exactly that – a story. The lack of a reliable secondary source prevents it from being considered an actual historic event. Yet so alluring is the tale that it deserves a summarized mention:

Jaddua was the High Priest of Jerusalem when Alexander was conducting his business in Tyre and Gaza. Jaddua's brother, Manasseh, married the daughter of Sanballat, the governor of Samaria. Manasseh faced constant pressure to end his marriage with the Samaritan as the Jewish council was wary of the gentile Samaritan's proximity to the highest Jewish office. Josephus Flavius accurately mentions the historic schism, lack of trust, and mutual disdain between Jerusalem and Samaria. Manasseh's father-in-law, vassal to Darius III, the King of Persia, promises to build a temple in Samaria and make Manasseh the High Priest in order to save his daughter's marriage. When Alexander is laying the siege of Tyre, Jaddua of Jerusalem decides to stay loyal to Darius, and refuses reinforcements for Alexander, whereas Sanballat of Samaria sends his army to help the Macedonian boy-king. Alexander sacked Tyre and was victorious in Gaza. The Samaritans were awarded their temple before Alexander turned his attention to Jerusalem. Alexander was known to be merciless toward dissent, his mercy reserved only for those who surrendered to him. Aware of the fate of Tyre – the city all but obliterated from the face of the earth – Jaddua threw open the gates of Jerusalem and went out to meet the Macedonian conqueror with a white flag. Contrary to expectations, Alexander forgave Jaddua on a whim and spared Jerusalem. Alexander was given permission to sacrifice at the altar of the Second Temple and was shown ancient Hebrew text that prophesized the arrival of a Greek conqueror who would usurp the Persians. Alexander left Jerusalem with the prophesy ringing in his ears – another propaganda feather in his cap. And Jerusalem lived happily and in peace – for maybe fifteen minutes.

I shoo away doves before I can sit under the portico near the Chain Gate, not far from the *sabil* – a public water fountain, which Sultan Qaitbey commissioned in the fifteenth century. An IDF commando loiters nearby, seemingly curious about my sketchbook. Or is he posing for me? I let my pen race over the paper, capturing an image here, a movement there. It is a breezy, cold and cloudy day. A handful of visitors are sprinkled across the Haram al-Sharif, where typically the visitors are in hundreds. These don't seem like the types who would let the weather change their plans. As a matter of fact, they do not look like *anything* could make them change their plans. These are not Instagram-tourists: no man-buns, no wanderlust tattoos, no vegan shoes, no selfie-drones, no insect-repellant trousers, no items being checked off a bucket list. No social media influencer creating targeted content for an audience. Men and women have draped themselves and their children in layers of rumpled clothes and are making the trip of their lifetimes. They are anxious people looking for a place where miracles happen, needing to touch and feel the places touched and felt by great men who have overcome extraordinary odds. For them, Temple Mount is not a tourist site, it is a pilgrimage.

I was reminded of another incident from my father-daughter trip. Not far from where I sit, I sat and sketched that day while Rhea patiently people watched. The Temple Mount was a lot more crowded than it is today. It was past noon and a stream of pilgrims had emerged into the scorching heat, having finished their afternoon prayers at the al-Aqsa mosque. Without warning, a group of pilgrims, in deep religious fervor, stood up and started climbing the steps of the platform, their cries of *Allah-hu-Akbar* – God is the greatest – ringing out across the Temple Mount. The IDF commandoes who had been lingering in the shadows, leaning against the aging walls, were suddenly alert. With minimal but very decisive movements they moved into formation, limbs taut, a word or two whispered urgently over their headpieces, eyes squinting behind iridescent sunglasses, chewing gum pinched between clenched teeth. Within a matter

Damascus Gate, Jerusalem

of a few seconds the atmosphere had tensed up. Rhea shot me a panicked look. *Leave?* Her eyes implored. I shook my head, my pencil hovering over the sketchbook. Sit back, I told her. If the situation were to inflame, we were as safe as we could be anywhere in Jerusalem. We were surrounded by trained soldiers, armed with the most advanced tactical weapons, whose jobs were to ensure the situation did not get out of hand. Despite my words, my perpetually composed, wise-cracking 14-year-old was visibly shaken. I can still see her worried face in my mind. Fortunately, the situation cooled off as quickly as it heated. The pilgrims stopped shouting and walked towards the Dome of the Rock, laughing as if they had pulled a prank.

The two incidents – the run-in with the Jordanian soldier at the entrance of the Temple Mount and the frisson caused by the spontaneous cries of *Allah-hu-Akbar* – had left a deep impression on Rhea.

Presently it starts to rain. Having concluded her exploration of the Dome of the Rock, Monica sits down next to me. I can see that she is ready to leave. Before I pack up, I tilt my sketchbook, allowing the IDF commando one final glimpse of my output that afternoon. He smiles and nods his approval, making an A-OK sign with his hand. Some art-lovers must also carry guns.

As we head to the exit, a small group of orthodox Jews also move toward the exit, barefoot and walking backwards, long white beards fluttering in the stiff wind, long black robes billowing like the sails of a boat gathering speed. The elder Jew waggles a finger at his companion. The two are walking in front of the rest of the group, and the body language indicates the conversation is at a critical juncture.

Jews are forbidden on the Temple Mount as per *Halakhic* restriction, a set of Jewish laws that only allow a High Priest to enter the Holy of Holies. Since the exact location of the original temples on the hillock is unknown, one school of thought prohibits all Jews from entering the Temple Mount to avoid accidental desecration of the temple. A different school of thought interprets the exact same *halakha* and insists that Jews visit the Temple Mount but only certain areas and only after the *mikvah* – a ritual bath. The two equal and opposite forces have essentially created a status quo, ensuring that people who do not ascend to the Temple Mount, do not have to, and the ones who do can continue to.

The youngest of the group of orthodox Jews, a boy of 15 or 16, brings up the rear; his eyes are repeatedly drawn to the golden dome. As the elders climb down the stairs of Bab as-Silsileh, the Chain Gate, he pulls out a black object from his robe, turns towards the Dome, raises his right arm towards the sky and pauses. He pauses, then he poses and clicks a selfie. The next moment the phone disappears back into the pocket and he walks out, head bowed, once again serious and grown-up.

From the Chain Gate, I stop to turn back and cast one last look at the Temple Mount. From the Old City, the Temple Mount looks like an inaccessible castle. From the Temple Mount, the Old City looks like a siege. It is a deadlock.

KING DAVID HOTEL

~~~~~

Ducking between the drops of rain that clatter onto Jerusalem's rooftops, we run-walk to the Jaffa Gate via the perennially busy David Street, where we flag down a taxi and direct him to King David Hotel. The colonial-era familiarity of Western hospitality at the hotel is a welcome change. Cypress logs crackle in brick fireplaces. A portly maître d'hôtel with a great white beard and a pristine white waist coat is seating elderly ladies. White-gloved waiters flit between tables, adroitly balancing breakfast trays on their fingertips loaded with continental treats. Seated at a window with a view of the weather and having sent half a mug of scalding Nescafe down my throat, I ask the twinkle-eyed maître d' – Captain Twinkles, I name him – to persuade the chef to make me a masala omelet. I give him my recipe – chopped onions, chilies and a dash of salt, whipped with one egg and fried on two drops of oil on both sides till it turns brown. And can I also have a copy of the *Jerusalem Times*, please?

Captain Twinkles returns within a few minutes with *The New York Times*. "It's the same," he winks and clucks his tongue, "New York or Jerusalem – both are run by the Jews anyways." I mentally give him five stars for the Jewish *juggad*.[9]

"See?" He points to an article below the fold. Scott Pruitt's visit to Jerusalem had been canceled. The head of the Environmental Protection Agency of Trump's administration was scheduled to arrive in Jerusalem that day. Pruitt had been embroiled in scandals involving extravagant spending and conflicts of interest. Apparently, the President had put the kibosh on the trip, tired of seeing Pruitt in the news headlines, a virtual real estate that Trump firmly believed belonged to himself.

"No wonder," Monica says, "*This* weather was meant for *him*."

To my delight, Captain Twinkles returns a few minutes later with a plate covered by a steel dome, which he taps with a gloved index finger and says, "The only dome that matters in the city." Under it is the best masala omelet I have ever tasted in the Middle East. The chef has thoughtfully added a dash of turmeric to the omelet and garnished it with crumpled cilantro, two ingredients I cannot do without at home but do not expect in a restaurant. King David Hotel is the kind of a place that does the little details well.

The hotel is accustomed to hosting heads of states, royalty, A-list film stars, and dignitaries. "Was Scott Pruitt going to stay here?" I ask conversationally, to which Captain Twinkles expertly and ever so slightly rearranges the lines of his face to confirm my theory without ever answering my question.

This is the first Western breakfast I have had on the road since the breakfast in Suez overlooking the canal. Monica and I polish off everything that is put in front of us – home-made granola laced with the massive raisins, crispy and spiced tater tots, four different berries mixed in homemade yogurt, three types of Danish pastries, several slices of toast, a glass each of blood orange, pomegranate, and cucumber juice.

[9] *Juggad* is a colloquial Indian word for hack

The table is cleared. The coffee mugs are topped-off. While we wait for our check to arrive, I pull out of my backpack the hardcover copy of James Ballentine's *The Life of David Roberts, R.A,* published in 1866. James Ballentine and David Roberts were close friends, and the book presents Roberts' adventurous life chronologically, using entries in Robert's handwritten journals and his day-to-day correspondence. I flipped to a page marked by post-it notes. They marked the passage when Roberts was in Jerusalem.

Roberts stayed in Jerusalem for a total of nine days, not counting his six-day excursion into the Judaean Desert. In Jerusalem, Roberts settled down to systematically document as many biblical sites he could. In the back of his head, he was ticking through a mental map of the locations he needed to sketch to satiate future readers that were hungry for a view of the biblical land. A fantastic panorama from the Mount of Olives. Various sites in the Kidron Valley with biblical significance, like the Tomb of Zachariah, Pillar of Absalom, the Fountain of Siloam and the Fountain of Job. The general view of the city from the four points of the compass, as was the prevailing practice of the time.[10]

Not only is Roberts able to see each individual drawing as a plate, but also as part of the book, the way it would be sequenced and bound in its final printed form. Roberts' book was slowly coming together. He was also getting ready for his six-day trip into the Judaean Desert with John Pell in tow.

We are too.

Mount of olives, Jerusalem

[10] Uzi Baram writes, "Art historians interpret the multiple perspectives as a quest for accuracy." "Images of the Holy Land: The David Roberts Paintings as Artifacts of 1830s Palestine." *Historical Archaeology*, vol. 41, no. 1, 2007, pp. 106–117.

MOUNT OF OLIVES

The Old City of Jerusalem looks timeless across the Kidron Valley. The raised platform of the Temple Mount on the south side, with the glittering Dome of the Rock and the grey domes of al-Aqsa Mosque, the blurry-grey dome of the Church of the Holy Sepulchre, and the white dome of the Hurva Synagogue are all enclosed in the tight hug of Jerusalem's ancient walls.

"Mount of Olives is the Switzerland of Jerusalem. You can see all religions from here," Gazi says. Our perch on top of the Mount of Olives has a sprawling view over the oldest cemetery in Jerusalem – some of the graves were already a thousand years old when Jesus Christ walked into Jerusalem.

We are test-driving Gazi, who is helping us finalize the details of a trip to the Judean Desert. The short trip to the Mount of Olives is a dry run – I am looking for a fierce guide and a sedate driver, not the other way around. I had taken the lesson learned in Petra to heart.

Gazi is crouched next to me, one knee resting on the ground, his other knee supporting his elbow. Broad-shouldered and heavily bearded, he contemplates the panorama with us and for a moment looks like Atlas with an invisible but heavy globe on his shoulder that he is ready to shrug.

Gazi is in his mid-thirties. He is part of the Palestinian diaspora – his family had to leave Jerusalem after the creation of Israel in 1948. He is Jordanian by nationality, lives in the Christian quarter in Jerusalem and carries an Israeli ID card. You can read all the books you want on the Israel-Palestine conflict, you can listen to all the experts who know all the details, you can let the

JERUSALEM FROM THE MOUNT OF OLIVES BY DAVID ROBERTS, R.A.
8TH APRIL 1839

philosophers and the theologians debate the nuances of right and wrong, morals and responsibilities, but there is nothing like the point of view of the guy on the street living it every day. I ask Gazi my questions – some are textbook, many are mine, a few are rhetorical – just voicing them out loud feels like they are being answered. Gazi speaks at length. He talks about driving past the house that once belonged to his family before they were evicted in 1948 and is today occupied by a Jewish family. He talks about his new bride – a Palestinian who lives in Jordan. He can't bring her to Jerusalem, nor can he stay with her long enough out of a fear that his Israeli ID card – and with it his ability to work in Jerusalem – will be revoked. His day-to-day struggles are that of a Palestinian who resents Israel but depends on it for his survival.

Across the Kidron Valley, a massive wall encloses the Temple Mount at the southwestern corner of Jerusalem, strikingly like the walls of the Tomb of Machpelah in Hebron. These are sites that King Herod fortified with cyclopean walls, as if the pagan king could foresee the issues of the future, trying to enclose it and seal it.

A Jewish temple stood here from 1000 to 587 BCE, built by King Solomon. The temple was destroyed by the Persians and a second Temple stood between 516 BCE and 70 BCE. From the late first century CE to the early part of the seventh century, Jerusalem was a Christian town and the Temple Mount lay ignored in its ruins. In the seventh century, Caliph Omar cleared the site of filth, and the Temple Mount started to be known as the Haram e-Sharif. The Dome of the Rock was built in the late 600s. The Crusaders arrived in the eleventh century, converted the mosque into a church, and left. After they left, the Haram e-Sharif was deserted until Saladin conquered Jerusalem in the thirteenth century and converted the church into a mosque. Suleiman ("the Magnificent") surrounded the entire city with walls in the sixteenth century, and Jerusalem has looked the same since.

These broad brushstrokes are the widely accepted and easily understood corpus of facts. Everything else is a jumble of opinion, perception, viewpoint, interpretation and conflicting accounts. Coming to a clear conclusion on any one issue is like trying to solve a thousand-piece jigsaw puzzle that has a different picture printed on each side. If one side of the puzzle is assembled correctly, the other side is scrambled.

I let Gazi fetch the car while Monica and I scamper down the hill between the grave markers. The Kidron valley is verdant and in full bloom. The valley floor is covered with blue and purple flowers bathed in the orange-yellow haze of sunset. A toddler is pestering a lamb with giggles and shouts of joy. Boys in long, loose shorts are kicking a soccer ball with their naked feet, showing a dexterity that would interest a talent hunter.

Up there is a mound surrounded by a wall that everybody is fighting for, and down here lies a valley worth all the enmity.

~~~~~~

On 1st April 1839, having hired horses, David Roberts and John Pell headed into the Judaean Desert, just two days after reaching Jerusalem. In those two days Roberts had completed a large collection of sketches already. Roberts and John Pell also found the time to meet the Ottoman Governor of Jerusalem, Ahmet Aga Dizdar, who was planning to lead a contingent of pilgrims into the Judaean Desert to the site of Jesus's baptism on Easter Sunday and accepted an invitation to travel with the pilgrim convoy.

Between 1st and 6th April, Roberts would travel to the traditional site of Jesus' baptism on the Jordan river, stop at the Dead Sea and Jericho, stay at the Monastery of Santa Saba for two days, and visit the most important of all biblical sites: Bethlehem.

~~~~~~

I am sitting with Gazi, a vintage map of Israel and Palestine laid out between us, like two generals at a war council. Except Gazi is having trouble spotting anything on the map.

"I have never gotten used to the bird's eye view," he laughs, "I know this area like the back of my hand. I know every road in and out of the mountains, but don't ask me to trace it on a map. My brain does not work in cartesian coordinates."

Gazi peruses Roberts' itinerary one more time.

"Do we have to follow his exact sequence?" he asks me.

I shake my head.

"That's a relief," he says, "To visit in the exact order in the face of unpredictable Israeli check points would take a lot more time."

Manger Square, Bethlehem

BETHLEHEM

~~~~~

While Roberts was sketching inside the Church of Nativity in Bethlehem, the Holy Fire – part of a ritual centered around the Church of the Holy Sepulchre – arrived from Jerusalem. His sketches ended up as two fantastic lithographs that show the entrance to the very underground cave where Jesus was said to be born. Roberts was readying to bid John Pell and Ismail Effendi goodbye, as they prepared to return to Cairo, but not before Pell, the adventurer, had one more adventure, which would have added a fun section to his book if he had ever cared to write one. Katherine Sim writes in Roberts' biography that the travelers heard a commotion in the street. The monks were called to mediate. The citizens who were refusing to part with supplies were being beaten up by soldiers. John Pell, armed to the teeth, jumped into the scuffle brandishing the Pasha's *firman and defused a situation that was getting out of control.*

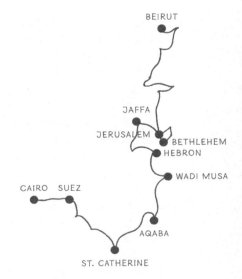

Roberts wrote in his journal:

> "MR. PELL AND ISMAEL EFFENDI TOOK LEAVE OF US THIS MORNING, GOING TO CAIRO BY WAY OF HEBRON..."[11]

~~~~~

The mood in the car is somber when Gazi parks near an overpass with a view of a school backyard. Middle school kids chase a ball, their tiny feet shod in black leather school shoes, scampering around a scaled-down soccer field. The sounds of their happy, carefree jostling and laughter are a tonic for the soul. That morning we read grim news of a high school shooting back in the United States. A teenager, armed with assault rifles, walked into his school in Florida and killed seventeen of his classmates. The country is in a state of shock. Monica points out that, at this moment, the kids in this playground in the middle of Palestine look at peace and safer than their counterparts in the United States.

[11] John Pell and Roberts would stay friends. They corresponded regularly, two travelers writing to each other from different corners of the world. Pell continued his swashbuckling life of an explorer, living out of the proverbial portmanteau. And like buccaneers often do – travelers who collect nothing but stories and fail to publish – he ended up destitute. He died in Devon in 1856, leaving behind many debts, which were only paid off by selling a painting he had received from Roberts.

In 2000, US President Bill Clinton, Israeli Prime Minister Ehud Barak, and Palestinian Authority Chairman Yasser Arafat failed to broker peace between Israel and Palestine at the Camp David Summit. The Intifada, an intense period of violence that lasted for four and a half years, kicked off. At the height of the Intifada, Israel built a concrete barrier – the Separation Wall – between Israel and Palestine (according to Israel) to protect Israeli soft targets that were being hit by Palestinian gunfire and rockets, and (according to Palestine) to isolate Palestine from the rest of the world and convert it into a ghetto.

Monica and I easily pass through Checkpoint 300 of the Separation Wall on the way to Bethlehem, the ten-kilometer distance to Jerusalem still taking us an hour plus a smidgen of time.

"The good boys of Israel become bad boys in Palestine," Gazi says, as he expertly swerves to get out of the way of a speeding Land Cruiser.

"How did you know the driver was Israeli?" The Land Cruiser is already a speck on the horizon.

"It is an Israeli car. Israeli cars have white plates, Palestinians have yellow. It allows the Israeli cops to know who to let speed."

The upkeep of Palestinian infrastructure lags behind Israel's, and the gap is never more evident than at the border. No prizes for guessing which side has more potholes on the roads, garbage on the roadside, dilapidated houses and buildings, and older, decrepit cars. The Palestinians blame it on the Israeli barricades that prevent the flow of trade and jobs, Israel blames Palestine for mismanagement and lethargy.

The Church of Nativity can easily be mistaken for a fortress. Emperor Justinian built the massive walls capable of withstanding the most ingenious siege engines of the sixth century. Justinian

Church of the Nativity, Bethlehem.

expanded the original church built by Queen Helena, much like his work at the monastery of St. Catherine in Sinai, both constructed simultaneously. The building, entered through a tiny niche, is cavernous inside. The walls are covered with scaffolding for a long running project to service the rotting roof, which is fourteen centuries old. We make a beeline for the stairs that take us into the belly of the grotto, where a metal fourteen-pointed star has been placed to mark the very spot where Jesus was supposed to have been born. The original manger where the baby was placed lies in a nearby nook.

Despite the sheer antiquity of the building – in continuous use for fourteen hundred years – the architecture does not enchant me, nor does the atmosphere propagate spirituality. The enormous space, despite the Doric columns and the soaring frescos, reminds me of an industrial warehouse.

Across the street in Manger Square, there is a mosque that looks to be of recent construction but claims a connection with Caliph Omar. Turns out that the mosque was built in the second half of the nineteenth century over a spot where, according to Muslims, there once stood a mosque that Caliph Omar built. According to the Jewish people, it is also the place where King David and King Solomon were buried. *Holy places remain holy.* If you want to find a demolished church, look for a tall minaret, a student of archaeology acting as our guide in Andalusia had once whispered in my ear.

An Arab man has set up his shop in the shadow of the mosque. He looks at my yellow *kaffiyeh* and clucks his tongue. "You are wearing it in Sinai style, *habibi*," he laughs, his gigantic belly moving like jelly. He picks out a red checkered scarf of the type made famous by Yasir Arafat and offers to drape it. While he is messing with my head, so is Gazi.

"This is the second example of Caliph Omar choosing to stop short of entering a church of high significance to the Christians. He did that with the Church of the Holy Sepulchre and he did it here. But when he reached the top of Haram in Jerusalem, he did not hesitate to clear the rubble." Gazi is trying to persuade me that Christians and Jews got interested in the Temple Mount only after the Muslims started using it in the late eighth century.

I ignore his diatribe, as I have a more pressing issue on my mind. "Is the Turkish coffee any good here or should I wait for Jericho?"

JERICHO

~~~~~~

Blowing towards the open horizon in the direction of the Judean Desert feels therapeutic. Getting down to the level of the sea and descending rapidly into the belly of the earth, the desert air, warm and devoid of humidity, feels salubrious. Gazi compliments us for picking the most pleasant season to visit the desert. Monica and I, sitting in the back of his vintage Mercedes, exchange a smile. We no longer look at the weather forecast or the prevailing season when we travel, or for that matter the ticket price or government travel advisory or travelers' reviews. Once we are fixated on a destination, we make a hole in our calendars, we pack our bags, and we move.

The town of Bethany even by Palestinian standards is dilapidated.

"If your car is stolen in Jerusalem you will probably find it in Bethany," Gazi says. "This is not a place where you stop to buy oranges. You don't stop here if you want to pee badly. You don't even stop here if you have a puncture. Especially if…" he completes the sentence by rolling his eyes in manner, the meaning of which (in the presence of an attractive woman) is innately understood by men across the barriers of language and culture.

We cross a mountain associated with the traditional Mount Temptation, which offers a cable car for tourists to experience the quiet and solitude that Jesus is said to have enjoyed during his stay of forty days and nights. The dust and heat eddies merge into the warm hues of the earth and the cool blue of the sky on the line of the horizon. The sighting of palm trees is the first sign that we are approaching Jericho, exactly as advertised in the Bible – the City of Palm Trees. Gazi skirts the town of Jericho and drives an extra kilometer to the Tell es-Sultan. While Gazi stretches his legs and lights a cigarette, Monica and I stop at the visitor center to watch a thirty-minute informational film on a loop – "Can we now claim we watched a movie in a theatre in Palestine?" – and take Instagram-friendly photos in front of a sign that claims Jericho as the oldest city in the world.

The ten-thousand-year-old mound is seventy feet tall and spread over two acres. At least twenty civilizations have successively inhabited this place since the end of the Ice Age, making it the oldest continuously inhabited city in the world. *Make that the oldest 'excavated' city in the world*, I say. There are countless mounds in the Levant that have not yet come under an archaeologist's spade.

At the top of the mound, an Asian woman in a short floral-print frock stands on the verge of a ditch, making a V for victory sign for the camera manned by her companion, who is wearing a floral-print shirt. "Where is anything?" I hear her ask their guide. I have the same question: *Where is everything?*

Gold diggers, grave robbers and archaeologists have beaten us to it. The hilltop is strewn with holes of all sizes, the place desecrated, the surface pockmarked and shorn of any ancient signs of life. I squat beside a trench that runs all the way to the bottom of the *tel* (a man-made hill created by successive generations building and rebuilding in the same place). Archaeology is also a type of destruction. Wave upon wave of archaeologists has spent season after season at this tel, leaving behind neatly dug and well-presented terraces, walls, foundations, embankments, and crisscrossing staircases that look like they are a part of an MC Escher painting. Areas where one can tread are demarcated from areas to stay away from. The place had been left clean as a whistle. The only things left behind are stories.

The bottom of the pit represents the soil from the beginning of the Holocene epoch when the glaciers started to retreat 12,000 years ago. A few feet above it is the telltale signs of the Natufian hunter-gatherers – early settlers who had stopped to quench their thirst at the plentiful spring of Sultan and never moved on. Above that, a layer on which lived a unique civilization sixty centuries before Christ, a civilization that mastered animal husbandry, agrarian living, and constructing houses, but had no pottery. The discovery of such a culture in the early 1900s had shaken the archaeological world. The civilization covered the skulls of the dead with a layer of adobe and placed painted seashell in the pits to depict eyeball, a bleak attempt to conserve the living features. The civilization also built a heavy stone wall several feet tall that gave Jericho the moniker of the oldest city. My eyes rake several feet up to the ancient brickwork of

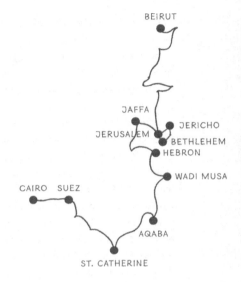

defensive structures and well-built houses, signs of prosperity, five hundred years on either side of the Great Pyramid, right about the time bronze was taking over from flint as the material of choice. Above that lived the vibrant Hyksos civilization, influenced by the rich tombs of Egypt and a lavish lifestyle that ensued. Sure enough, the walls got thicker and taller, a sign of economic disparity and fear of being invaded by enemies from across the desert. Then, the soil is silent for a few feet, indications of the lull after the fall of an ostentatious civilization, possibly an abandonment of Jericho but not permanently. Because past the midway mark would be the time when Mark Anthony gave away Jericho to his beloved Cleopatra. A jutting brick wall marks the time Emperor Constantine embraced Christianity. The Byzantine era arrives years later, and a dark swath of soil represents the waves of Crusades. A poking stick marks the time Suleiman built the walls of Jerusalem. A few inches below the surface they found beer bottles and condoms left by British soldiers in WWI. But just before that Roberts stood here and saw none of this.

On 1st April 1839 he wrote:

"...THE PRESENT TOWN HAS NO PRETENSION TO THE ANTIQUITY..."

The Bible says that Jesus passed through Jericho on his final journey to Jerusalem where he would be crucified. At the time the oasis was a flourishing town on an important trade route between Damascus and Jerusalem. The spring of Ain-e-Sultan pumped a thousand gallons of fresh water per minute, converting Jericho into a lush oasis where orchards of citrus fruits kept the air fragrant. Jesus stopped at Jericho and converted Zacchaeus the tax collector into a believer. There are no physical markers of the event. The city has been buried under gravel for the last two thousand years. Jericho is probably the only place in Palestine that enjoys peace and solitude despite being touched by Jesus, Herod and the Crusaders.

CONVENT OF ST. SABA BY DAVID ROBERTS, R.A. 4TH APRIL 1839

What is the future of Jericho? Abundant water of the Ain-es-Sultan, palm trees plentiful, a trade route between Jordan and Jerusalem, proximity to the Dead Sea. "We come back to the same old places to do the same old things," writes Craig Childs, author of *House of Rain*, in which he follows ancient migration routes on foot, pursuing early pueblo passages across the American Southwest. Holy places stay holy. New battles are fought on old battle fields. New civilizations live on top of old civilizations. Great cities are built on top of the ruins of great cities. That's the future of a city with a great past.

St George Monastery

JORDAN RIVER

~~~~~

As the sun reaches its highpoint overhead, Gazi takes us to a patch of the Jordan River favored by tourists and guides as the spot where Jesus was baptized. Israeli soldiers stare at their Jordanian counterparts across a muddy part of the river that an Olympian long jumper could ford without getting her feet wet. Men and women dunk themselves in the yellow water in a show of religious hysteria amidst much chanting and clapping.

So docile is the Jordan today that it is difficult to imagine the horrific scene that Roberts witnessed. Roberts followed the Governor of Jerusalem early in the morning to the banks of the river. The procession of traveling pilgrims rushed to the river in a religious fervor, all wanting to be the first to take a dip. In that ruckus, a youngster was pulled into the vortex of the eddies and lost his life, the wails of his mother's loss universally every parent's nightmare.

The traumatic event did not prevent Roberts and Pell from accepting an invite to the Governor's tent for lunch. Trying his best to merge into the colorful local scene, a trend T E Lawrence would set years later dining with the chiefs of the Arab Revolt, Roberts struggled to eat rice and mutton with his bare hands. The amused governor noticed his discomfort and called for spoons and forks, confessing that the Pasha had instructed him to extend the best hospitality to the European, particularly the English. (Despite Roberts' proximity to the governor and despite the governor's willingness to go above and beyond, Roberts was not able to secure permission to enter the Temple Mount. If nothing else, it gives us a frame to appreciate the risk Frederick Catherwood took to map and sketch the Dome of the Rock.)

MONASTERIES OF THE JUDAEAN DESERT

~~~~~

Gazi drives us along Wadi Qelt, a tremendous ravine that cuts through the Judean Mountains and wiggles its way through the Judean Desert to Jerusalem. We are roughly following the path that Jesus is said to have taken on his way to Jerusalem before he met the good Samaritan. After driving through the mountains for 30 minutes, we are flagged down at an Israeli checkpoint. Soldiers open the hood and the trunk of the vintage Mercedes. Gazi shows his identity card. We are asked for our passports. The suspicious look from the soldiers, the way they move about, tells me something is awry. The atmosphere is tense. Gazi tells us a plane has crashed in the Zagros Mountains in Iran the previous day. All the passengers on board have been killed. I remember reading the news article on Reuters in the morning, but I could not connect the dots. It was a commercial plane, the crash caused by a combination of fog and the age of the aircraft. Why would that lead to a terse ID check in Palestine?

Gazi says, his smile wry, "Anything can trigger a situation here. It does not take much for something to turn into an event where people lose lives."

Gazi pulls over. From a viewpoint he points to a monastery with whitewashed walls and blue domes halfway down the ravine. I grab a bottle of water and follow Monica down the trail to the Monastery of St. George of Choziba.

Under the sweltering Judean sun, Palestinian boys follow us on foot and mule, offering cold water bottles, freshly squeezed pomegranate juice, handmade bead necklaces, tattered picture postcards, travel books, and a ride on the donkey *down* to the monastery. Cleverly, not one of them impart the information that the monastery is closed to visitors that day. After we reach the massive monastery gates, we read the typewritten notice and turn back for the hike out of the canyon, the Palestinian boys reappear offering cold water bottles, freshly squeezed pomegranate juice, handmade bead necklaces, tattered picture postcards, travel books, and a ride on the donkey *up* to the car.

The monastery clings to the steep cliffside. From the bottom of the canyon, the perilous location of the structure on a narrow ledge, teetering on the edge of the ravine halfway down a cliff, reminds Monica of the cliff dwellings of southern Utah, deep in the American cowboy country, where we had spent time on our honeymoon. Built in the twelfth and thirteenth centuries by the people known as *the Anasazi* – the ancient ones – houses and villages were tucked into south-facing alcoves in the rugged red sandstone cliffs high above the canyon floor. Thousands of these structures lie in the backcountry of the American Southwest, some of them still undiscovered and in pristine condition, after they were abandoned about eight hundred years ago, the reason for the abandonment still an unsolved mystery. Structures built fifty to seventy-five years before the mass abandonment were situated in increasingly precarious locations, higher on the cliff face, difficult to reach from below.

"Weren't those structures defensive?" Monica asks, her hands akimbo, face tilted up, eyes squinting in the sun.

So are these monasteries. The ascetics and the early Christians came here in the early fourth and fifth centuries to live the desert life their saints and prophets had lived. These were perilous times. The rugged terrain abounded with brigands and mercenaries and tribal militia and religious bigots. The monasteries and churches needed to be first and foremost military structures before they could be religious places.

"How come David Roberts didn't sketch the Monastery of St. George?" Monica asks me. I am wondering myself.

Later, I find out that the monastery – originally built in the late fourth century, destroyed by Persians in the seventh century, rebuilt by Crusaders in the twelfth – had since fallen derelict and was reconstructed only in early 1900s by Greek monks. The monastery wasn't here when Roberts passed by. That's why.

We race against the setting sun to make it to the monastery of Mar Saba before it closes. Alas, by the time we cross all the IDF roadblocks, the doors of the fourth century Greek Orthodox monastery have been shut and bolted.

But it is not too late to walk down a sheep path and see the final rays of sun shroud the ancient walls in sublime golden light. That's when Monica discovers that the monastery does not allow entry to women.

Shocked, she turns to me and asks, "So, what was your plan, babe? Were you going to dump me outside?"

"I was never going to go inside," I say lying through my teeth. She bursts out laughing, not believing a word I said. There is a reason she is a top lawyer in town.

"You chose to visit the St. George monastery first because St. George allows entry to women. You were gambling on either me being too tired or me not minding being left outside Mar Saba. *It's pretty much the same monastery, babe."* The last line is a very good impression of me, and I join her laughter. And yes, that was kinda-sorta my evil plan.

We push a 'to-do' pin on the two monasteries of the Judaean Desert, leaving them to be explored on the next visit. After all, one must leave some things for next time. It is a way of not saying goodbye to a place.

David Roberts, on the other hand, enjoyed two days of wonderful hospitality at the Monastery of Mar Saba. Roberts was offered comfortable rooms despite the quarantine and was fed austere but nutritious monastery meals. Roberts' sketches of Mar Saba are extraordinarily well-composed. He picks

AL AKSA

MUGHRABI BR.

PLAZA

angles that show the jaw-dropping architecture and the setting of the monastery set close to the edge of the cliff, the buttresses tumbling down the face of the mountain like molten chocolate from a birthday cake. In one sketch, Roberts even attempts an aerial composition, as if photographed from a drone in which he once again knocks out an entire mountain to show the relative position of the monastery to the Dead Sea.

BACK IN JERUSALEM

〰〰〰

Jerusalem is colder than Satan's heart on our last week there. Grey days follow inky nights. The skies are dark by five o'clock. Only when the sun finds a gap in the clouds, sometimes just for a few minutes, do the walls glitter amber as if honey has been poured over them. Otherwise, they are a shapeless grey lump. The cold winds blow ceaselessly, the buildings are stone cold inside, the frigid air creeps up the floor, up wooden furniture and iron beds, up slippers and legs, until everything is as cold as a tomb.

The walls of Jerusalem, they tower over you, adding claustrophobia to the gloom. Streets become trenches. You no longer walk at your own will. The walls push you through the narrow lanes.

WESTERN PLAZA

~~~~~~

Everything is within walking distance from our hotel in the Old City. This statement, while one hundred percent true, is also misleading, because everything in the Old City is within walking distance of everything else in the Old City. Such is the charm of old Jerusalem that is merely one square kilometer in area, less than two hundred and fifty acres. There is barely a day in Jerusalem when we do not walk on every major thoroughfare and cross at least two gates.

On the day Monica and I stand in line to enter the Western Plaza, everybody around us smells of shampoo, soap and cologne. Monica points to a signboard and asks me what it means.

The signboard reads:

> ENTRANCE TO THE WESTERN WALL IS POSSIBLE ONLY AFTER A SECURITY CHECK. THE MAGNETOMETER IS SET TO SABBATH MODE. YOU CAN REQUEST A CHECK.

Per my basic knowledge of *Halakha* – the definitive Jewish law, Jews are not allowed to work on the day of *sabbath*, the day

of rest. They are restricted from doing even basic things like cooking a meal or fixing a broken radio or hammering a nail in the wall or even turning a switch on or off. A magnetometer is a device that measures the strength and direction of a magnetic field. My tenth-grade physics reminds me that a metal object changes the strength of the magnetic field it is introduced into. The airport-scanner is a magnetometer detecting the presence of metal on the person passing through it – looking for a gun or a knife – and the magnetometer mode, I am guessing, is a switch that allows the laws of physics to bypass the laws created based on the edicts Moses heard on Mt. Sinai.

It turns out I am on the right path. Jews have been tinkering with basic sabbath modes since probably the day after the *Halakhic* rule came into place. For example, instead of switching off a lamp, an opaque cover would be used to cut out the light. But as the electronics got complicated, bypassing became complex too. Finally, an engineer with a deep understanding of *Halakha* figured out a loophole. If the lamp could be left burning during sabbath, the act of burning not considered work, then an appliance could also continue to function without altering its state. All that had to be done was to disable all the switches that operate the sounds and the lights. The sabbath mode was thus invented. Practicing Jews could now cook a meal and put it on a hotplate before sabbath and switch it to sabbath mode. The meal would stay warm until the hotplate was taken out of the mode. Since the mode disabled all displays, lights and sounds, no "work was done" during sabbath. A simple but elegant solution for an otherwise prickly problem.

A refrigerator in sabbath mode would not switch on the light if the door was opened and would not show the temperature inside the fridge if it had an LCD display; it would turn off the icemaker and would ensure the compressor was not triggered by a door opening but would continue to keep the inside cold. The focus was on ensuring that the status remained unchanged.

"The sabbath mode is just another Middle Eastern status quo then," Monica accurately summarizes.

We step in and out of the sabbath-mode governed scanner. The visual display is switched to a magnetic compass that deflects only if metal is detected on the person. It passes muster with *Halakha* since no circuit is switched on or off.

I have never seen the Western Plaza this empty. A few dozen Orthodox Jewish families dressed in their finery offer their prayers at the wall, the only remaining part of the Second Temple accessible to the Jews. Men wearing kippah wedge handwritten notes in the cracks of the ancient walls. A soldier rests his assault rifle against the wall before leaning on it himself, his forehead resting in the crook of his arm, a desolate and forlorn pose of helplessness.

Back in 2015, Rhea and I met Uri in the Plaza to take us through the underground tunnels of the Old City. Uri was a student at the Hebrew university. I had connected with him online after reading an insightful blog he published.

A bit further north from the Western Plaza, Rhea and I followed Uri into the belly of Jerusalem, climbing down wooden stairs and navigating narrow passages, the air getting dustier, our breath heavier. In one dark corner, a trench about 10 feet by 20 feet had been dug about 40 feet deep. Conveniently placed lights showed several layers of ruins stacked one on top of another. *Holy places on top of holy places. Cities on top of cities.*

We walked along the Herodian walls, following the foundation of the Temple Mount. All around us were residences, hallways, passages, shops, water cisterns – the rocks and adobe bricks revealed their size and shape when the lights from our headlamps and handheld torches fell on them. Once the light turned away, the ruins seemed to sit down, lean back and relax. *Layers on top of layers. Civilizations on top of civilizations.*

In an hour and a half, we were back in broad daylight, following Uri up staircases, across passageways and around corners to a terrace with a sweeping view of the Western Plaza and the Temple Mount. In broad daylight it struck me that everything we had seen underground was on the surface once upon a time, every layer a result of hope, ego, and greed.

Uri was in his thirties. Pencil thin, with razor-sharp light eyes and pale skin, he wore a baggy stonewash shirt and trousers. Out of his well-used sling bag he pulled out a black and white photograph of the Plaza taken in 1929 – the Plaza is unrecognizable in the faded period photograph. In it a jumble of buildings extends almost all the way to the Western Wall.

During our underground tour, I asked Uri questions that books and articles did not answer – I needed a joe-regular insight. Uri was telling me, without a lot of emotion:

"In the 1500s, Suleiman was trying to get Jews to come back to Jerusalem from Europe. He reserved a strip adjoining the Western Wall for the Jews to pray. The strip was only fifteen feet wide.

"The Jews had to make an arduous circuit though the labyrinths and filthy streets of Jerusalem. They were heckled and ragged on their way, taunted and tortured, drenched in dirty water and sprayed with feces as part of a cruel game. The narrow strip of praying area available to the Jews would get crowded on special days and festivals.

"After the creation of Israel in 1948, Jerusalem came under Jordanian control and the Jews lost whatever little access they had to the wall. During the Six Day War of 1967, the Israeli army under General Dayan entered East Jerusalem and seized control of the Temple Mount. Overnight, the buildings adjoining the Wall – the Arab Moghrabi Quarter – were razed. Houses, shops, mosques hundreds of years old were flattened by bulldozers

Old City of Jerusalem.

working under floodlights. By morning, Dayan had created the Plaza. Dayan prayed at the wall, pushed a prayer note in the ancient crevices of the *kottel* and relinquished control of the Temple Mount to Jordan for governance."

He went on, "Dayan created a secular space in the Old City. The only open space in the city that is not on the Temple Mount. This is not just a plaza, it is peace. It is the sign that we are secular. That night Dayan could have flattened the *entire* Muslim quarter along with the Moghrabi Quarter if he wished. That would have exposed the *entire* Wall of the Second Temple along the west and north side of the Temple Mount. He could have let Jews fly the Israeli flag on the Temple Mount. He did not. General Dayan averted World War III."

~~~~~~

I told Uri a story I read in a book about another Israeli army general, General Ariel Sharon, who went on to become the Prime Minister of Israel. He was gifted an ancient rifle that was found in the mountains of the area he helped liberate in the war of 1967. He brought the rifle home to add to his collection of antiquities, for General Sharon was an antiquarian. While fooling around with it, his son accidentally pulled the trigger and was killed – the tragic irony of losing a child to an artifact that would have never been found had the father not been such a brave heart.

Back came Uri's reply, "Nothing big can be achieved without a bit of sacrifice." He wasn't being philosophical or trying to sound grandiose. He believed in it as if it were plain old truth.

In the two hours we spent with Uri, an entirely new layer was added to my understanding of Israel.

LIONS GATE

~~~~~~~

Every street corner in Jerusalem either has a story steeped in history or a fruit-seller selling fresh pomegranate juice – often both. We are at one such corner, just inside the Lion's Gate in the Muslim quarter, where the northern edge of the Temple Mount meets the Walls of the Old City.

The *keffiyeh*-clad juice-seller feeds a cut pomegranate the size of a coconut into a yellow hand-press, pours the juice into plastic cups – sweet nectar exchanged for a small Israeli denomination. The Via Dolorosa starts at the Lion's Gate. It is said that Jesus entered the city through this gate on the day of his crucifixion. As did the Israeli paratroopers in 1967 when they finally breached the walls of the Old City. The Lion's Gate in the Muslim quarter is Jerusalem's intricately intertwined knot of culture, religion, and history.

The kids are returning home from school. They are swathed in bright puffy jackets and carry backpacks as big as their torso – the heavy accoutrement failing to prevent them fooling around. A trampled can of coke is kicked around like a football amidst the banter, pushing and shoving, and a lot of giggles and laughter. The shops lining the Via Dolorosa have settled down into the post-lunch lull, their owners ensconced in thick Bedouin blankets slumped deep into their chairs, pulling on their water pipes and cigarettes, their sock-covered toes pointed at smoldering charcoal stoves. Women, covered head-to-toe in black hijabs, are hurrying home carrying a leg of lamb, onions and oranges in thin polythene bags. A curio displayed in a shop draws Monica inside; I stay outdoors, sitting on a narrow ledge balancing my sketchbook on my knee. As I put pencil to paper, I am suddenly surrounded by devotees carrying crosses on their shoulders, heading to the next station of the cross. They walk past me, bent low, singing a hymn in a language that I cannot identify, the only familiar words being Yeshu Christa.

Issamo
Jerusalem

A few feet from the Homo Ecco Arch is a little coffee shop run by Essam, a self-described Afro-Palestinian. The interior of Essam's shop is decorated like a Bedouin tent – walls covered in colorful blankets, furnished with low inlaid mother-of-pearl tables, chairs and divans made of cedar and covered with burgundy-colored velvet cushions. The wall behind the counter is covered with vintage prints and the shelves are stacked with vintage books. Issam has created around him a Palestinian bubble from which he sells Illy blend espresso made in a shiny *La Favorita* espresso machine.

I order a Turkish coffee, Monica a ginger tea. If Essam's burly shoulders, black curly hair, and floral silk shirt don't make him look Caribbean then his drawl would, except his English comes with a strong Arabian lilt like his coffee. He speaks slowly, he moves slowly, he turns slowly. He even does slow slowly.

I ask him how safe it is to travel to Nablus. I am exploring driving through the second largest city in Palestine on our journey northward. I ask the question, but the answer is meant for Monica's ears.

"Nablus is peaceful," Essam says, "and beautiful this time of the year."

"Is it easy to get in?"

"Yes, easy," pat comes the response.

"And getting out?"

"No problem," he says, smiling ear to ear.

Easy. Safe. Beautiful. Peaceful. No problem. No worries – I quickly figure out that's Essam's world.

"The bathroom? It's in the back. It does not have a lock. It's safe. Just sing loudly. Ha Ha."

An hour later, as we step out of the coffee house, a swerving car almost runs us over. That brings us back to the present. We are now outside Essam's sanctuary. Not everything is safe.

By the time Roberts returned from the Judaean Desert, his interest in Jerusalem had started to fade.

Jerusalem does that to you. It takes you a day or two to see all the mega-sites: the churches, the mosques, the walls, the pools, the gates, the bazaars. Then a switch flips and you start to see the ugly side. The imperceptible but indisputable stench of stagnant water. The garbage accumulating at street corners.

second station, Via Dolrosa, Muslim Quarters, Jerusalem

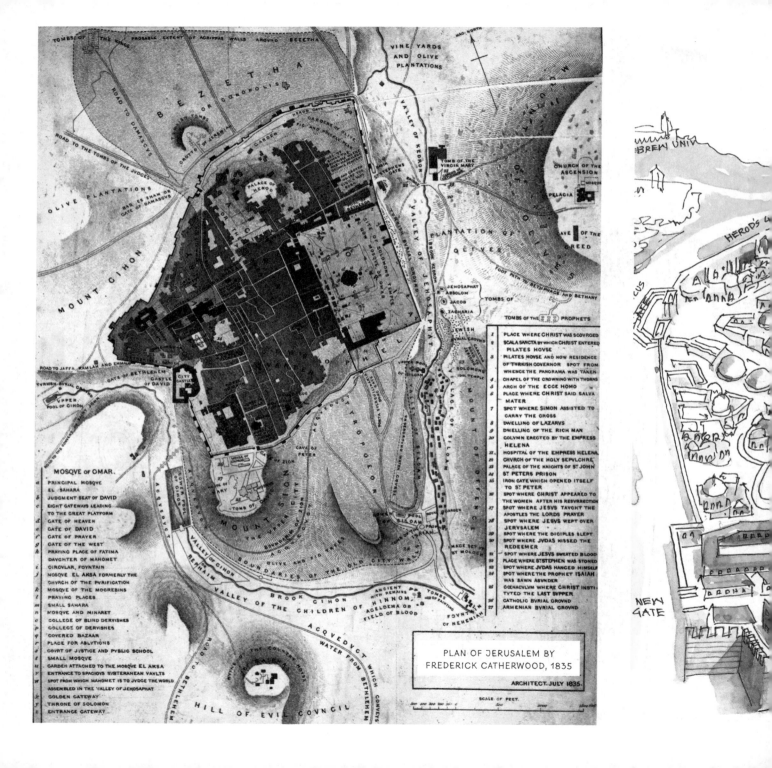

PLAN OF JERUSALEM BY
FREDERICK CATHERWOOD, 1835

ARCHITECT. JULY 1835.

SCALE OF FEET.

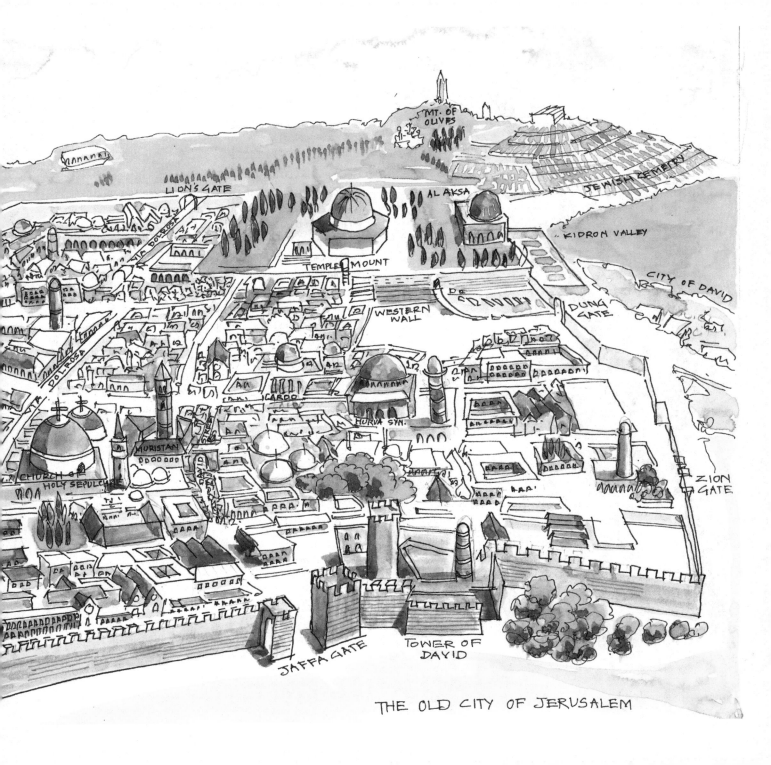

THE OLD CITY OF JERUSALEM

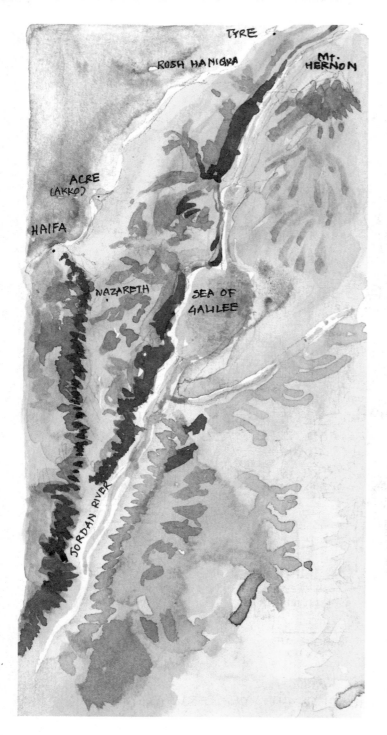

The fetid smell of sweat and tobacco mingling with the religious odors of myrrh and frankincense. The idiosyncrasies of the big-three monotheist religions and their subsects. Their intolerance to each other starts to exasperate the senses. Claustrophobia sets in.

Once, and *if*, you brave through it, a second Jerusalem shows up. You learn to ignore the blockbuster sites and the tourists and pilgrims they attract; you see past the front that residents put up for the short-term visitors. You start to notice kids going to school. Women hurrying to the markets. Men at barber shops. Markets selling spices, unlabeled and certainly not in three languages. The girl at the hotel reception, wearing a *hijab* and reading *Vanity Fair* on her mobile phone. Gawky teenagers bunking classes. Lovers walking in the streets, hands lightly touching. Street dogs zealously guarding their territory. These everyday scenes show the gritty side of a city that is anything but mundane. Amidst the stones that have been placed and displaced for hundreds of centuries and the ghosts of caliphs and messiahs that have come and gone (and may come again), in a place where religion is a way to live and a reason to die, Jerusalem comes alive for me in these innocent, everyday moments.

NAZARETH BY DAVID ROBERTS, R.A. 28TH APRIL 1839

NORTH ISRAEL

~~~~~~~

David Roberts left Jerusalem for his onward journey to Nablus on 16th April 1839. The servants who started with him in Cairo were still with him. His other companions had dispersed – John Kinnear departed from Jaffa to his original destination of Beirut, where he was traveling on business. John Pell and Ismail Effendi returned to Cairo from Bethlehem, one seeking his next adventure, the other happy to get back home. Roberts retained a Jewish guide in Jerusalem to accompany him and a new fellow traveler – identified only as "R" in his journals. Roberts' release from the confines of the walls of Jerusalem into the countryside is reflected in his sketches. He incorporated hues of green to paint olive, fig and pomegranate orchards in the fertile lands of Syria (now northern Israel). He followed a path that took him through some well-known but lesser-preserved sites named in the Bible – the Well of Jacob, Samaria, Jenin and Mount Tabor; it is a route Monica and I avoid, despite Essam's assurances. En route to Nazareth, Roberts deftly captured in his sketchbooks the interiors of smoky churches and dark chapels – beautiful studies of chiaroscuro – quaint villages with deep biblical connections, and the unmistakable layer of Roman architecture – capitals, columns, and colonnades, swarthy men draped in colorful *djellabas* and *kaffiyeh*, water-carrier women and soldiers with long muskets.

On a foggy winter morning, Monica and I throw our bags into the boot of a rental Fiat and sneak out through the Dung Gate while the city still sleeps. We are headed north towards the towns of Nazareth, Haifa and Akko. Once outside, I look in the rearview mirror at the walls of Jerusalem and after making a particularly tricky turn on the wet road, look again a minute later to see that the mighty walls have disappeared, as if a magician has delicately yanked the handkerchief away, whispering *abracadabra*.

We drive west and then north, tracing the shape of a butterfly with its wings open, the boundary of West Bank. On our left, the Mediterranean plays hide and seek, its mood changing like a teenager's – shimmering in the sun one minute, dark and brooding the next.

After an hour of sedate driving through a serene landscape that is gradually gaining elevation, we crest a hill and enter the limestone bowl of Nazareth. Roberts accurately captured this topography in a study he made on 19th April. The biblical village is situated in a depression in the earth next to an open space in which a camp is being set up most likely his own. A shepherd wearing a striped *djellaba* and riding a mule drives a herd of sheep down a path towards the village – the viewer's eye effortlessly glides along their anticipated path.

At the bottom of the hill, now chockablock with low rise buildings and narrow streets, I find the only open spot for the rental on a street packed with parked cars. My driving skills, sharpened by the tiny backstreets of India, come in handy when navigating the rental into the tight spot without causing any damage. We follow a woman wearing red high heels and pushing a stroller up the hill. All roads in Nazareth lead to the Church of the Annunciation. The Holy Land formula – built by Queen Helena in the fourth century, destroyed by Muslims in the eighth, built by Crusaders in the eleventh, destroyed by Ottoman in the fifteenth – has ended up in a strikingly modern building with an inverted funnel-shaped cupola. The church is built over the spot Gabriel announced to the Virgin Mary that she was going to become pregnant with the son of God. Within the bowels of the modern church and in its immediate vicinity are the remains of houses dating back to when Mary and her tribe lived in Nazareth.

Under light filtering through the stained-glass windows, the interiors of the church are lit up in psychedelic colors like a dancefloor. A service is in progress; the choir sings dutifully. I stay in the shadows, preferring to watch without being seen. Later we buy coffee and candied sesame squares from a street vendor, retrieve our car, and continue. Sagi, our guide in Hebron had warned me, "Nazareth is adult Disneyland for the devout Christian. You are going to get bored." I was beginning to see what he meant.

Staying in Robert's footsteps we drive on, only stopping to buy water at a shop with a board painted in English.

"If you keep it overnight, it may turn into Chardonnay," the shopkeeper guffaws. You cannot buy water in Cana without hearing a mention of Jesus' first miracle of turning water into wine at a wedding dinner.

Roberts stopped at the deserted town of Tiberias on the shores of the Sea of Galilee on 21st April where…

> "…NOT A BOAT IS NOW TO BE SEEN ON THE SEA OF GALILEE, THE SCENE OF SO MANY OF OUR LORD'S MIRACLES, AND WHERE HIS FOLLOWERS PLIED THEIR HUMBLE CALLING…"

Just two years prior to Roberts' arrival, in 1837, the area was devastated by an earthquake that killed hundreds of people in the area, the nearby town of Safed being hit the worst. All the building lay in heaps of stone and mud, which Roberts dutifully sketches with his usual élan:

Nazareth

"TO-DAY I MADE SEVERAL SKETCHES OF THE TOWN, OR RATHER OF ITS REMAINS..."

Monica and I are seated on a bench overlooking the Sea of Galilee, digging into 100 percent kosher ice cream. Colorful boats bob in the harbor. A tour guide leads a group from Scotland, the youngest in the group a septuagenarian. A motorboat splutters to life on the water, scaring a flock of double-crested cormorants. Twin sisters sit next to each, canvas frames propped up on easels. One paints the boats, the other paints her sister.

The Sea of Galilee is an important location in the Bible and an important stop on the Christian pilgrimage. This is where Jesus is said to have walked on water and netted his first disciple, Simon the fisherman. The Sea of Galilee, known by many other names in the New and Old Testaments – the Sea of Tiberias and the Sea of Chinneroth – is described for its abundant fish, trade routes, and violent storms. An armchair reader of the Bible, which, until the mid–1800s was practically everybody in the West who could read, visualized a body of water that stretched from horizon to horizon, temperamental and churning. In short, a challenge worthy of Jesus the savior.

The reality is different. Discounting the drought in the region since 2013 leading to the lowest-ever sea level in the last hundred years, this grandiosely named body of water is at best a medium-sized lake. From our seat on the western bank of the lake, we can see the east bank with our naked eye. The smallest island country in the Mediterranean Sea, Malta, is twice the size of the Sea of Galilee. The smallest sea in the world, the Baltic Sea, is 2,300 times larger than the Sea of Galilee. Not one to debate religion, Monica listens without taking her eyes off her ice cream. I am complaining about the gigantic proportions mentioned in the Bible and the Sea of Galilee happens to be a

handy exhibit for my tirade, which has been building up since the beginning of our Levant adventure.

I must confess I have only read highly abridged, summarized versions of the Old and New Testaments. My rare run-ins with the Bible are in hotel rooms, often on a phone-call and looking for a pen to scribble notes. Even with a hefty pinch of salt, the scales mentioned in some Bible descriptions are stunning: the mountain that Moses climbed is made to be of epic proportions, while the traditionally identified Mount Sinai, the mountain behind the monastery of St. Catherine, is hiked everyday by pilgrims who start early in the morning and return back to base in time for lunch. The Israelites wandered the desert for forty years – forty years! – despite the Sinai Peninsula being just 200 miles at its widest point and in spite of the abundant trade routes from Egypt that crisscrossed the desert all the way to the Promised Land.

"If the two million Jews that followed Moses out of Egypt walked five people in a row, keeping ten feet between two rows, the column would be a hundred miles long. When Moses, who was at the head of the column, reached Mount Sinai, the last person in the column would still be crossing the Red Sea." I reconjured a visualization that Edward Robinson had once proposed.

The guide of the Christian tour from Scotland confidently points out a spot where Jesus recruited Simon the fisherman. The sun sets and we have many miles to go before we sleep. We leave for Haifa, where we spend our last night in Israel.

On the way, we pass the Horns of Hattin, where Saladin's army defeated the knights of the Second Crusade in 1187, a battle that would change the course of world history. Saladin (whose Citadel in Cairo was the starting point of my journey in the footsteps of Roberts) soon conquered Jerusalem, after which

Muslims controlled the Holy Land for the next seven hundred years. Jews could no longer pray at the Cave of the Patriarchs in Hebron. Muslim also has a stranglehold on the tangle of key trade routes through the region until Vasco da Gama showed a new route to the east by going around the Horn of Africa. This disrupted the Egyptian economy in the sixteenth century, requiring the Egyptian Sultan Qaitbey to build Khan el Khalili and establish a navy in the Red Sea, a distraction that allowed the Ottoman the time and opportunity to deepen their roots in Turkey. Suleiman the Magnificent built the walls of Jerusalem and established a four-hundred-year monopoly over the region, which was challenged by Napoleon in 1799, and whose defeat enabled Muhammed Ali to come into power, modernizing and stabilizing the region and allowing Roberts to complete his 1839 Near East adventure.

"Babe, the whole adventure started with the Battle of Hattin," I say to Monica, proudly.

"And just an hour ago you were complaining about exaggerations in the Bible," she replies, trying not to roll her eyes.

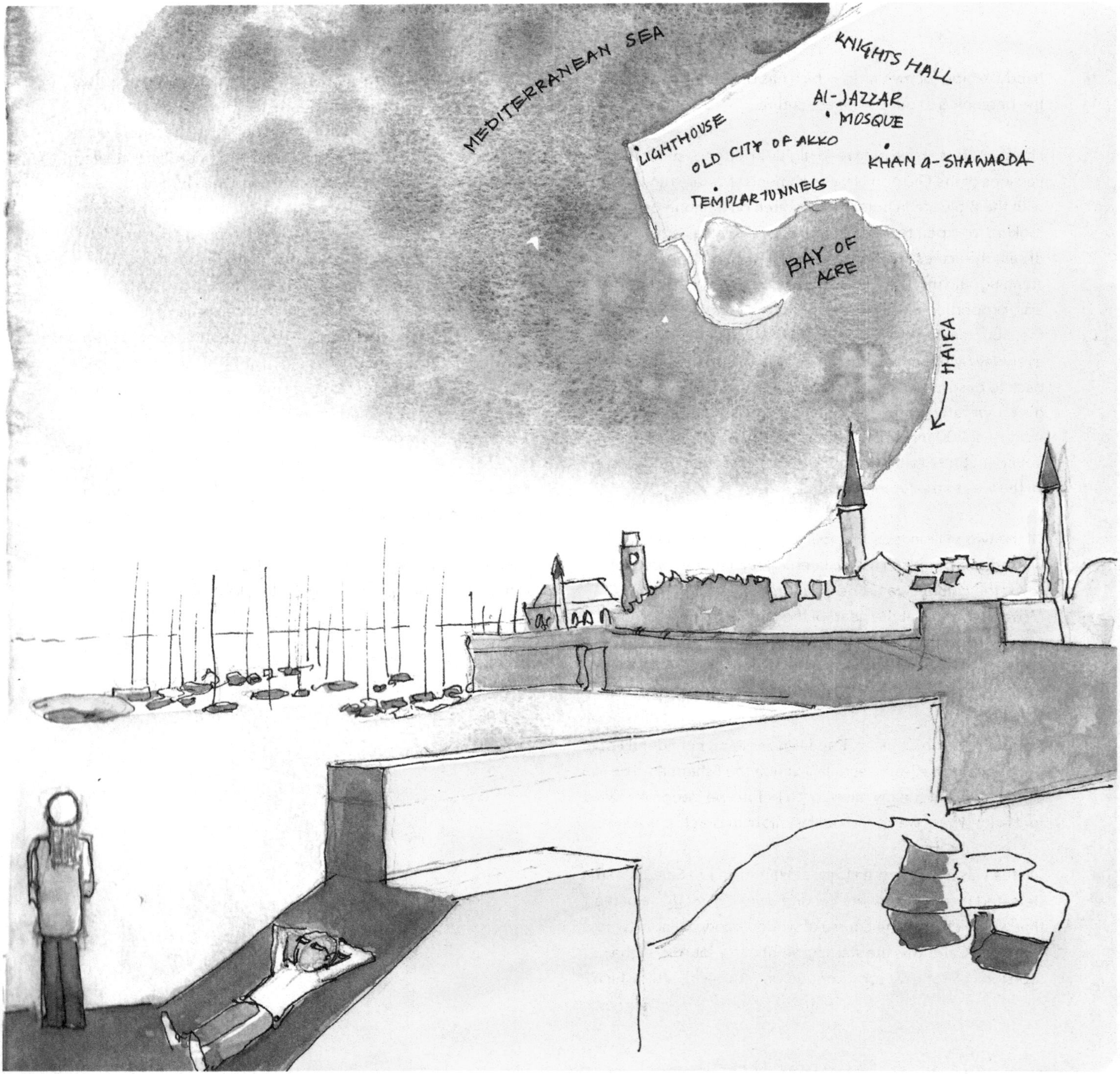

MEDITERRANEAN SEA

KNIGHTS HALL

AL-JAZZAR
· MOSQUE

LIGHTHOUSE
OLD CITY OF AKKO
KHAN a-SHAWARDA

TEMPLAR TUNNELS

BAY OF
ACRE

HAIFA

ACRE/AKKO

〰〰〰

It is dark by the time we reach our hotel in Haifa. We are welcomed by teenage girls behind the reception, their hair arranged in stylish bobs. They give us a room on the top floor and gush about the "tiptoe" view of the Mediterranean it has.

"Did they mean a tiptop view of the Mediterranean?" I ask Monica in the elevator.

It is only the next morning, when I stand on the tip of my toes to see the glint of the morning sun on the Mediterranean, that I fully comprehend their description. We polish off a sumptuous breakfast in the company of Gal Gadot, who looks fresh and lively on television – a piping hot *shakshuka* (caramelized onions, tomatoes and peppers baked with eggs), an Israeli salad of chopped cucumber, tomatoes and pepper doused in lemon juice, fresh olives marinated in – umm – olive oil, and *challah* – a soft ceremonial Jewish bread, sprinkled with poppy seeds.

We head north to Acre, also called Akko in Arabic. We pull over on the side of the road to let Monica wet her feet in the saltwater – her first contact with the warm Mediterranean. The Crusader city of Akko shimmers on the horizon.

The sound of the word Akko invokes in me a romance that is undoubtedly fueled by its association with legendary travelers – Alexander the Great, Marco Polo, Richard the Lionheart. The name of the city inspires *fernweh*, invoking in me a distant land that is accessible only through a lot of hardship and persistence, and once reached, it is loved because of what one knows about it, not just what one sees.

We find parking near the souk; the lot is filling fast as the sun climbs overhead. I walk in Monica's wake as she cuts a path through the twisting lane and up a series of stone stairs to the top of the splendid ramparts. Within fifteen minutes of arriving in Akko we enjoy a sweeping view of the Mediterranean – a view that Napoleon failed to see despite a two-month siege. Before Waterloo, Akko happened to Napoleon. His cigarette of the conquest of Palestine was stubbed out in the Akko ashtray.

Port of AKKO, Israel

ST. JEAN D'ACRE BY DAVID ROBERTS, R.A. 24TH APRIL 1839

We walk through the souks, which sell a variety of fish and seafood, spices and everyday household items – clearly a souk that caters equally to locals and visitors. We stop at a local grocer to restock for the drive ahead. The shopkeeper's craggy face turns ebullient when I greet him with a *salaam-aleikum* and then thank him with a *shokran*, exhausting my fifteen-word Arabic vocabulary in five minutes.

Monica and I visit the ancient medieval tunnels where the soot on the ceilings was deposited by Crusader torches. We duck into a bakery that displays trays crammed with sweets, choosing items to eat by visual cues – the taste unknown to us. The sweets come with a side of polythene gloves, a marvel of forward thinking in a place where finding water is not easy. We sit on the rocks of the ancient promontory to eat the treats and watch motorboats carrying passengers splutter to life. They are keen to see the city from the sea, a view Roberts painted.

During the two hundred Crusader years – the twelfth and thirteenth centuries – the Akko horizon swarmed with boats ferrying people and goods between the northern Mediterranean coast and the Holy Land. On the seaside, the fortification is a tangle of minarets, domes, towers and lighthouses, successive attempts to find higher and higher ground in order to keep an eye on the boats appearing on the horizon. High ground was the radar of the medieval world. Arriving on these boats were Christian warrior-pilgrims marching to Jerusalem to liberate the city from its Muslim occupiers. They arrived in waves that historians have since numbered like sequels of the Rocky movies. In Crusade I, Christians gained control over Jerusalem. In Crusade II, Muslims led by Saladin defeated the Knights Templar at the battle of Hattin. In Crusade III, Richard the Lionheart landed in Akko, built a beachhead at Jaffa, and signed a peace treaty with Saladin. Crusade IV ended in Istanbul, never reaching Jerusalem. Like the movies after Rocky IV, Crusades V to VII were soon forgotten by the masses except by academics and diehard nerds (the two often one and the same).

Roberts reached Acre during tumultuous times. Mahmud II, the Ottoman Sultan at the time, was on his deathbed, and the colonial vultures were circling over his empire. Ismail Pasha, the governor of Syria and Muhammed Ali's son, was assembling an army to go after the weakened Ottoman Porte. In the meantime, Syria was in open revolt against Mohammed Ali Pasha's harsh taxes and conscription practices. Roberts had seen firsthand the citizens being conscripted in Hebron and soldiers sacking a bazaar for provisions in Bethlehem. He had seen the Pasha's soldiers assembling in Gaza. Roberts made two principal studies at Akko. In the one he made from the sea, a three-masted warship with a high superstructure looms on the horizon, a symbol of brewing troubles. The other shows the Pasha's modern army marching in perfect files, sketched from the promontory leading to the ramparts.

By mid-afternoon we leave behind the Crusader city, the Ottoman fort, the Templar tunnels, the Arab bazaars, the caravanserais, and the most famous harbor of medieval times to head north towards the Israel-Lebanon border. Monica will be going back home to Seattle from there.

Souq Al Abaid, Akko Israel

KFAR ROSH HANIKRA

~~~~~~

Eighteen kilometers north on Highway 4 brings you to Kfar Rosh HaNikra, the last town on the Israel side of the Blue Line. A cable car follows a 60-degree decline to take you halfway down the face of massive white limestone cliffs at the base of which the Mediterranean churns and crashes. The waves have carved grottoes and caves into the soft limestone cliffside over millions of years. During World War I, the British Army connected the caves and laid the Cairo–Istanbul train track.

After the independence of Israel, the tunnel was sealed. A trade route described in the Old Testament has been crimped. A major north-south communication line has been snipped.

We are at the impenetrable Israel-Lebanon land border.

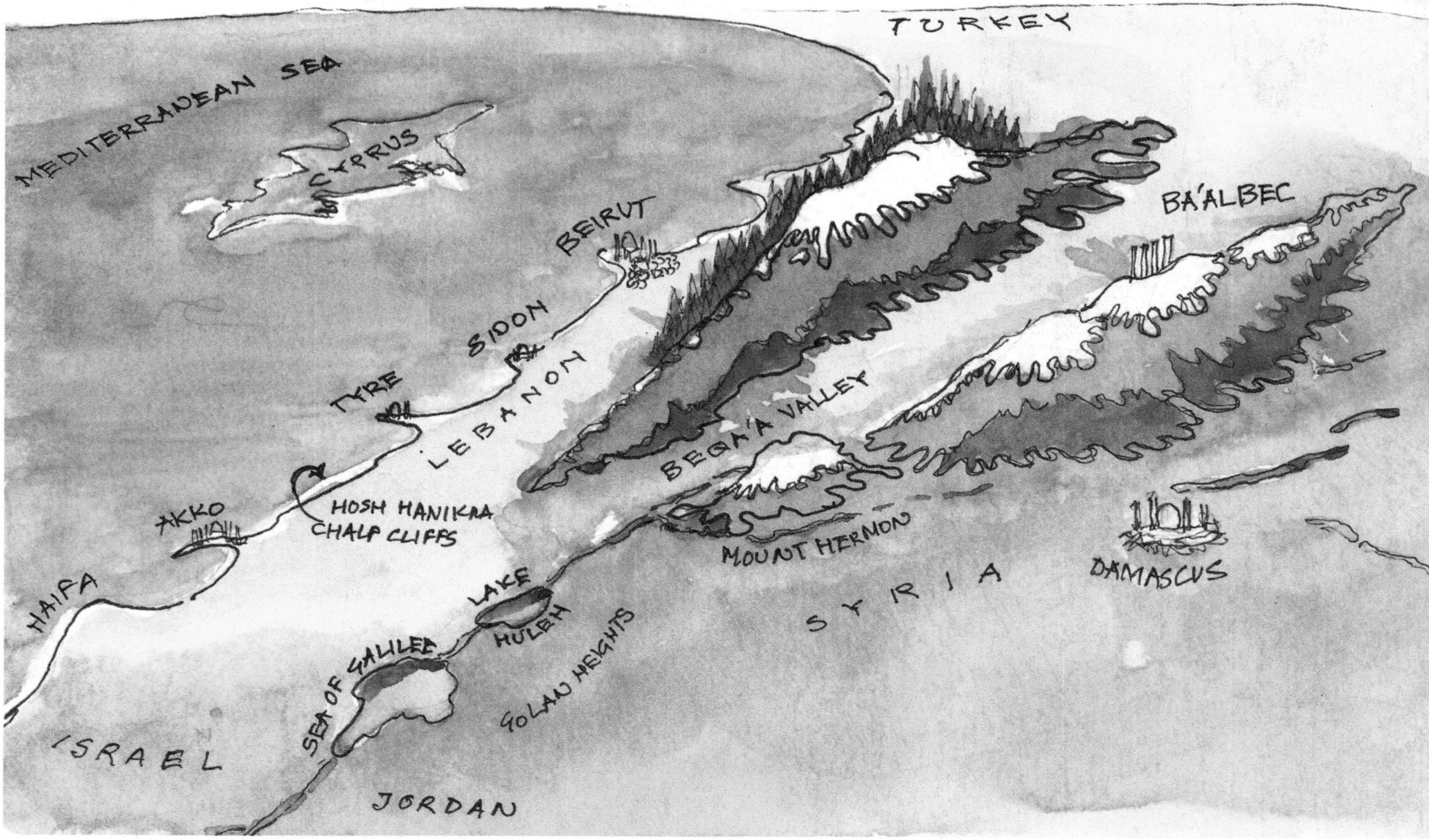
TURKEY
MEDITERRANEAN SEA
CYPRUS
BEIRUT
BA'ALBEC
SIDON
TYRE
LEBANON
BEQA'A VALLEY
HOSH HANIKRA
CHALK CLIFFS
AKKO
MOUNT HERMON
DAMASCUS
HAIFA
LAKE
HULEH
SYRIA
GOLAN HEIGHTS
SEA OF GALILEE
ISRAEL
JORDAN

LEBANON

‧‧‧‧‧‧‧‧

"...the city that sent out colonies to found Carthage
is now little more than a naked rock in the midst of the sea..."

— DAVID ROBERTS, 26TH APRIL 1839, TYRE.

"The beauty of its form, the exquisite richness of its ornament,
and the vast magnitude of its dimensions, are altogether unparalleled."

— DAVID ROBERTS, 4TH MAY 1839, BA'ALBEC.

NAQOURA

~~~~~~

Natural borders follow geography. Natural borders separate
fundamentally different ways of living. People of the mountains
and people of the valley. Cliff dwellers and the ones in the
canyon. Coastals vs inlanders.

Ras al-Abaid, also known as Capo Blanco, is mentioned in
the Old Testament as the northernmost tip of the Holy Land,
separating the Philistines from the Phoenicians. When the
word is not capitalized, philistine refers generically to people
without taste or sophistication. The Phoenicians, on the other
hand, they were maritime traders, street-smart coastal dwellers
who knew the ways of the world. When Roberts crossed Capo
Blanco, the border was more traditional. Roberts felt this
topographical border innately; there was no need for a barbed
wire barrier between Palestine and Syria – both regions were
already past their prime.

Just a few decades ago, an accomplished travel writer standing
at this melding point would describe the turquoise waters
of the Mediterranean, the sheer white limestone cliffs, the
bountiful orange groves, the verdant valleys of the Litany River,
the fragrant fields of marigold, and the blue skies picturesquely
dotted with cumulus clouds on the horizon. Today, that writer
will need to mention the drab grey concrete wall of a military
compound covered by barbed wire, ditches and foxholes, sniper
watchtowers, armed men in battle camouflage riding Humvees –
men of war riding beasts of death.

After World War I, as the colonial powers retreated, the boiling
cauldron of the Middle East was stirred once more. Iraq, Jordan,
Israel and Lebanon were carved out of Syria and Palestine.

Naqoura border, Lebanon.

The border between Israel and Lebanon is one of the most sensitive, complex and complicated in the world.

"That's the Blue Line," says Ananth, who is back with me in Lebanon, pointing at a map spread on the hood of a car. We are parked in the village of Naquora in Lebanon, outside a shack that sells cigarettes and cold drinks. "There's the Green Line. A Red line. A Purple line. There are more lines here than in a palmistry chart."

Every line marks an armed conflict, a mad rush over a few hundred yards, a pile of dead bodies, all followed by a status quo. The United Nations Interim Force in Lebanon (UNIFIL) took control of the border in 1948. The 'I' in the acronym standing for 'Interim' communicating a status that is not changing anytime soon.

Nothing here is ever allowed to settle; nothing changes either.

"Who says we have a border problem? We have a problem of borders," Ahmad says. Ahmad is an Urban Sketcher from Beirut who agreed to be our translator and companion in Lebanon. He is in his mid-twenties, tall and curly haired. It is difficult to say if his stylishly curly beard is a result of the millennial hipster fad or the Middle Eastern penchant for facial hair.

In researching my logistics for Lebanon, I reached out via email to Amira, who is an active member of the Lebanon Urban Sketchers group. After she patiently answered my questions and introduced me to Ahmad, I asked her if she knew anything about a place called Cape Blanco. David Roberts had mentioned crossing a Capo Blanco, but I could not locate that placename on Google maps.

"There is no Cape Blanco in Lebanon," she replied in her email, "It must be in another place." Only later would I understand that "another place" is a Lebanese code word for Israel, the place that cannot be named.

On 26th April 1839 Roberts wrote in his journal:

"THIS MORNING WE DESCENDED ON A SMALL VILLAGE CALLED NAKHURA, AND TRAVELLED ALONG THE OLD ROMAN ROAD, STILL IN MANY PARTS IN EXCELLENT PRESERVATION. ON A HEIGHT WE FOUND THE REMAINS OF AN EXTENSIVE GREEK TEMPLE, SOME OF THE CAPITALS BEING IONIC, AND OTHERS DORIC... IT IS SINGULAR IT HAS PASSED UNNOTICED."

Ananth, Ahmed, and I had driven to Naqoura to pick up Roberts' spoor. We also wanted to locate the Roman ruins Roberts mentions in his journal. On cue I sight a hill on the right side of the road on the outskirts of Naqoura. I pull over besides a vintage sign painted in Arabic and English, acknowledging an archaeological site in the vicinity. The English text promises Phoenician, Roman, and Crusader-era ruins at Oum Almed, Om Al-Omad and Om I Omad – the name was spelled in three different ways within just a few dozen words. In the true spirit of adventure, the sign did not provide a direction. Anyone with curiosity had to do their own finding.

I turn the car into the single-lane gravel road next to the sign and drive for several minutes along a verdant south-facing slope bursting with vineyards. I am looking for a second signpost, a breadcrumb trail to the ruins. When I don't see one and don't know how far is too far, I decide to return to the military check-post we passed ten minutes prior. The swarthy soldier has an expression of utter irritation emblazoned on his face for making him walk fifteen feet to the car. Fortunately, Ahmad's Arabic breaks the ice. The soldier knows of ruins up the mountain, and he dispatches us by pointing a nicotine-stained finger up

a fork in the road that I hadn't noticed. At the end of a rocky road that the rental car barely manages, we come across a clearing covered by undergrowth, sheep droppings and human garbage.

The Phoenicians plied this area with markets, store houses, shops and bazaars. The Romans probably added a villa, a vineyard, olive press, and winemaking implements. Crusaders contributed a watchtower to keep an eye on the ships headed towards the Holy Land. None of this remains. A once-major street weaves down the mountain side, lined with ruins in specked black and white stone that barely reach my ankle. The site has been excavated clean, there is no chance of discovering a potsherd or an ancient coin, though that doesn't stop me from exploring for several minutes. No signs of Roberts' Doric columns, though. The ruins are too far away from the well-planned route Roberts was taking. Even in such early days of exploration, Roberts was already unwittingly following an itinerary: every day had been plotted, the route chalked out.

We drive down the mountain, past large flocks of sheep and weather-beaten buildings. In one such building in the region, an Indian restaurant that served tandoori cuisine is now shuttered, a reminder of the large Indian Army contingent participating in UNIFIL.

TYRE

〜〜〜

The scenery gets greener with every kilometer we drive north. We are headed along the coast of the Mediterranean towards the town of Tyre, or *Sour* in Arabic. Flags in different shades of green flutter in the salty breeze. Massive cardboard cutouts of men with lush beards and huge turbans are placed strategically by the roadside. Ananth asks Ahmad about the men in the advertisements.

"One of those guys is named Sadr. I can't remember his surname," Ahmad says, "He was kidnapped in the '80s and his whereabouts are not known. The other is a member of the parliament and a candidate in the election. They are both canvassing for a party called the Harkat-e-Amal."

"How can the guy who was kidnapped and disappeared be canvassing?" Ananth says, "Is Harkat-e-Amal the party in power?"

"No. That's Hezbollah."

"What is the difference between Amal and Hezbollah?" Ananth asks conversationally.

"Amal is light green while Hezbollah is dark green," Ahmad says after a pause. I can see him mentally scratch his head searching for pearls of wisdom but coming up with peas. Green peas.

Ananth and I exchange a quick glance. I picture this: we are in the backcountry of Lebanon, a few miles from the Syrian border. A bearded guy has us pinned down, a gun pointed at our heads, his hand shaking, index finger on the trigger. Tempers are frayed, emotions are running high. Arabic is flowing back and forth. Our guide keeps a calm head. He uses his nuanced understanding of tribal alliances of Syria and the prevailing political alignments, unhesitatingly utters carefully chosen words that help calm the situation.

With a deep sigh I realize Ahmad is not that kind of a guide. We are in a land where one can die for not knowing the Druze from the Maronite. Our only hope is that we avoid getting into such situations which, incidentally, was Ananth's third condition for the trip.

Felafel Samhat
SOUR, LB

"I don't want to be on Amanpour," he said, laughing, referring to Christiane Amanpour, the famous BBC anchor who covers the Middle East. "I hope we don't create a political situation that is broadcast on international TV."

Later I find out that Ahmad even had his colors wrong. The correct colors for Amal are dark green and black and, for Hezbollah, bright yellow and green.

I suddenly realize that I am responsible for bringing Ahmad back home safely.

~~~~~~

We are seated in Ahmad's favorite restaurant in Tyre, not far away from the glittering water of the Mediterranean. The table in front of us is covered with a dozen dishes, big and small, beautifully presented, no two plates alike – an explosion of colors, visual textures, and aromas. Finally, here is one positive outcome of the Christians, Byzantines, Crusaders, Arabs, Turks, and French repeatedly crossing paths and swords.

The liberal use of olive oil and fresh local produce comes from Italy, the cuts of meat are a gift from the Turks, the hint of cheese, herbs, and spices from Syria, and the yogurt and lemon are the French contribution in this medley of Lebanese cuisine – a healthier, more refined version of Middle Eastern and Mediterranean cuisine with a bias for presentation, small-sized portions, and assortment. Even my palate, brought up on Indian spices, can detect the subtle sophistication and the nuanced use of herbs and spices here.

I am not a foodie by any stretch of imagination. When faced with too many choices, my narrow taste palette searches for bread and a dip. I can survive an evening on just that. As such, I have already spotted a platter of *khubz*, the round flattened

Syrian flatbread, lathered with virgin olive oil and *za'atar*. Cubes of potato sautéed with garlic, coriander, lemon and salt hit the right spot too. The familiar flavors of *khubz* and the *batata harra* having taken the edge off my hunger. I watch Ahmad and Ananth chomping through the *mezze*. In my books, the Mediterranean *baba ghanouj* is the opposite of the Thai Swimming Rama. I like the former because of how it sounds and hate the latter for the same reason. *Baba ghanouj* tastes like the Indian *baingan bharta* despite the two dishes only sharing on major ingredient – the charbroiled eggplant. The Lebanese mash it with tahini sauce, while the Indians mix it with diced onions, crushed peanuts, green chilies and yogurt before topping it with a seasoning of cumin, sesame and asafetida.

"If you liked the Baba, you should try the Mama," says Ahmad. *Mama ghanouj* is made from zucchini instead of eggplant, otherwise the recipe is the same. Ahmad is in his element in this setting.

As I am getting ready to throw in my napkin, Ahmad insists I try one more item. What looks like lightly fried fingers of mashed potato turns out to be meat laced with pomegranate juice, an enjoyable experience for my tongue. It is so tasty and crunchy that I demolish a small pile.

"The dish is called *Fawaregh*, which is rice and goat meat stuffed inside goat intestine and served with mint pomegranate sauce," Ahmad says, watching me eat with gusto.

I stop in my tracks.

"You take a goat, get to its gut and turn it inside out until the goat is in the gut?"

Within a span of a hundred miles, I have enjoyed a Jewish breakfast in Haifa, an Arabic lunch in Akko and now a Lebanese supper in Tyre. Later we stroll beside the Mediterranean. Families lean against the stone balustrade enjoying the evening breeze slurping the salty water out of boiled corn. A group of teenage coeds lick an ice-cream cone, eyes glued to their phone screens. Half a dozen men dangle fishing lines in the water, waiting for a bite. A few hundred feet to my left is the public beach of Tyre, which I am told is jam-packed in summer. It is one of the few public places in the Middle East where locals and tourists, men and women, can turn out in swimming trunks and bikinis without fear of harassment.

We are now on the last leg of the journey. From Tyre, we will follow the coastal route via Sidon and turn east towards Zahle in the mountains of Lebanon. After the pass, we will drop into the Beqa'a Valley, one mountain range away from Syria. We will continue north to Ba'albec, following David Robert's route to a T.

Three months have flown by. My daughters are clamoring for me to get back home. Domestic duties have piled up. My sabbatical is almost over. I have landed a job at an exciting startup. Work emails have already started piling in my inbox. The realities of life are itching to claim me back.

But all this will have to wait its turn, because right now the sun is putting on a show, its translucent light cloaking the city in a golden hue that can only be experienced in the Middle East. I am sitting where the famous southern harbor of Tyre once used to be. My seat on the cobbled wall along the Mediterranean is made possible by Alexander the Great.

RUINS OF AN IONIC TEMPLE BY DAVID ROBERTS, R.A. 25TH APRIL 1839

Twenty-four-year-old Alexander rode into Tyre in 332 BCE. When he took the reins of the Macedonian Empire from his father four years prior, he inherited some very interesting things. From his father, King Phillip II of Macedon, he got the means to fulfill the ambition in the form of the most advanced army of its time, capable of the lightning-fast attacks. From his mother, Olympia, he acquired limitless ambition and chutzpah to conquer all the known world. And from Aristotle, he received the wisdom and philosophy to rule the lands he was about to conquer.

With his victory over King Darius III of Persia at the Battle of Granicus and then, in the battlefield at Issus (both in modern day Turkey), the young Alexander stepped out of his illustrious father's shadow and planted the Greco-Macedonian flag in Asia. In his quest to march to "the end of the world and to the Greater Outer Sea," he turned south towards Phoenicia. The coastal cities of Byblos and Sidon quickly surrendered.

spice shopping at
SOUK AL-KADEEM „ TYR Lebanon

Azemilcus, the King of Tyre and vassal of the Persian empire, grudgingly followed suit and pledged allegiance to Alexander. In a celebratory mood, Alexander graciously asked permission to make a sacrifice at the famous Phoenician temple at Tyre, which lay in his way to the ancient land of Egypt. Azemilcus, already facing ignominy due to his abject surrender to the boy-commander, decided to put his foot down. Aware that no back-up would arrive from Darius anytime soon (Darius was himself licking wounds inflicted by Alexander's army twice in the past twelve months), Azemilcus devised a simple plan that he hoped would hoodwink the warrior-prince. The city-state of Tyre was dual-shored: the old city was situated on the mainland, and the new city, the capital, was built on an island a kilometer offshore in the Mediterranean Sea. Since both cities had a Phoenician temple, Azemilcus invited Alexander to participate in an elaborate pagan ritual in the old city, hoping that would satiate him and keep him at bay.

No such luck. The astute Alexander realized instinctively that he was being denied entry inside the famous walls of the new city. Known for his ability to see the bigger picture, Alexander rejected the invitation and insisted he be permitted to visit the *other* temple situated in the new city, the Temple of Merqat, dedicated to a Phoenician god who was closely associated with the Greek hero, Heracles. When the parley went nowhere, Alexander threatened to sack the city. The Tyrians, secure inside their towering walls

OLD TYRE

ALEXANDER'S CAMP

ALEXANDER'S MOLE

SIEGE ENGINES

EGYPTIAN HARBOR

TEMPLE

TYRE

FINAL ASSAULT

PHOENICIAN FLEET

SEIGE OF TYRE

and confident of their unassailable defense, decided to stand their ground.

The irresistible force of Alexander met the impregnable walls of Tyre. And thus began the famous siege of Tyre: one of the most tactically complex battles in the history of warfare, and the longest and the most terrible of Alexander's sieges.

A dashing young warrior stuck outside the fabled walls of a legendary city – was Alexander unwittingly enacting the climactic scene of the *Iliad*, casting himself as his childhood hero, Achilles at Troy?

Alexander had solved the riddle of the Gordian Knot and now faced another one: how does one lay siege to an island after all? Alexander had unleashed his sword, slashing though the clump of wool, unraveling the famous knot; at Tyre he would need to patiently work at the tedious tangle, strand by strand, for the next seven months.

Putting into use his penchant for planning intricate campaigns, Alexander decided to build a causeway from the mainland to the island. After all, the best way to lay siege to an island is to ensure it is not an island. The story follows the pattern of Alexander's battles. Despite severe resistance from the Tyrians and overcoming impossible odds – engineering, morale, manpower, supply-chain, politics – Alexander led a vanguard of troops to the walls of Tyre. He ransacked the city, destroying

Tyre, Lebanon

every standing wall and building (except the temple), killing all soldiers and selling everybody else into slavery. This total dominance and no mercy attitude towards a city that did not surrender would become a major weapon in Alexander's armory. It gave Callisthenes, the historian who accompanied Alexander on his Asiatic campaign, another chapter to write on the futility of resisting Alexander.

Alexander was known to have repeatedly changed the course of world history in fourth century BCE. At Tyre, he also permanently changed the geography. The causeway has sedimented and grown over the years and converted Tyre into an isthmus.

~~~~~~

The next morning, our first stop is at the other remaining port of Tyre. The port used to be called the North Port and is closest to Sidon; the South Port, closer to Egypt, silted up after Alexander built the mole. The day is windy. Fishing boats bob on choppy water. A waterfront area with restaurants and residential buildings seems devoid of activity on this winter day. Ananth, Ahmad, and I walk through a labyrinth of streets with buildings painted purple and blue, with bright yellow and green doors and windows. A nineteenth-century lighthouse, now abandoned, guards the mouth of the port. I sketch the scene from a coffee shop, inhaling the smell of the strong Turkish tobacco that a woman at the next table incessantly puffs.

I am still contemplating Alexander's tactical masterpiece. Having spent several hours in the pre-dawn hours poring through my research material, I am now familiar with the minute details of his seven-month campaign.

As temperamental as Alexander appeared in attacking the island in retaliation for being snubbed by the Tyrians, his motive behind the siege was purely military. Alexander wanted to break the spine of the Persian fleet before he headed east, where Darius had fled after being stunned at Issus. Having subdued Cyprus and Sidon, Tyre was the last remaining stronghold of the Persian fleet.

While the causeway was being built (Alexander had personally led a seven-day expedition to collect cypress and cedar lumber) he barricaded the seaward route towards Carthage, in present day Tunisia, by mustering a fleet of 220 vessels from his new allies – Cyprus and Sidon. This inadvertently strengthened the Tyrian resolve, as their wives and children were now trapped inside the walls, ensuring it would now be a fight to death. The final naval battle – galleys ramming each other and sinking, battering rams pounding the once-untouchable walls, Alexander leaping on to the walls from his flagship, the screams and shrieks of the Tyrians as they realized all was lost, oily smoke, burning flesh – all of this happened right here in this harbor, which looks so serene today. I think I can smell the smoke until I remember the chain-smoker behind me.

The North Port looks tiny. I count half a dozen mid-sized private yachts and a couple of dozen small fishing boats swaying in the stiff, freezing wind. Once again on this trip the size of the landscape throws me off. I am expecting a larger port to accommodate the fleet of Cypriot galleys, which must have moored not too far from where I sit. Once again, I remember that the real-life proportions don't match the epic scales of these written accounts.

The wrath of Alexander wiped away the 150-foot walls. Streets, homes, palaces – all gone. The great Phoenician city was erased. What remains is the isthmus and the outline of the city – what was once the new city is already the old. A new city is already spawning on top of it.

TYRPORT
LEBANON

The area between the colonnaded walkway and the Roman necropolis is overrun with blonde marigolds. A carved stone arch bends over cobbled stone, commemorating a victory – exactly which one has long since been forgotten. Buried underneath is a city that was old even when Alexander rode into Tyre, and there must be other cities beneath it. On the edge of the archaeological site, prefab buildings have sprouted, as if feeding from the ruins; colorful clothes flutter on the balconies – civilizations turning the wheels of history again.

In the old souk, *shawarma* is turning over a spit and honey is being poured over pistachios. Spices are stacked in gunny bags. Carcasses of goats and cows hang from metal hooks. We are sitting in a quiet spot, sketching a photogenic corner of the spice market when a shopkeeper yells at us to disperse. The sight of strangers looking at his shop and scribbling in their notebooks has probably intimidated him. Shocked with the shopkeeper's behavior, Ahmad approaches with the intention of showing him the sketchbook but is dismissed summarily by a wave of hand. Fortunately, the shopkeeper next door comes to our aid.

"He is getting old. He is always angry," says the neighbor, shushing the recalcitrant troublemaker.

A child is dispatched and returns with freshly made falafel, wrapped in an old newspaper, a peace offering we accept with glee. The ice is broken. Other shopkeepers now crowd around to watch us sketch. They point out improvements and offer suggestions.

"Why do your people not have eyes?" one shopkeeper asks, pointing to my sketches.

"People should have eyes," he says, not interested in my explanation and waits until I add eyes to every one of the figures in my sketch. Then he proceeds to provide me with their names and stories. Abhu moved here recently. Karim is newly married. Salama is having a baby. She is a tigress. Nobody messes with her.

The sketch I made in the souk that day still smells of spices and I can still hear all their stories.

~~~~~

David Roberts, in the meantime, was tangling with the locals too. Having arrived in Tyre on 27th April, a *janissary* (a member of the Turkish infantry) decided that Roberts had illegally escaped the quarantine in Jerusalem. The janissary took it upon himself to walk in front of the party with a flag in hand, warning the locals to get out of the way of Roberts' party, a scene Roberts dutifully captured in one of his compositions. This unfortunate incident led to Roberts needing to find a spot in the cemetery to set up camp for the night. He could not find a merchant in the local souk to sell them provisions.

Tyre, Lebanon.

Crusader Castle, Sidon, Liban

SIDON

~~~~~

After a typical Lebanese breakfast of *labneh*, honey, fresh apricots, and cucumbers sprinkled with *za'atar*, we race the clouds. Just as it starts to drizzle in Tyre, we reach Sidon, where glorious Mediterranean sunlight bathes the Crusader-era castle that had so captivated Roberts.

Roberts was disillusioned by the appearance of Tyre, "the city that sent out colonies to found Carthage is now little more than a naked rock in the midst of the sea," evident from the barebones backdrops of his painting, but he was quickly enamored with Sidon. He made three large studies that show the citadel situated on an island, and a bridge that connects it to the mainland, using his trademark colorful characters in the foreground.

Ananth, who can find 12 differences playing the game "Find 10 differences between the two pictures" is comparing Roberts' lithograph with the scene in front of him and says, "Is it just me or has the citadel taken some beating since Roberts was here?"

Indeed, the sea castle today is a small fraction of what Roberts' saw. A turret, a gate with an arc, a dome and a few rooms are all that remain. The rest was destroyed by the British bombardment of 1840 – widely known as the Oriental Crisis – which was a culmination of the escalating arms race between the Ottoman Empire and the Egyptian warlords. The Turkish Navy surrendered to Mohammed Ali, but the French withdrew their support, and the British settled the issue by banishing Ismail Pasha from Syria in exchange for independence for Egypt from the Ottoman Empire. The tottering Ottoman Empire bought itself a few more decades until the end of World War I, becoming a pawn in the Great Game between Britain and Russia.

THE CITADEL OF SIDON BY DAVID ROBERTS, R.A.
28TH APRIL 1839

We cross the road to stand beneath the beautiful arches of the
Khan-al-Franz – The Inn of the Foreigners. The seventeenth
century khan is a typical square structure with an enclosed
courtyard. Ancient trade caravans camped here, camels and
all, a medieval motel where the trader slept within a few feet
of his "truck." Nobody leaves Sidon without eating Abu Rami's
falafel sandwiches – certainly not Ananth. The falafel is wrapped
in flat bread and garnished with herbs, tomatoes, turnip,
radish, tahini and a generous helping of hot sauce, topped with
pickled chili peppers. We wolf down the sandwiches in the
parked car, keeping the doors open, wanting to take with us
the taste, but not the smell.

Crusader Castle, Sidon Li

THE BEQA'A VALLEY

~~~~~~

By the time the rain catches up with us, we are a third of our way into the mountains. First a dense fog and then the persistent spray bouncing off the road reduces our visibility to a few feet. We stop outside a roadside shed with a pulsating light over its door. A man hurries from inside to make us strong viscous coffee shots served in what look like mouthwash cups.

We follow in the wake of Syrian lorries lurching towards Damascus, grumbling in low gear, engines working against the grade of the treacherous pass. We pass a convoy of military-green Humvees, occasionally catching a glimpse of a soldier behind bullet-proof glass. Every so often we pass abandoned buildings that were devastated in the civil war of the 1980s. They are riddled with bullets, some pock marks as large as dinner plates. When we descend into the Beqa'a Valley, we have once again pulled ahead of the rain clouds and the scenery is bathed in the honey-colored sunlight that Lebanon is famous for. We are traveling on top of an ancient Roman road that reached the eastern boundary of the Roman empire in the Syrian desert. The Roman road in turn follows the topographical contours of the Great Rift Valley – a series of geographical trenches that divide the Lebanon and Anti Lebanon mountain ranges. The valley continues further south, separating Galilee from the Golan Heights. The River Jordan forms in the rift and flows between present-day Israel and Jordan, terminating in the Dead Sea. The trench continues through Wadi Araba and then into the Gulf of Aqaba, where it plunges underwater and flows to the tip of the Sinai plateau through the length of the Red Sea. For the past two months, I have been crisscrossing this rift in David Roberts' footsteps.

If the seismic activity that created the Sinai Peninsula, separating Africa from Asia, had been any larger in magnitude, it would have ripped along the Great Rift Valley. The chunk of the land between the Mediterranean and the River Jordan – a narrow corridor that is the birthplace of the world's three largest monotheistic religions – would have been lost underwater, the Mediterranean pouring into the Indian ocean. The nature went as far as it could without tearing things up. Is that a divine design?

On both sides of the road, we see the snowcapped peaks of the Lebanon and anti-Lebanon ranges. Beyond the peaks on my right, due east, lie parts of Syria that were burning until three months ago; it was the ceasefire in this area that propelled me towards putting my adventure in motion, sliding through a short window of peace before the cauldron in the Middle East stirred again. President Trump was already reaching out for the wooden spoon when I landed in Egypt, recognizing Jerusalem as the capital of Israel.

To our left, we pass through beautifully laid out fields, lined by long lines of tents that are full of Syrian refugees waiting to return to their homeland. I recall a heartbreaking segment on the radio about a seven-year-old Syrian child who had never slept a night without hearing a bomb blast.

As we hurtle towards Ba'albec, on the road Alexander followed after his successful campaign in Egypt, we pass through some of the most fertile regions in Lebanon: orange and lemon groves, beautiful vineyards and boutique wineries, picturesque villages with quaint cottages and signs of developing infrastructure. This is not the Lebanon that worried my mom when I outlined to her my hurriedly put-together itinerary. Growing up, in the '80s and '90s, the images that the word Lebanon triggered were of an extreme warzone.

We had made the journey from Sidon to Ba'albec in about three hours – what had taken Roberts and his team a very rough three days over the mountains. They were soaked in torrential downpours, their mules repeatedly bogged down in the wet mud. Their bedding and clothes were often saturated with water, which, in the bone-biting November cold, caused the body aches and sniffles that Roberts was experiencing. In Zahle, Roberts heard rumors of a Druze revolt in the Beqa'a Valley and was afraid that they might not be able to make it to the famous ruins of Ba'albec after all the effort. The treatment meted out to Robert's troupe in Sidon left them demoralized and without supplies, which they could replenish only in Zahle.

"THE ONLY LIGHT LEFT WAS A RAG IN A DISH OF BUTTER."

Roberts' journal entry on 29th April is an evocative description of the state of his travel party. By and by, they saw the same snowcapped peaks and the fertile valley that I am traveling past. Roberts reached Ba'albec on 2nd May 1839.

BA'ALBEC

~~~~~~

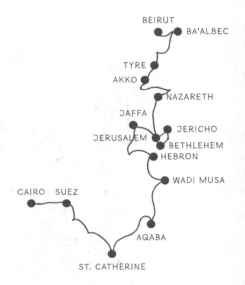

You would never want to be held in a head lock by this man, is my first thought when I see a bulldog of a man flag down our car in Ba'albec. Broad shouldered, barrel chested, and with strong, stubby legs, he is wearing dark jeans and a dark sweater. His beard reaches his belly button. My heart skips a beat until Ahmad waves back at him and yelps in delight, "That's Omar!"

Jumping out of the car, Ahmad's thin frame disappears into Omar's bear hug as the friends touch cheeks three times. Omar graduated in Fine Arts from the University of Beirut studying under Ahmad.

"Omar commuted to Beirut daily from Ba'albec," Ahmad tells me, describing the strenuous ninety-minute drive on the Lebanese backroads.

Leaving our rental parked in the space allocated by Hotel Palmyra, we set out on foot, making best of the few hours of light left in the day to explore Ba'albec. This is Ahmad's first visit to Ba'albec, too, and Omar is excited to show us the wonderful sights of his town. We fall in line with Omar's military stride, his head thrown back majestically, his beard blowing in the evening breeze, leaving behind a trail of mild cologne. His swagger is as much a part of his attire as is his neatly wrapped Syrian style turban.

Ba'albec is a frontier town. We are ten miles away from the border with Syria if we could cut straight through the mountain to our east. There is a delightful rural coarseness in everything around me. The terrain is rugged. Ancient, weather-beaten, lifted 4x4s and dirt bikes ply the streets. The bearded men, unkempt and loud, wear loose *kurta* and thick jackets – attire favored by the working class. They are all broad shoulders and have massive hands that could do serious damage. Guns are everywhere – inside the cabs of pickups or slung casually on shoulders. In this region, the firearm is a necessary tool, like a hiker's walking pole.

We walk past a row of shops on the way to the souk. Omar raps the shutters of one with the heel of his fist.

"This one is mine. Someday, it will be my studio," he says with a hint of pride.

Ba'albec Old Sonqs

"What is this?" Ananth asks, poking at a circular scar on the massive wooden doors.

"That's a 7.62," Omar says nonchalantly. In this part of the world, you know the caliber of NATO cartridges like teenagers in US know the version of iOS on their iPhones. "Hezbollah was angry at me. They tried to shoot me. That was a few years ago. Nothing to worry. Hezbollah is cool with me now."

We are deep inside Hezbollah country. The party's yellow-green flags are visible every few yards and turbaned leaders smile down at us from billboards at every corner. Ba'albec is the Hezbollah capital of Shi'a Islamists, who are looking to transition from militancy to politics. Hezbollah, openly backed by Iran, vehement opposes the state of Israel, an ideology it shares with the Sunni, backed by Saudi Arabia. But the two parties cannot see eye-to-eye despite this critical alignment. Politics aside, I am relieved that the monopoly of the yellow-green flag leaves no room for a competing set of colors that could put Ahmad's political nous to the test.

We walk through the old souk behind Omar who is on a mission to get us fed. The souk is a sensation for the nose. At the grocer's, gunny bags of spices are laid out in the front of the shop like perfume bottles at Macy's – an olfactory bait for passerby trudging with heads bent low. Aleppo pepper, sumac, dried Turkish chili pepper, Indian saffron, cumin seeds, and za'atar are flaunted in big piles but sold in little polythene pouches as if they are contraband. At the poultry souk a couple of streets over, a chicken is picked, plucked, and chopped in a matter of minutes. Gathering the chunks in a polythene bag, we head to the bakery, where a tall baker uses his muscular arms to rub the spices we just bought over the chicken we had butchered and spread it over a flatbread he has just baked. Within a few minutes, we are walking out with the best take-away pizza I have ever seen made.

Back in the hotel, our luggage has been taken to our rooms. A smiling Ahmed Kasseb takes charge of our passports and leads us down a passage and up a grand staircase. The paint on the walls has peeled and the hallways smell of mothballs. Lights magically switch on ahead of us and off after we pass them, a sign that electricity is being used judiciously. We reach a lounge that has a panoramic window framing the ruins, which are lit up by flickering halogen streetlamps across the streets. The room itself is a museum. Walls are adorned with black and white photos of the rich and the famous who flocked to Ba'albec in an era gone by. Statues carved in stone, missing limbs and noses, are lined up against the walls. Massive capitals stand guard in every corner.

We are led to the sitting area sprinkled with period furniture draped in velvet. A woman and two men occupy a divan and armchairs adjoining ours. Kasseb fusses around us. He gets the heat going in a wood-burning stove in the corner. Gnarly pipes emanate from it, and it dispatches heat to various parts of the room – a centralized heating system of sorts – apparatus that befits any Frankensteinian lab. It may have been in place since 1874 when Hotel Palmyra first opened. The hotel has been open every single day since, and Kasseb has worked here for the past 75 years – longer than the average life expectancy in this area.

Kasseb flits to a diner at the next table, tops up the wine glasses with the elegance of a Parisian waiter, and makes a comment that elicits a laugh from the woman. She must be in her early forties, tall and copper haired, wearing fashionable jeans and a checkered shirt cinched at the waist. From what I can see, she is not a local. She has the two men sitting with her wrapped in her aura.

Kasseb peeps into my sketchbook. I tell him about my David Roberts project. Roberts had ridden into town on 3rd May. The ride across the mountains had been the hardest journey for the troupe. The weather had not been kind: incessant cold

Ba'albec, Liban

and rain, the mules getting bogged in the mud repeatedly, tent malfunctions. One night a ton of water cascaded down onto the sleeping inhabitants. Roberts was aching all over and feverish when he reached Ba'albec but was "so much struck by the magnificence of the temple" that he could not resist visiting and exploring. Despite his sickness, he spent several hours making several studies of the ruins of Ba'albec. In the middle of all this, the governor confiscated his mules as part of the conscription and Roberts had to use his *firman* to get the mules rescued. And while he was there with the governor, he managed to wrangle a *firman* to travel to Damascus, which was an additional two-day journey across the mountain.

"When was he in Ba'albec?" Kasseb asks, "1839? That's before my time." His laugh culminates in a bout of coughing. Kasseb's long years of service at Hotel Palmyra is part of the folklore of the hotel, his frail but elegant personality now very much a part of the scenery. He happily poses for photos, pulling himself tall and straightening his weathered leather jacket.

"Will I be in you book, Mr. Sunil?" he asks, "Will you write nice things about me?"

The steaming hot *sfisa* (the pizza we had made in the souk) is laid out on plates, and the plates go around the room. The lady holding court at the neighboring table is an archaeologist restoring the ruins at Ba'albec. She has excavated in Cairo and Karnak and Sinai. She is happy to see visitors in Ba'albec.

"We have not had tourists for ten years now," she says, the archaeologist in her probably not complaining too much.

She gives us a virtual tour of the ruins telling us what to expect. She warns, "Trying to imagine the temple of Jupiter using the six remaining columns is like trying to imagine the Golden Gate bridge by holding a rivet in your hand." She is referring to the

AA battery-sized metal rivets that were extensively used in the construction on the bridge in San Francisco, copies of which can be bought in a gift shop.

The subject turns to Syria and I cannot resist asking how one can enter the war-torn country.

"Very easy," Omar says, "A bus leaves every hour from the souk. You buy a ticket and you are in Damascus in four hours. With your Arab looks no questions will be asked."

"They won't check my passport?"

"Only on the way out," he says.

"And?"

"Then you are screwed," he laughs. "Especially if you can't speak Arabic and have an American passport."

I have always believed that my American passport and my brown skin are my two best travel accessories. The passport gets me in, my brown skin gets me out. Not here, apparently.

After dinner, Kasseb shows me to my room. It is tastefully decorated, a benchmark of luxury in its heyday. Kasseb lights up a stove at the foot of the bed. He tells me about the days when the hotel teemed with customers and warmth. Today they are struggling to make ends meet. The bedroom is freezing. An effort has been made to clean the bathroom, but the patina betrays months of neglect. It is the kind of a room where you touch as few things as you can.

"Please understand, we are trying our best," Kasseb says, his smile apologetic, "Hotel Palmyra was the grandest hotel in the world. Albert Einstein slept in this very room. In the morning,

THE GATEWAY TO THE GREAT TEMPLE AT BAALBEC
BY DAVID ROBERTS, R.A. 7TH MAY 1839

you will know why he was given this room, Insh'Allah," he smiles. "You won't see me in the morning, but you will thank me."

I have a huge tolerance for discomfort. But the night at Hotel Palmyra is perhaps the most uncomfortable night I have spent in a hotel room. The plumbing gurgles all night. The room is cold to begin with and gets colder. The bedsheets are so low in thread count that if the naked bulb in the room would stay lit, I could count them myself. But all of this is forgiven at first light. The sun peeps over the Anti Lebanon range, bathing the ruins outside the window in a surreal light, like pure honey poured over marble. Who knows what this view inspired in Einstein?

Ba'albec, Liban

I thank Ahmed Kasseb with all my heart. I wish I had insisted on meeting him in the morning. Kasseb passed away a few months after my visit, another Ba'albec icon dimmed, lost forever in the flow of time. I keep my promise to him and put him in my book.

Our bags in the car, passports in our pocket, we cross the road to the ruins. For several hours we roam the site at will. We are the only visitors that day, but the news is out that tourists are in town. A few sellers have set up stalls, but they aren't in our faces. Maybe the recent tourist hiatus has eroded their hard-selling skills. One stall displays lemon yellow T-shirts with a green insignia, which on closer inspection is an AK47 in a clenched fist. I am glad I listen to my inner voice, the one I invariably ignore to purchase one. For I can only imagine the shock on the face of US customs officers to see Hezbollah souvenirs in my bags.

The ruins are a blatant display of power, technology, resources, and the strong economy of their time. Three massive monoliths were measured and hacked out of bedrock in a quarry half a mile away. They were pushed, hauled, lifted, and wedged into place. They had been maneuvered, laced, and dressed until they looked like they had grown out of the ground. These monoliths are the largest known stone blocks to have been moved by mankind ever. Built on top of this platform are columns of such magnificent proportions that the engineering feat is only surpassed by the artistry. Each capital is the size of a kitchen fridge, carved and detailed despite knowing the work would never really be seen at close quarters. The scale is unprecedented.

Roberts felt challenged to accurately depict the scale and the beauty. Despite his sickness, Roberts was exhilarated by the ruins and threw himself feverishly into his work. Roberts sat on a fallen pediment outside the Temple of Bacchus and sketched to his heart's content the composition of a doorway with a falling capstone. The composition had been sketched before: by Charles Barry in 1819 and by William Bartlett in 1834, almost from an identical spot (artists follow artists!) but without the drama Roberts was able to create. Roberts tips his hat at travelers who had visited the ruins before him – Burkhardt, Wood and Dawkins, Irby and Mangles – by inscribing their names in his image of the entrance the stonework.

Briony Llewellyn, art historian and an expert on David Roberts, makes an interesting observation in an essay: Ba'albec struck a particular chord in Roberts, perhaps because the mountain scenery and classical forms of the provincial Roman architecture were more assimilable to his Western understanding that the ancient temple of Egypt or even the rock-cut tombs of Petra.

It is also likely that he knew he was at the end of his peregrination. Whether it was the incessant rain or the biting cold or the rumors of the Druze revolting in that part of the world, I am thankful for whatever made Roberts cancel his onward journey. Perhaps Roberts simply realized he had already done his best work and that it could not be bettered. He knew how to quit while he was still ahead.

Perhaps he had already made up his mind not to continue to Damascus "owing to the unsettled state of the country," as he wrote in his journal on 8th May 1839. Through his sickness and fatigue, he maximized the time and opportunity available to him, as he was known to do, and produced a masterpiece. The composition titled *The Doorway of the Temple, Baalbec* went on to earn him his fellowship at the Royal Academy in 1841.

BEIRUT   BA'ALBEC

SIDON

TYRE

AKKO

NAZARETH

JAFFA

JERUSALEM   JERICHO

BETHLEHEM

HEBRON

GAZA

PETRA

CAIRO   SUEZ

ST. CATHERINE

BEIRUT

〜〜〜〜

Paint flowed freely from Roberts' brush, but ink from his pen was sparse. "The unsettled state of the country…" was an inadequate description of the massive unrest brewing in the regions along Roberts' route. In 1838, the Druze had attempted – and failed – to topple the iron-fisted rule of Ibrahim Pasha, the Governor of Syria, and son of Muhammed Ali. They were rebelling against Ibrahim Pasha again. The Pasha, backed by the French, was himself getting ready to fight the Ottoman Empire, backed by the British. The vultures of war were circling the sky.

Ibrahim Pasha's men were reaching out to the leaders of the tribes of Syria and Palestine to renew the pledge of allegiance. A draft was in progress. Food and fuel were being stockpiled. John Kinnear describes in his journals the conscriptions and its impact that he witnessed: villagers being shackled and dragged away amidst shrieks and screams of devastated family members; young men gauging out an eye or cutting an arm to avoid fighting somebody else's war; mules and camels being confiscated for military duty leaving the citizens without a means to earn their daily bread. Robert accurately depicted in his paintings the Pasha's army marching in rank and file, in Gaza and Acre (Akko). In the harbor of Acre, Roberts painted a warship ominously looming on the horizon, hidden in plain sight. Those are the only clues Roberts gives his readers of the impending war in his wanderings through Syria, instead painting idyllic, bucolic scenes.

On 8th May 1839, Roberts left Ba'albec and reached Beirut after a tedious two-day crossing over the mountains. On his way, he saw trains of mules lugging food to Ibrahim Pasha's army in Damascus. In Beirut, Roberts briefly reunited with John Kinnear one evening over dinner. They continued to remain in touch for many years after.

The dice rolled in Roberts' favor one more time. The sick Ottoman Sultan Mahmud died within days of Roberts departing from Alexandria. Ibrahim Pasha defeated the distracted Turks in the Battle of Nezib in 1839. The British had to intervene to halt the Ibrahim Pasha's victory march to Constantinople, the intervention itself leading to another conflict known in the annals of history as the Oriental Crisis of 1840. The British needed the Turks as a buffer against the Russians – a canny move in the Great Game that was being played out between the great powers across Asia. By the time the British bombarded Acre, Tyre, and Sidon, Roberts was safely back in

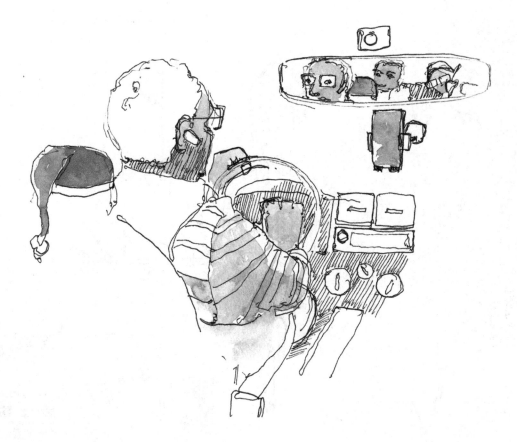

London. Ibrahim Pasha, having lost the support of the French, handed Syria over to the British, but only after he had negotiated the liberation of Egypt from the Ottoman Empire.

In early 2010s, the epithet of "unsettled state ..." still applied to Syria. Sunni rebels – backed by Turkey and Saudi Arabia, were locked in a civil war with the Shi'a Alawite regime – backed by Russia and Hezbollah (and Iran, by proxy). In 2014, a breakaway faction of al-Qaeda formed Daesh – better known in the world as

ISIS. A year later, the United States jumped into the melee and the battlefield was rearranged: the now formidable ISIS was pitted against three powerful, but comically uncoordinated, coalitions: the Kurdish forces backed by the US, the Syrian regime backed by Russia, and the rebels backed by Turkey. In October 2017 the Kurdish SDF (Syrian Democratic Forces) defeated ISIS in al-Raqqa, marking the beginning of the end for the militant organization, and prompting me to launch my expedition to the Levant. By February 2018, the fire had been extinguished, but the ground

Beirut, Liban

still smoldered – too hot for me to attempt crossing into Syria to go to Damascus. Roberts' description of an "unsettled state…" still applies to Syria in 2020, where a humanitarian crisis looms large over this once prosperous and liberal nation.

I feel grateful to Roberts for aborting his plan to proceed to Damascus. I would have struggled to follow the proverbial last mile in his footsteps.

~~~~~~

After spending the afternoon amidst the ruins of Ba'albec, Ananth, Ahmad, and I also set out for Beirut. The return journey always feels shorter. The blue expanse of the Mediterranean comes quickly into view as we descend the slopes of the Lebanon Mountains, and I know the expedition is all but done.

Beirut. The name still evokes images that I remember seeing on black and white TV sets in the '80s: bullet-ridden city blocks, tottering superstructures that somehow survived the bombs, the burning metallic shells of cars strewn amidst a talus of concrete debris, oily smoke emanating from tires on fire, the sound of gunfire echoing in empty streets.

Beirut today is a far cry from those grainy images. Instead, I see the city returning to its pre-civil war opulence. A Zaha Hadid designed shopping mall rises between gunshot-pockmarked buildings, a Lamborghini is parked outside a Ferrari showroom as the owner peruses another shiny roadster, hipster coffee shops offer free Wi-fi and sell za'atar croissants, Hermès and Louis Vuitton boutiques are crowded, and Ed Sheeran croons over expensive speakers at a midday party on a yacht moored in Zaituna Bay.

Like an inebriated patron ordering one more round at the bar, less for the alcohol and more for the reluctance to end the evening, we put together one more impromptu adventure.

Ananth and I follow the Lebanon Urban Sketchers group to the ancient city of Byblos. The first city built by the Phoenicians and continuously inhabited since the fifth millennium BCE, Byblos was famous for its papyrus and lent its name to books, the most popular of them being the Bible. We sketch from the balustrades of the Crusader castle, descending through the ancient souk to a picturesque port lashed by the Mediterranean as the sun tilts towards the horizon. Back in Beirut, after bidding Ahmad goodbye, Ananth and I tuck into some delicious Lebanese food and enjoy the sunset over the Corniche.

"Ready to go home?" Ananth asks me.

The cool breeze from the Mediterranean flutters on my face. The last fifteen weeks flicker through my head, images flashing bright for a second, then fading into the dark, like a movie reel whirring out of control. I have meandered through labyrinthine Cairo and its spice markets under the watchful eyes of John. I have traveled with the effervescent ex-commando Showqi across the Eastern Desert to the oldest living monastery in the world. I have stood at the easternmost tip of Egypt and traveled along an ancient trade route through the desert of Wadi Rum to the rock city of Petra, where nutty Issa showed us a side of the Nabataean city that tourists tend to miss. With my wife Monica, I visited the biblical sites of Palestine and Israel in the company of Sagi and Gazi, who showed us that a coin has three sides – your side, my side, and the truth. Ananth and I regrouped in Lebanon with Ahmad and followed the Mediterranean coast back in time to discover Alexander's battles, Crusader castles, souks, and the best cuisine west of Mumbai. We forged on to the frontier town of Ba'albec and its alluring Roman ruins and crossed the Beqa'a valley to Beirut.

I have accomplished what I set out to do. A journey through the timeless landscapes of the Middle East, along the contours of ancient civilizations, following the indelible ridges of history. You can't judge a place until you have seen it in three lights. I

FRIDAY PRAYERS Md. Al Amin.
Musano

have done exactly that, traveling at a pace set by no one but me, lingering in settings long enough to see the sagas unfold in the eye of my mind, connecting old stories with even older stories.

David Roberts has been a great travel companion. We both took the long way around, never missing a scenic detour, stopping at wonderful sights, leaving behind the well-trodden path. Only when safe travel was not possible, like in Gaza and Ramallah, did I avoid a place Roberts visited. I stood in every one of his compositions, give or take, lining up his sketches of the ancient sites with the modern sights. Time and again, I was astonished at how little things have changed and yet how everything is different. The landscape and the architecture Roberts so skillfully captured with his fine eyes and deft fingers can still be experienced and enjoyed without needing to stretch one's imagination too much.

David Roberts has been a good teacher, a "do as I do" type. I picked up a myriad of little nuggets from him, lessons that can only be learned the hard way, by walking in the shoes of the teacher. Here is a minor example: the buff-colored paper on which Roberts sketched in the Holy Land was better suited for sketching in bright sunlight. I used white paper. The white shines beautifully through the thin glazes of watercolor, but it also reflects the desert sun, and the eyes begin to hurt within a few minutes of sketching. No book nor workshop gave me this heads-up.

Roberts' discipline in carrying his sketchbook with him everywhere and sketching every single day has inspired me. His prolific productivity at a consistently high quality is a thing every artist must aspire to.

But the single largest contribution to my art journey was seeing Roberts' use of human figures in the foreground of his majestic compositions. My early sketch compositions were rooted in the years I had spent photographing landscapes. As I sketched more, my compositions evolved to embrace the constraints and facilities of the new medium. Still, I avoided having people in my frames, exactly as I did in my digital landscapes, because human subjects cannot hold still long enough to be properly captured. They also have opinions – about light and angle, about location and poses. I found myself gravitating more and more towards compositions that could be accomplished without the human element. (My friends warned me it was just my introversion.) As I studied Robert's paintings of Egypt and the Holy Land, I discovered the depth and color that the figures in the foreground brought to the scenes. I started experimenting with human figures in my own compositions. Early attempts, clumsy silhouettes, soon evolved into something that looked like a balloon tied to a pillow. Then the lumpy shapes grew a neck, hands and feet. The figures learned to sit upright and hold a pose. Like studio mannequins, they started holding things awkwardly in mitten-covered hands, before growing fingers. The heads started to tilt, the backs started to curve, the arms started to flex. The figures stood up and turned and walked and kneeled and leaned. They are still evolving. Even to my ever-critical eyes, having human figures in the foreground brought my sketches alive, and with them the memories of places, their very raison d'être.

For this lesson, I forgive David Roberts for his occasional bigotry ("Visited the tombs of the Caliphs, which are in ruins and inhabited by poor squalid wretches" *5th January, Cairo*), for being such a fusspot ("...bitten cruelly by mosquitoes and ants" *7th December, Giza*), for his ignorance ("The tomb called Belzoni's is in excellent state" *22nd October, Valley of the Kings* – it was the tomb of Seti I, discovered by Giovanni Belzoni, a circus strongman and explorer), sensationalism ("A lean hungry dog and two immense white eagles were gorging themselves on a dead camel"), or what we would now recognize as his Islamophobia ("The only difficulty will be contending with the prejudices of the Mohammedans, who will not allow an infidel to enter their mosques, and certainly not to sketch them"). Katherine Sim, the author of Robert's authoritative biography,

Beirut, Liban

writes, "His sometimes violent comments on the subject should be regarded only as in accord with pretty well all other superficial English travelers of that era. He simply did not have the time then, not the desire, to learn, judge and inwardly understand. He had gone to draw, and that he did superbly."

The only thing I hold against David Roberts is that once he boarded the boat headed for Malta in May 1839, he never looked back. It was as if he had experienced everything he wanted to experience in Egypt, Palestine, and Syria, seen everything worthy of seeing and had stored it in his photographic memory. Once he left the shore, he washed his hands of the Holy Land and moved on.

Not me. The Middle East has a special place in my heart; it is a place I can never bid goodbye. I often find myself planning my next trip to the Middle East while I am still in the Middle East. The juxtaposition of densely packed humanity in cities surrounded by vast deserts that the horizon can't contain, the constant commotion and perpetual solitude, the waste and the sparseness, a place where history is inseparable from geography. It is a magical place.

The ruggedness inherent to the Middle East and other regions of the world where some of the oldest civilizations once thrived – the Indian Subcontinent, Central America, South East Asia, North Africa – the lack of polish is attributed to the lack of development and, by extension, to a lack of ambition and initiative. I disagree. Change is the sum of progress and regress. Change happens through successive waxing and waning, expansion and contraction. One step forward, two steps back. Then three steps forward and two steps back. Progress is not linear. Civilizations that made rapid progress in a short span of time are now relegated to the history books; civilizations that made *absolutely* no progress for a century lie in dust, too. It is the ones in between that have survived. Small changes have survived. Slow and steady. Like in the fable, the turtle wins in the long run. Successive waxing and waning, expansion and contraction. Back and forth, back and forth.

"Yes, I am ready to go home," I tell Ananth.

〜〜〜〜

On our last night in Beirut, Ananth and I watch *The Post*, which is showing in theatres on the weekend. We sit in a multiplex with a crowd of Lebanon's cognoscenti, who understand the nuances of American politics. After the movie, we leave the theatre in search of spice – my tongue is craving not just flavor but also heat – something Sichuanese, I am thinking.

I am in a tremendous mood, having successfully concluded the adventure. I am also deep in the middle of a debate with Ananth. The *Washington Post*, the newspaper that was praised for publishing the Pentagon Papers, the premise of the movie we had just watched, was also known for asking for Edward Snowden to be prosecuted. Edward Snowden is an American whistleblower who is on the run from the USA for having leaked classified information about government sponsored surveillance programs. I find the *Washington Post*'s hypocrisy stunning; I tell Ananth. We wait in a line snaking into a metal detector to enter a mall. When our turn comes, a soldier wearing a crewcut and a Browning automatic on his hip asks us casually, "What are you doing here?"

Deep in the middle of enunciating my point of view, I blurt, "We are having a blast!"

Only later do I understand the strange look the soldier gave us and only because Ananth points it out. In the Middle East, "having a blast" does not translate to "having fun."

Ananth is laughing. "The soldier did not understand your accent, Sunil, or we would have been on Amanpour."

MAHER
T5012

MAHER

FARAS EL BAHAR
TA317

Byblos Star
3284T

SAT 20 JAN 2018 PORT OF BYBLOS, LEBANON

EPILOGUE

From Beirut, Roberts sailed to Alexandria where he met Mohammed Ali Pasha on 16th May 1839. He memorialized the event into a painting done entirely from memory as he hadn't carried his sketchbook with him to the meeting.

In the center of the composition, titled *Interview with Mehemet Ali in his Palace at Alexandria 1839*, the ailing Pasha sits cross-legged, pensive, and slumped. On the right, bathed in bright sunlight streaming through a huge window, are the British in their spiffy red and white uniforms – Lieutenant Waghorn, the mastermind for the overland route from Suez to Alexandria; Colonel Campbell, the British Consul, and David Roberts himself, hat in hand, looking awkward and unsure. On the left, the Pasha's men are relegated to the shadows, their faded red *tarboosh* hats an unmistakable symbol of the Ottoman Empire, also fading. The yin and the yang, the Orient and the Occident face each other like boxers in a ring, each in their corner, a sign of the impending crisis that has gripped the region, accentuated by the view through the window, where the Pasha's fleet is visible, swarming the horizon, getting ready for war, the air acrid with gun powder.

Eager to get back home, Roberts found passage to Malta. He was quarantined for three weeks, but spent the time well, correcting his drawings, before proceeding to Gibraltar along the coast of Africa, then to Cadiz and finally to London in June 1839. He reunited with his daughter, Christine, after eleven months. Meanwhile the ailing Ottoman Sultan Mahmud died on 30th June, while Roberts was still in Malta. By the end of July, the Pasha's army was at full scale war with the Ottoman Porte. David Roberts had got out of the Near East in the nick of time.

INTERVIEW WITH MEHEMET ALI IN HIS PALACE AT ALEXANDRIA BY DAVID ROBERTS, R. A. MAY 1839

Roberts returned home with 272 sketches, a large panorama of Cairo, and three full sketchbooks. "One of the richest folios that ever left the East," he wrote. He started work on his book almost immediately. Learning from his previous experience of selling the book to a publisher without much thought,[12] this time he signed a lucrative contract with Francis Moon for exclusive rights to his pictures for £3,000 (approximately £310,000 in 2020).

David Roberts partnered with Louis Haghe, a thirty-four-year-old Belgian lithographer. The technology to reproduce hand drawings on a mass scale without losing the finesse and detail was still in its infancy. Louis Haghe had to etch the mirror image of each of David Roberts' compositions onto a stone. The mold this created had to be dipped in paint, one color at a time, and pressed against paper carefully to transfer the image. The process was extremely tedious and complex, and the result

---

[12] Hodson and Graves published Roberts' *Picturesque Sketches of Spain* in 1837 and sold 1,200 copies in two months but was stiffed by his publishers out of the fortune. The publishers made approximately £4,800 ($600,000 in 2020) while Roberts was paid £300 ($3,600 in 2020) making Robert's write in frustration: "The conduct of this firm to me is I think without exception the most ungrateful and base I have ever seen in my life met with" (Katherine Sims, *David Roberts RA: A Biography*)

breathtaking. The lithographs we enjoy today – which sell for hundreds of thousands of dollars each – are as much Haghe's skills as Roberts' artistry.

Moon invested a large amount in creating the volumes that matched Roberts' lavish vision for the book. 247 tinted lithographs were published serially in 41 parts and as six volumes between 1841 and 1849. The first of the two three-volume sets were titled *The Holy Land: Syria, Idumea and Arabia* and contained lithographs of the second part of Robert's journey starting with the Sinai. The second set, titled Egypt and Nubia, captured his journey to Upper Egypt via the Nile and his stay in Cairo in 1838-39.

Roberts' book had a long list of advanced subscribers including Queen Victoria, the Prime Minister of England, the Archbishop of Canterbury, the Duke of Wellington and hundreds of notables. It was an instant bestseller of its time.

~~~~~

In February 2018, I was back in Seattle and, within a month, back in the grinder – a 40-mile daily commute through treacherous traffic, school drops-offs, PTA meetings, demanding customers, board meetings, business presentations, and the perpetual quest for more revenue. In the midst of all this, I started to work on my book. A 4 o'clock alarm was necessary to put in an hour of writing before an eighteen-hour day vanished in front of my eyes. My weekends were spent completing the sketches and painting them. Despite all of this, and within just a few months, my own expedition of the Middle East seemed to be a thing of the distant past.

The economy was booming. They say a booming economy hides all ills. I started to wonder if some of David Roberts' experiences in the first five months of 1839 – the xenophobia,

racism, political unrest, war, revolt, economic uncertainty, plague, draft – did these things only happen *back then*? Only in the far away *Middle East*?

Life sighed philosophically. Then it uncorked a series of events in unrelenting and quick succession. The US embassy opened in Jerusalem in October 2018, leading to massive unrest in the region. A flash flood killed eleven tourists in Petra in November of the same year. The medieval church of Notre Dame in Paris was destroyed by fire in April 2019. After 178 years of operations, Thomas Cook, the world's oldest travel company collapsed later that year. Donald Trump was impeached. Popularity of Tesla's electric cars started to slowly push Germany towards recession, new money eating the lunch that the old money took for granted. Britain exited the European Union. Nationalism grew in the West, leading to the rise of several far-right movements. Lebanon's economy melted down in January 2020. The United States assassinated an Iranian general in February 2020, bringing humanity to the brink of another world war. In March 2020, the world went into the largest voluntary lockdown on the back of a pandemic, the global economy teetering on the edge of a recession that could last a decade. By July 2020, the 1,500-year-old Hagia Sofia was converted back into a mosque, thereby annulling an eighty-four-year-old decree. In August, Beirut was returned to rubble when a forgotten cache of ammonium nitrate exploded.

Xenophobia, racism, political unrest, war, revolt, economic uncertainty, plague.

Progress and regress. Waxing and waning. Two steps forward, one step back.

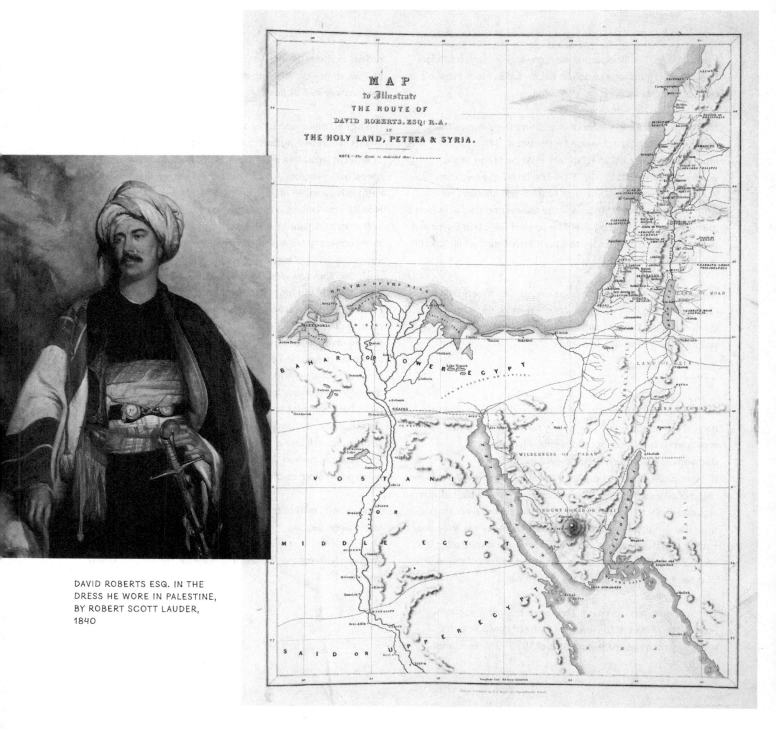

DAVID ROBERTS ESQ. IN THE
DRESS HE WORE IN PALESTINE,
BY ROBERT SCOTT LAUDER,
1840

DAVID ROBERTS' BIO

~~~~~~

Roberts was born on October 24th, 1796 to a shoemaker in Stockbridge. His mother spotted his artistic talent early when he covered the walls of their family homes with pictures whose quality surpassed his age. In 1808, at the behest of a family friend, Roberts was apprenticed to a house painter named Gavin Beugo. For the next seven years, he mixed paints every day in the back of an oil-paint-scented studio for long hours. It gave him a chance to understand different mediums and surfaces, which came in handy later in his career. In 1815, aged 19, he was hired as a set designer by a small theatre company in Edinburgh.

A year later, Roberts joined a traveling circus as a scene painter. Every day after work, Roberts watched *Ali Baba and the Forty Thieves* in the circus theatre. He painted the scenes in intricate detail later at night starting his lifelong fascination for the Orient. He traveled all over Scotland with the circus and learned to draw on a large scale and to sketch fast – covering large areas rapidly with detail and drama. When the circus disbanded a year later, Roberts went back to house painting where he perfected the skill of accurately depicting wood grain and marble.

In 1820 he married actress Margaret McLachlan. Their daughter Christine was born in 1821, and in 1823 he moved permanently to London. His first oil painting was exhibited to good reviews at the British Institution, a nineteenth century art society. He traveled in Europe – Belgium, Antwerp, Brussels to paint romantic travel sketches, which were exhibited and sold to critical acclaim. He also continued to paint sceneries in Edinburgh and Glasgow.

In 1829 JMW Turner convinced Roberts to give up painting scenery. Roberts started his own studio in order to focus on painting commissions for the clientele he had garnered. He soon painted the first of his historical paintings: *The Departure of the Israelites from Egypt*. He needed to refer to the work of other artists who had traveled to Egypt. The time he spent researching the illustrations and texts of other travelers undoubtedly fanned the flames he had burning for the Orient. As it did the need to make the drawings on the spot and from direct observation.

In 1832, Roberts had traveled to Spain. Over the next two years, he visited Madrid, Toledo, Granada, Malaga, Seville and Gibraltar. The wonderful portfolio he assembled made him famous. The associated riches unfortunately escaped him because of a lopsided contract with his publisher. Nevertheless, the experience of sketching of mosques in the Moorish cities stood him in good stead for his trip to Cairo.

In the early 1838 he was inducted as an associate to the Royal Academy, one step short of becoming a full member. In the same year he finished all his commercial commitments, cashed out his investments, packed his bag and belongings, shipped his sixteen-year-old daughter off to stay with friends in England and, in August 1838, set off on the expedition to the Near East that would make him famous. He returned home to London in June 1839. Between 1842 and 1849, the lithographs based on the sketches he made on the journey from Cairo to Beirut were published as "The Holy Land, Syria, Idumea, Egypt, Nubia". In 1942 Roberts was made a full member of the Royal Academy.

Roberts continued to travel abroad to make paintings and etchings that were by now sought after because of the fame and glory his work in Egypt and the Near East had garnered him. Successful and famous, he died of a heart attack at the age of sixty-eight on the 25th of November 1864 and was buried in the cemetery of Norwood.

AUTHOR BIO

Sunil Shinde is an ardent urban-sketcher since 2013 and is a correspondent for the Urban Sketchers blog, urbansketchers. org. Over the last twenty years, Sunil has travelled to over thirty countries, tracing stories of history, religion and culture. When he isn't travelling, he is dreaming of travelling. He is also building an AI-based population health product in stealth mode. SHHH! He lives in a cottage in the woods in Redmond, WA, with his wife, two daughters and their golden retriever, Oscar.

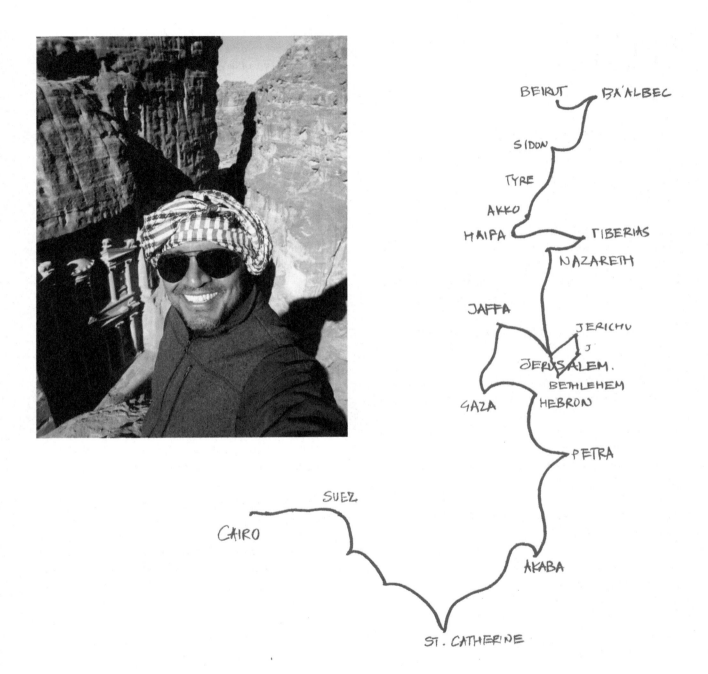

BEIRUT   BA'ALBEC

SIDON

TYRE

AKKO

HAIFA   TIBERIAS

NAZARETH

JAFFA

JERICHU

J

JERUSALEM.

BETHLEHEM

GAZA   HEBRON

PETRA

SUEZ

CAIRO

AKABA

ST. CATHERINE

CREDITS

~~~~~~

Page 11: *Temple called Khazneh, Petra*, by David Roberts, R.A. March 1839, source: Library of Congress

Page 12: *View from under the portico of Temple of Edfou* by David Roberts, R.A. 23rd November 1838, source: Library of Congress

Page 26: *Tombs of the Khalifs, Cairo* by David Roberts, R.A. January 1839, source: Wikipedia

Page 33: *The Mosque of Sultan Hassan, Cairo* by David Roberts, R.A. 12th January 1939, source: Library of Congress

Page 44: *Bazaar of the silk mercers, Cairo* by David Roberts, R.A. January 1839, source: Library of Congress

Page 47: *Interior of the mosque of the Sultan El Ghoree* by David Roberts, R.A. January 1939, source: Library of Congress

Page 95: TK

Page 117: *Entrance to Petra* by David Roberts, R.A. 10th March 1839, source: TK

Page 123: *El Deir Petra* by David Roberts, R.A. 8th March 1839, source: Library of Congress

Page 124: *Triumphal arch across the ravine leading to Petra* by David Roberts, R.A. March 1839, source: Library of Congress

Page 137: *Gaza* by David Roberts, R.A. 21st March 1839, source: TK

Page 146: *Entrance to the Holy Sepulcher* by David Roberts, R.A. April 1839, source: Library of Congress

Page 164: *Jerusalem from the Mount of Olives* by David Roberts, R.A. 8th April 1839, source: Library of Congress

Page 172: *Convent of St. Saba* by David Roberts, R.A. 4th April 1839, source: Library of Congress

Page 186: Plan of Jerusalem by Frederick Catherwood, 1835, source: Wikipedia

Page 189: *Nazareth* by David Roberts, R.A. 28th April 1839, source: Library of Congress

Page 197: *St. Jean d'Acre* by David Roberts, R.A. 24th April 1839, source: Library of Congress

Page 209: *Ruins of an Ionic Temple* by David Roberts, R.A. 25th April 1839, source: Library of Congress

Page 222: *The Citadel of Sidon* by David Roberts, R.A. 28th April 1839, source: tk

Page 231: *The Gateway to the Great Temple at Baalbec* by David Roberts, R.A. 7th May 1839, source: Library of Congress

Page 246: *Interview with Mehemet Ali in his Palace at Alexandria* by David Roberts, R. A. May 1839, source: Library of Congress

Page 248: David Roberts Esq. in the dress he wore in Palestine, by Robert Scott Lauder, 1840, source: Wikipedia. Map to Illustrate the Route of David Roberts Esq: R.A. in The Holy Land, Petrea & Syria, source: Oscar I. Norwich Collection at Stanford University

BIBLIOGRAPHY

〜〜〜〜

Abdul-Hakim, Sahar and Manley, Deborah *Traveling through Sinai, From the Fourth to the Twenty-first Century* (The American University in Cairo Press 2006)

Ballantine, James. *The Life of David Roberts, R.A.* (Adam & Charles Black, 1866)

Bar, Doron and Cohen-Hattab "A New Kind of Pilgrimage: The Modern Tourist Pilgrim of Nineteenth Century and Early Twentieth Century Palestine" *Middle Eastern Studies* 39:2, 131–148

Baram, Uzi "Images of the Holy Land: The David Roberts Paintings as artifacts of 1830 Palestine" *Historical Archaeology* Vol. 41, No. 1, Between Art & Artifact (2007), pp. 106–117

Ben-Arieh, Yehoshua Painting the Holy Land in the Nineteenth Century (Yadlzhak-Ben-Zvi Pubns 1997)

Ben-Arieh, Yeshoshua *Jerusalem in the 19th Century: The Old City* (Palgrave Macmillan 1985)

Ben-Arieh, Yeshoshua *The Rediscovery of the Holy Land in the Nineteenth Century* (Sefer VeSefel 2007)

Bentley, James *Secrets of Mount Sinai* (Doubleday 1985)

Bourbon, Fabio *Egypt: Yesterday and Today: Lithographs and Diaries by David Roberts* (Stewart, Tabori and Chang 1996)

Bourbon, Fabio *Holy Land: Yesterday and Today: Lithographs and Diaries by David Roberts* (Stewart, Tabori and Chang 1996)

Duggan, Alfred *The Story of the Crusades 1097-1291* (Faber & Faber 1963)

Friedman, Thomas L. *From Beirut to Jerusalem* (Farrar, Straus and Giroux, Doubleday 1990)

Guiterman, Helen, Llewellyn Briony *David Roberts* (Phaidon/ Barbican, 1986)

Hunt, Patrick "Artist David Roberts and Near Eastern Archaeology" *ArtWis Kunstpedia*, January 2014

Karabell, Zachary *Parting the Desert: The Creation of the Suez Canal* (First Vintage Books 2000)

Kinnear, John Gardiner *Cairo, Petra, and Damascus in 1839: With Remarks on the Government of Mehemet Ali and on the Present Prospects of Syria* (1840)

Larison, Kristine Marie "Mount Sinai and the Monastery of St. Catherine: Place and Space in Pilgrimage Art"

Lunn, Richard Francis *Frith's Egypt and the Holy Land* (Frith Book Co Ltd, 2004)

Mooreland, Alan *The White Nile* (Harper Perennial 2000)

Murray, John and Wilkinson, John Gardner *A Handbook for Travellers in Egypt: Including Descriptions of the Course of the Nile to the Second Cataract, Alexandria, Cairo, the Pyramids, and Thebes, the Overland Transit to India, the Peninsula of Mount Sinai* (J. Murray, 1858)

Proctor, J. Harris "David Roberts and the Ideology of Imperialism" *The Muslim World*, January 1998

Said, Edward *Orientalism* (Vintage 1979)

Sim, Katherine. *David Roberts R.A. 1796–1864: A Biography* (Quartet Books Ltd, 1984)

Sim, Katherine *Desert Traveller: The Life of Jean Louis Burkhardt* (Phoenix, 2001)

Schuler, Wolfgang *In the Holy Land: Paintings by David Roberts* (Studio Editions, 1995)

Siliotti, Alberto *Guide to Exploration of the Sinai* (White Star Editions 2001)

Starkey, Paul, Starkey, Janet *Travellers in Egypt* (I.B. Tauris 1998)

Vyse, Howard *Operations Carried on at the Pyramids of Gizeh in 1837* (John Weale, High Holborn and G. W Nickisson 1842)

Wiemers, Galyn *Jerusalem: History, Archaeology and Apologetic Proof of Scripture*

ACKNOWLEDGMENTS

~~~~~

To Bruce Rutledge at Chin Music Press for putting his faith in this idiosyncratic book. To Mary Bisbee Beek for showing this debuting author the ropes of the publishing industry. To Tatiana Wilde and Kayla Kavanaugh for giving the manuscript the shape it has today and to the indefatigable Liliana Guia for waving the wand of design.

To Gabi Companario, Stephanie Bower and Suhita Shirodkar for showing me how to be a better Urban Sketcher. To Sid Gavandi, Vanita Mascarenhas and Justin Hamacher for setting the visual tone of the book from its early days. To Susan Parman for asking the provocative questions that changed the arc of my story and to (artby)Radha whose commentary is as beautiful as the human being she is. To Sankara Subramaniam from Bangalore, Shannon Ngono from Senegal, Judy Abi Roustom from Lebanon, Aamira Al Tabbaa from Syria, Ammara and Kubaib in Karachi, Dr. Steve Overman, Vijya Patel from Seattle, and Daiva Chesonis from Telluride for pointing me in the right direction when all felt lost. To Sunny Neogi, Ankur Teredesai, Vani Mandava, Kuljinder Dhillon and Loring Cox for cheering me on. To John Emad, Captain Showqi, Ananth Kumar and Ahmad Gadar for being such fabulous travel companions.

To Fabio, who himself followed David Roberts, for taking me under his wings. To Professor Uzi Baram for taking this unacademic body of work seriously. To Craig Childs for the written and spoken words, my North star in the southwest.

To Dr. Nitin Paranjape who taught me to learn. To Gauri Shringarpure who can spin it without failing to land it straight. And to Kanishtha Gavandi for always having my back.

To Amol Brahme and Lakshmi Krishnamurthy for not letting go of me. Without you I could not have gotten off that ledge alive.

To Dr. Chandra Kaup and Vinoda Kaup, my in-laws, for your words of wisdom and unfettered support

To Dr. Sweety Shinde, my sister, who reminded me that you are not done if you have not rewritten. She was right, as she always is.

To my mom Saral Shinde, for showing me how to always live in the present.

To my daughters Asha and Rhea: You are the light in my life – sometimes the torch in a dark cave, other times – an interrogator's high wattage bulbs.

And finally, to Monica for tolerating my crazies. I love you, babe.

~~~~~

There is a longer list of people who did not respond to my reasonable call for help. I remember each one of you.

~~~~~